# VOLTAIRE IN LOVE

*Also by Nancy Mitford*

*Novels*
HIGHLAND FLING
CHRISTMAS PUDDING
WIGS ON THE GREEN
PIGEON PIE
THE PURSUIT OF LOVE
LOVE IN A COLD CLIMATE
THE BLESSING
DON'T TELL ALFRED

*Non-Fiction*
MADAME DE POMPADOUR
VOLTAIRE IN LOVE
THE SUN KING
FREDERICK THE GREAT
THE WATER BEETLE (essays)

*Edited*
THE LADIES OF ALDERLEY
THE STANLEYS OF ALDERLEY
NOBLESSE OBLIGE

# VOLTAIRE
# IN
# LOVE

*BY*

## NANCY MITFORD

Innumerable high-dressed gentlemen are gone to
inorganic powder, no comfortable or profitable
memory to be held of them more; and this poor
Voltaire, without implement except the tongue
and brain of him, he is still a shining object to all
the populations and they say and symbol to me:
'Tell us of him, he is the man.'
                                    THOMAS CARLYLE

'Ce siècle à perruque est celui où l'homme s'est le
moins masqué.'          FRANÇOIS MAURIAC

## HAMISH HAMILTON
### LONDON

First published in Great Britain 1957
by Hamish Hamilton Ltd
90 Great Russell Street London WC1B 3PT
First published in this edition 1976

Copyright © 1957 by Nancy Mitford

SBN 241 89154 X

PRINTED IN GREAT BRITAIN BY
THOMSON LITHO LTD, EAST KILBRIDE, SCOTLAND

TO
VICTOR CUNARD

# ACKNOWLEDGMENTS

I OWE an enormous debt to Mr Theodore Besterman. Although he does not, I think, quite approve of this enterprise, he has helped me in every possible way. I have had access to all the material in his possession including the newly-discovered letters from Voltaire to Mme Denis which reveal the full extent of their clandestine love affair. Mr Besterman also had the goodness to read my book in typescript and to make many valuable comments on matters of fact and style.

Comtesse Carl Costa de Beauregard had me to stay at beautiful Fontaines where I wrote much of the book. I am also grateful to Signor Cipriani and everybody at Torcello where I worked for two months. M. de Gandarillas in whose house at Hyères I also worked was a very kind host as always.

Comte Jean de Baglion and Princess Chavchavadze lent me some scarce and valuable books. The Librarian of the London Library has been kind and helpful; so have Mr Heywood Hill, Mrs St George Saunders, Miss Irene Clephane, Comte Charles de Breteuil and Mr Roderick Coupe. Miss Henrietta Lamb found most of the illustrations for me.

# AUTHOR'S NOTE

THERE are many hundreds of books about Voltaire. This one is not a biography, still less a study of his literary and philosophical achievements (which would indeed be above my station) but simply an account of his relationship with Mme du Châtelet. Voltaire's work as a reformer only began after her death. His campaigns for the rehabilitation of Calas and Lally Tollendal; his contributions to the *Encyclopédie*; his quarrel with Jean-Jacques Rousseau; *Candide* and his reiterated '*Ecrasez l'infame*' all belong to his old age.

In order to reduce the number of footnotes I have put the full names and dates of the characters in the Index.

# CONTENTS

# ILLUSTRATIONS
*Between pages* 128 *and* 129

# Chapter One

## Voltaire and Emilie

THE LOVE of Voltaire and the Marquise du Châtelet was not an ordinary love. They were not ordinary people. Voltaire's *Mémoires* begin with their meeting which he regarded as the turning point of his life: 'I found, in 1733, a young woman who thought as I did, and who decided to spend several years in the country, cultivating her mind.' It is rather mysterious that he had not found her sooner, for they moved in the same world; his father was her father's man of affairs; the Duc de Richelieu, one of his greatest friends, had been her lover. Voltaire used to say that he had 'seen her born' but this was a literary convention he often used; another one was 'he (or she) died in my arms'.

However, as soon as they saw each other, the famous love affair began and was soon announced. Love, in France, is treated with formality; friends and relations are left in no doubt as to its beginning and its end. Concealment, necessitating confidants and secret meeting places, is only resorted to when there is a jealous husband or wife. The Marquis du Châtelet always behaved perfectly.

Writing to Cideville, companion of his schooldays, Voltaire said of Mme du Châtelet: 'You are a male Emilie and she is a female Cideville.' He could not have praised her more highly, for Cideville was one of his great friends. So frivolous, so volatile in his likes and dislikes, Voltaire was unshakeable in friendship. He also compared her to Newton, the master of his thought. He said that though she was a genius and inclined to require a metaphysical approach at moments when it is more usual to think only of love, she fully understood the art of flirtation. From the first he wrote of her, in letters to his intimates as well as in the many poems he addressed to her, as Emilie. This was another literary convention; in those days Christian names were not used, even between brother and sister, and Voltaire certainly never spoke to her as anything but Madame. Sometimes, in his writings, she is Uranie, because Mme du Châtelet, though she moved in the thoughtless circles of high society, was learned and a scientist. The Breteuil family, whose glory and whose shame she is, speak of her to this day as Gabrielle-Emilie, her real name.

While Voltaire's friends were left in no doubt as to the new relationship, Mme du Châtelet herself went even further. She declared that she was planning to spend the rest of her life with him. Among the first to be informed was the Duc de Richelieu. We do not know when and how the news was broken to M. du Châtelet.

The lovers were not young. Voltaire was thirty-nine, Mme du Châtelet twenty-seven. She had been married eight years and was the mother of three children, one of whom was only a few months old. Each had had a chequered past. Emilie was a passionate creature, excessive in everything. Her physical attraction for men was not great enough for the demands of her own nature and this often made her restless and unhappy. To look at she was quite unlike the general idea of an eighteenth-century Marquise. Mme du Deffand, who never forgave her for carrying off the greatest entertainer of the age, has left a description of her which is certainly too catty but may have some truth: thin, dry and flat-chested, huge arms and legs, huge feet, tiny head, tiny little sea-green eyes, bad teeth, black hair and a weather-beaten complexion, vain, overdressed and untidy. Cideville, on the other hand who, like most of Voltaire's men friends, was attracted by Emilie, speaks of her beautiful big soft eyes with black brows, her noble, witty and piquant expression. Calling on her one day and finding her in bed, he wrote:

*Ah mon ami que dans tel lit,*
*Pareille philosophie inspire d'appétit!*

Over and over again she is described, in letters and memoirs of her day, as beautiful; reading between the lines one can conclude that she was what is now called a handsome woman. She was certainly not a beauty in the class of Mme de Pompadour, nor, in spite of a great love of dress, was she ever really elegant. Elegance, for women, demands undivided attention; Emilie was an intellectual; she had not endless hours to waste with hairdressers and dressmakers.

She was born, 17 December 1706, a Le Tonnelier de Breteuil. Her immediate ancestors had risen to power and riches in the magistracy. France was governed by such families, many of which had plebeian origins whereas the Breteuils were of the minor nobility. The great territorial nobles had had their wings cut by Louis XIV and now, powerless but decorative, they only had two professions open to them: the Court and the Army. Magical Versailles was their reward for this loss of power; a hundred useless privileges bolstered up their pride and self-esteem. They heartily despised people like the Breteuils, whose men-folk had administrative posts at the Court, but whose women never went there. Madame de Créquy says that it was during a long visit to her cousins the Breteuils that she learnt not to mention the *noblesse de robe* (the nobles of the magistracy) without first looking round to see that none were present, as one does with hunchbacks and red-headed folk.

The Paris society in which Emilie grew up was extraordinarily democratic. It consisted of the magistrates and the *fermiers-généraux*, each with a circle of friends and dependants. The *fermiers-généraux* ran the country's finances and made enormous fortunes for themselves in the process. They often came from the lowest strata of society. Old Poisson, Madame de Pompadour's father, once burst out with a vulgar guffaw, at the dinner table of one of these magnates: 'I can't help laughing when I think that if a foreigner dropped into this party he would take us for an assembly of princes! Yet you, M. de Montmartel, are the son of an inn-keeper; you, Savalette, the son of a vinegar merchant; you, Bouret, the son of a servant, and as for me—everybody knows what I am!' Yet Poisson's daughter was one of the most civilized women of her time.

These men were not too busy coining money to educate themselves. They patronized literature and art, made magnificent collections, built splendid houses and financed the most beautiful editions of the French classics that have ever been produced. Courtiers from Versailles, especially those with intellectual tastes, such as the Ducs de Nivernais, La Vallière and Gontaut, accepted their hospitality, made love to their wives and sometimes even married their daughters.

France was prosperous, having recovered from the wars of Louis XIV and not, as yet, embarked on those of Louis XV. Money flowed in the capital. Voltaire, describing life in Paris under Louis XV, makes it clear that magistrates of quite ordinary means lived in a style that few people could afford today. Their wives were covered with diamonds and dressed, as they were themselves, in embroidered clothes worth a small fortune. Nothing could exceed the elegance and beauty of their possessions; their furniture, silver, china and pictures were of the finest quality; their gardens were bedded out with rare plants; their carriages and coaches a joy to behold. A good cook in Paris received as much as 1,500 livres a year.* Voltaire reckoned that five or six hundred big supper parties took place every night, and that after each of them thousands of livres would change hands over the card tables without anybody being the least perturbed. More poultry and game was consumed in one night in Paris than in a week in London, and innumerably more wax candles were burnt.

The Breteuils lived in a big house looking over the Tuileries gardens. It was divided, as French houses generally are, into apartments inhabited by various members of the family: the Marquise, the Comtesse (both widows) and the Commandeur de Breteuil, the Bishop of Rennes and the Baron de Breteuil, with his wife and five children, of whom Emilie was one. The Baronne, sister of the Marquise, was born Froulay, and was a member of the old nobility. Emilie's father was a fashionable but slightly ridiculous figure, well known in Paris and at Versailles where he was 'Introducteur des Ambassadeurs' (head of the protocol). Nobody liked him very much; but his wife used to say that for her part she was grateful to him for taking her out of a convent and giving her children. Although she had been brought up in this convent and had never, says Mme de Créquy, had the opportunity to breathe the good air of Versailles, her manners were those of a great lady, and she taught her sons and daughters to mind theirs. 'Do not blow your nose on your napkin—you might think it unnecessary for me to tell you this; but I have seen the Montesquiou brothers blow theirs on the tablecloth which is really too disgusting. Break your bread and do not cut it. Always smash an egg-shell when you have eaten the egg, to

* Mr Besterman says that the purchasing power of the livre was that of the U.S. dollar in 1956. There were twenty-four livres to a louis, which was the equivalent of an English guinea.

prevent it from rolling off the plate. Never comb your hair in church. Be careful with the word Monseigneur, it is pronounced differently for a Prince of the Church and for a Prince of the Blood. If there is a Priest in the room always give him the chair nearest the fire and serve him first at meals, even if he has modestly set himself at the bottom of the table.'

Emilie did not benefit much from all this. She was too much taken up with her own thoughts ever to be polite, and indeed was famous in later life for her ill-breeding. But her intellectual instruction was another matter. Her father was shrewd enough to realize that he had produced a marvel. Whereas most young women of her class were left to pick up what knowledge they could from the servants (practical knowledge as a rule, later to be very useful to those who fled penniless to England and America from the Revolution) Emilie was well educated by any standards. She learnt Latin, Italian and English; Tasso and Milton were as familiar to her as Virgil. She translated the *Aeneid*, knew long passages from Horace by heart, and studied the works of Cicero. She refused to bother with Spanish, having heard that the only book in that language was frivolous. Her real aptitude was for mathematics. In this she was encouraged by M. de Mézières, a friend of the family and grandfather of Mme de Genlis.

The Breteuils entertained lavishly, they were never less than twenty to supper and, although their house was by no means a centre for intellectuals, certain literary figures were to be seen there. Fontenelle, the nephew of Corneille, came every Thursday. He was secretary of the Académie des Sciences and as a popularizer of scientific thought was a dim fore-runner of Voltaire. Born in 1657, he was in his middle age when Emilie was a child. He used to say: 'I would love to see one more strawberry season'; and noted with satisfaction on his death-bed that he had seen ninety-nine. Other habitual callers were the Duc de Saint-Simon and the Marquis de Dangeau, who were both considered rather dreadful old men. Saint-Simon's eyes were like dead cinders in an omelette, according to another friend of the house, Jean-Baptiste Rousseau. The Duke never came to supper for fear of being obliged to return hospitality; in his memoirs he did indeed bite the hand that had not fed him: 'Breteuil was by no means without parts, but was eaten up with love of the Court, of ministers, of anybody fashionable. He made money whenever he could, by promising his support [in matters of protocol]. We put up with him, laughed at him and teased him unmercifully.'

'Who wrote the paternoster?' M. de Breteuil was asked at a dinner-party. Pause. M. de Caumartin, his cousin, whispered to him, 'Moses.' 'Well, but of course, Moses,' said M. de Breteuil brightly, amid general merriment. He was better informed on the events of his own day and is presented as an infallible gossipmonger by La Bruyère, in his *Caractères*, under the name of Celse.

The Breteuils were related to Lord Clare, who brought many exiled Jacobites to their house. The Old Pretender himself once spent several nights there, disguised as an Abbé. Emilie, whether from a spirit of contradiction or because she had seen too much of the Jacobites, used to say that she was for good King George of Hanover.

When she was nineteen Mlle de Breteuil married the thirty-year-old Marquis du Châtelet, colonel of a regiment and the head of one of the great families known as *les chevaux de Lorraine*. He was distantly related to the Guises, and bore the *fleur-de-lis* on his coat of arms; his wife enjoyed the privilege, usually reserved for Duchesses, of sitting in the presence of the Queen and of travelling in her suite. His ancestors had been soldiers; his grandfather a Marshal of France. The family estates were neglected, the château of Cirey, his country house, an empty, ruinous shell, and the revenue from his land less than it should have been. He was, in fact, far from rich. Emilie, however, had a good dowry.

Two children, a boy and a girl, were born during the first years of their marriage. Du Châtelet's only interest was the army; he was generally absent on garrison duty and Emilie was left very much to her own devices. Like her father she loved society and the life at Court; she acquired a taste for gambling and plunged into amorous adventure. In spite of her careful upbringing and the outlet provided by a diversity of interests, she always had something of the whore. A man engaged as footman in her house has told how, on the first morning, he was sent for to her bedroom. While she was giving him orders she took off her nightdress and stood naked as a marble statue. On another occasion she rang for him when she was in her bath, told him to take a kettle of hot water from the fire and pour it into the bath which was getting cold. As she did not use bath salts the water was clear and she was naked in it. Without any embarrassment she separated her legs so that he could pour the water between them. Eighteenth-century manners may have been free and easy, but this was not the ordinary behaviour of an honest woman. The proof is that the man was perfectly horrified.

Mme du Châtelet's first declared lover was the Marquis de Guébriant. After a while, he left her for another woman. Emilie took it very badly. When she realized that he had no intention of returning to her she asked for a final interview. This passed off calmly. Emilie made Guébriant pour her out a cup of soup which she drank; then they said farewell. He left the house with a last note from her in his pocket. Luckily he read it at once; it was to say that the soup was poisoned and she was now dying at the hands of her beloved. The beloved, seriously alarmed, lost no time, rushed back to her and found her indeed very ill. He took energetic measures which saved her life. The love affair, however, was not resumed. Emilie's next lover was the Duc de Richelieu whose worldly wisdom and knowledge of the human heart enabled him, when the time came, to extricate himself from the situation without any such painful scene. He and Mme du Châtelet remained close friends for the rest of her life. When she was twenty-seven she had a third baby, a little boy, after whose birth she settled down to the study of mathematics. She was waiting, unconsciously, for that revolution which often comes in the life of a woman no longer young and directs the future course of her existence.

# Chapter Two

## The Young Voltaire

VOLTAIRE'S LIFE, too, had been agitated, though not by love. François-Marie Arouet was born in Paris 21 November 1694. This fact was not known until recently. He himself pretended that he had been born in the country in March and hinted that he was a bastard. He loved mystification and had no wish to dwell on his origins. When he grew up he changed his name. A sickly baby, he was the third surviving child of delicate parents, neither of whom reached old age, nor did his brother and sister. At no time during his long life did Voltaire expect to last more than a few weeks. Mme Arouet died when he was seven; the children were brought up by their father, who never married again.

The Arouets, established in Paris, originally came from Poitou and belonged to a good old bourgeois family. Voltaire's father was a prosperous notary with a middle-class outlook and an aristocratic clientèle. He wanted his sons to follow safe and honourable professions in his own walk of life; the elder son conformed, the younger did not.

He was the bad boy of the Jesuits at their school of Louis-le-Grand. 'Arouet, give him back his glass; you are a tease, you will never go to Heaven,' says one of the fathers.

'What's he talking about, with his Heaven?' says little Arouet. 'Heaven is the great dormitory of the world.'

His confessor said he had never known a child so

devoured by a thirst for celebrity. But he had an affectionate nature, and the companions of his later life
were nearly all friends he had made at school: the Comte
d'Argental (his 'guardian angel'), Pierre-Robert de
Cideville, a bourgeois from Rouen, the Duc de Richelieu,
the brothers d'Argenson, Marquis and Count. He kept
in touch with the priests who had educated him, and
cherished their praise. When the time came for him to
choose a profession he told his father that he was going to
be a man of letters. 'In other words,' said Arouet, 'you
want to be useless to society, a charge on your family and
eventually to die of hunger.' The child had been in the
hands of money-lenders from the age of thirteen; Arouet
was not very hopeful about his future. He put him to read
for the law, but Voltaire did not settle down to that. He
stayed up too late at night and generally made a nuisance
of himself.

At last young Arouet's high spirits and contempt for
office-hours got so much on his father's nerves that he
packed him off, as unpaid attaché, to the French embassy at The Hague (1713). Here he fell in love, more,
perhaps, than ever again, with a girl he could not marry.
He caused a scandal by trying to elope with her and
came home in disgrace. His father then put him into a
solicitor's office where, without much enthusiasm, he
acquired a knowledge of business and legal matters
which was to be invaluable during the rest of his
chequered, quarrelsome existence. He also acquired a
crony. Nicolas-Claude Thieriot was a fellow-clerk in the
office; the two boys soon became inseparable. Thieriot
was a charmer; a funny, lazy, cynical, dishonest ne'er-do-
well. Of Voltaire's other intimate friends, Cideville and
d'Argental were exceptionally high-minded, while
Richelieu was a Duke; he was slightly in awe of all three,
for these different reasons. Thieriot appealed to the lower
side of his nature. He could boast and brag to him about

things which would not have impressed the others in the least; could engage in doubtful transactions with him, and shriek with laughter at doubtful jokes. For years the two young men were so close that if one were ill the other would have a sympathetic fever. In Voltaire's youth Thieriot and Cideville were his chief correspondents; the worthlessness of the former, the goodness of the latter, are evident in every line.

From the age of ten, when he first went to Louis-le-Grand with a tutor and a man-servant, as boys used to go to Eton, Voltaire began to gravitate towards high society. At twenty-one he was its darling. He had every qualification, except that of birth. His appearance was delightful, a droll, impertinent, inquisitive look, dancing black eyes, a turned-up nose, elegant little figure, beautifully dressed, nothing out of place, he was like a creature of spun glass. His conversation matched his looks, droll, impertinent, inquisitive, dancing, elegant and brittle. He was the greatest amuser of his age and all history does not record a greater. Dukes and Duchesses, Marshals of France, Ministers and Royal Princes fell over themselves to invite the lawyer's clerk to their supper-parties and country-houses. Only the Church hung back. There were rumours that young Arouet's impertinence extended even to sacred matters. Cardinal Fleury, who knew and liked him, and the Fathers at Louis-le-Grand, said with sorrow that this excellent material was being spoilt. Poor Arouet thought so, too. It seemed to him that his son did nothing but get into scrapes with the kind of friends who do a young man no good, older than himself and far above him in rank. As for the poetry which the idle fellow scribbled from morning to night, it brought in no money and led to trouble. Voltaire was often to say that those who make names for themselves in literature and the arts have generally cultivated them against the wishes of their parents.

The first of Voltaire's writings to get him into serious difficulties was a satirical poem called *Le Bourbier* (muddy ditch) attacking the fabulist, Lamotte-Houdar. He had given a poetry prize, which Voltaire coveted, to somebody else. There was such a to-do about *Le Bourbier* in Paris that it was thought prudent for its author to make himself scarce. A rich old magistrate, the Marquis de Saint-Ange, offered to shelter him in his country house near Fontainebleau. He was the uncle of Voltaire's two friends, the d'Argenson brothers. Voltaire stayed with him several months; it was a profitable sojourn. M. de Saint-Ange, having held important political posts, had been in and out of Versailles all his life. He knew every detail of the long reign, now (1714) drawing to its close, from his own experience, and a great deal about the reigns of Henri IV and Louis XIII from his father, who had been a friend of Cardinal de Retz. He loved to tell about old times, and Voltaire loved to listen. The idea of writing history came to him at Saint-Ange and it was there that he began his *Henriade*, the epic poem on Henri IV which brought him fame and fortune.

Voltaire's troubles with the authorities all followed much the same pattern. He would write a play, a short story, a poem or an epistle pouring contempt on some branch of established authority, either of Church or State. He knew that he was exposing himself to severe risks. The poet Jean-Baptiste Rousseau had been in exile since 1707 for writing libellous verses; nearly all men of letters with anything new to say cooled their heels from time to time behind bars. Voltaire, in his perpetual game of Tom Tiddler's Ground with the government, ventured further than most of his contemporaries. His intolerance of stupidity and superstition, his hatred of cruelty, his love of teasing and his desire to be read combined to make him intensely rash. He thought his own work stunning, especially the manuscript on which he was engaged, and longed to see the effect it would have on his friends. He could never resist reading it aloud, under the seal of secrecy. The friends, particularly Thieriot, who offended in this way over and over again, could never, in their turn, resist talking about Voltaire's latest masterpiece, quoting and misquoting as much of it as they could remember. Voltaire always pretended to be furious, but publicity was the breath of life to him, and his fury was apt to be much exaggerated.

Men's thoughts were becoming a valuable commodity and the publishers would prick up their ears; another best-seller was in the making. Then came the dingy and complicated business of stolen sheets and pirated editions and soon a garbled version of the work, sometimes with chapters added by an alien hand, would be for sale under the counter. Had Voltaire himself arranged for the sheets to be 'stolen'? The whole affair was apt to become so involved that even his close friends could make neither head nor tail of it. When the work had been read by everybody that mattered and made its full effect, the police would step in. According to how tendentious it was supposed to be, it would be confiscated, or burnt by the public hangman; the publisher warned to be more careful, fined or sent to prison; and a *lettre de cachet* issued against the anonymous author. Voltaire would become more and more agitated, and tell more and more lies. 'As soon as there is the slightest danger,' he wrote, on one of these occasions, to d'Alembert, 'I beg you to warn me, so that with my habitual candour and innocence I can disavow the work'; and again: 'It is not exile that I mind, but that such infamous verses should be attributed to me.' He would fly for shelter to the country house of some Prince or Duke, so powerful that the police were unlikely to make an arrest there without due warning. After a while, largely owing to the efforts of Voltaire's friends at Court (Richelieu, the d'Argenson brothers or, later on, Mme de Pompadour, prodded into action by the faithful d'Argental) the affair would blow over; he would creep back to Paris and presently settle down to write his next attack on authority.

It was two years after the exile to Saint-Ange before Voltaire was in trouble again. The reign of the Regent, the Duc d'Orléans, had begun, scandalous from a moral point of view, a reaction from the old King's sternly religious rule. Verses and libels about the Regent's private life circulated in the capital and some of these were attributed to Voltaire. They went too far, with references to Lot, insinuating that d'Orléans was having an affair with his daughter, as indeed he was. Voltaire strenuously denied having written them, at the time and ever after, but nobody believed him. He was formally exiled from Paris by the Regent, who ordered him to go and live at distant Tulle. Voltaire pulled strings and got himself sent to Sully, on the Loire, instead. It was understood that he had relations there whose example would correct his impudence and temper his vivacity. We hear no more of these excellent folk, for as soon as Voltaire arrived at Sully, he moved into the château. The Duc de Sully was then forty-seven, a brave soldier but an unprincipled man. Member of a set known in Paris as *les libertins du Temple*, which had taken up Voltaire when he was hardly more than a child, the Duke loved the company of intellectuals. President Hénault said there was an odour about him, of having lived with clever men, like the odour which clings to a bottle that has contained scent. Voltaire, who loved the company of Dukes, was perfectly happy at Sully where there were continual balls and fêtes, hunting-parties and every sort of amusement. He said it was only fair that he should be allotted such an agreeable exile since he was innocent of the crime for which he was being punished. Before long the good-natured Regent allowed him to go back to Paris;

he immediately began to cook up more mischief. He bore
a grudge for the very mild correction he had received
and soon the police were reporting that young Arouet
could not speak of the Duc d'Orléans without transports
of rage, and that he was given to reciting virulent rhymes
about him all over Paris.

Everything that appeared in print against the government began to be laid at Voltaire's door. There was a
satire entitled 'J'ai vu'. 'I have seen the State prisons
crammed to bursting point. I have seen poor soldiers
dying of hunger. I have seen the whole population
crushed by taxes. I have seen the Jesuit worshipped as if
he were God'—etc. This was immediately attributed to
him, and for once, wrongly attributed. The real culprit, a
certain Le Brun, confessed years later to having written
it. Voltaire's denials of its authorship, however, were
again disbelieved. One afternoon the Regent, walking
in the gardens of his Palais-Royal, came face to face
with him. 'Monsieur Arouet,' he said, 'I'm going to
show you something that you have never seen before:
the Bastille.' 'Ah! Monseigneur! I'll take that as seen.'

On the morning of Whit Sunday 1717, 'twenty
scavenging, starving black crows' (in the poet's imagination, really two policemen) appeared in his bedroom and
carried him off to gaol. This, in the parlance of the time,
was his first Bastille. Voltaire was familiar with the inside
of the fortress because the Duc de Richelieu, having got
out of hand at the age of fifteen, had been sent there with
his tutor for a year. Voltaire used to visit him. A spell in
the Bastille could hardly be described as durance vile for
anybody rich or important. Such 'guests of the King'
were made very comfortable in a special part of the
prison. There was room for fifty but this number was
seldom reached, and there were generally about thirty.
During the reign of Louis XIV they furnished their own
apartments; in Voltaire's time the rooms contained the

necessities of life, but the prisoner was expected to provide tapestry, silver, books, cushions, screens, lookingglasses and lamps. (Richelieu arrived with family portraits, musical instruments and a backgammon board.) Women took their maids with them. Food and wine in vast quantities and of excellent quality, heating, light and laundry were provided by the King. The prisoners were only shut in their rooms at night; during the day they were at liberty within the walls; they paid each other visits and received their friends from outside. It need hardly be said that Voltaire dined at the governor's table.

Captivity, however, is bad for those of an excitable nature. Although Voltaire lived well at the Bastille and managed to do a great deal of work there, he retained a nervous dread of prison to the end of his days. On 11 April 1718 he was set free but forbidden to stay in Paris. He went to Chatenay to a delightful house belonging to his father. But he was insensible to the charms of this summer in the country; he had a particular reason for wishing to be in Paris. His first play, *Œdipe*, had been accepted by the Comédie-française and was about to go into rehearsal.

It was at this point that young Arouet decided to take another name. He said that he had been unhappy under his own and furthermore did not wish to be confounded with the poet Roy. (Roi, in Court parlance, was pronounced Roé.) Younger sons often changed their names in order not to be confused with their brothers; there was also the precedent of Molière, born Poquelin. More pretentious than he, Voltaire gave himself a particle and called himself Arouet de Voltaire. He never told anybody why he chose that name; probably it was an anagram of Arouet l.j. (le jeune); J's and I's, U's and V's being then interchangeable. The first letter of his that exists with the new signature was written to an Englishman, Lord Ashburnham, and concerns the loan of a horse. It is dated from Chatenay, 12 June 1718. The change of name was accepted quite calmly in society; no mockery or laughter is heard of until the silly insolence of the Chevalier de Rohan-Chabot seven years later. Even the Minister responsible for his exile from Paris, the Marquis de La Vrillière, addressed him as Arouet de Voltaire, in October 1718.

*Œdipe* came on in November. Voltaire was not quite free to live where he liked, but, largely owing to the good offices of the Baron de Breteuil, he was allowed to go to Paris for a few days at a time to help with the production. Always apt to fall in love with his leading ladies, he was having an affair with Mlle Livry, who played Jocaste. *Œdipe* contained some passages that would never have been allowed under Louis XIV, but it got the author into no further trouble and was a startling triumph. It received the kind of publicity that makes for success, pamphlets either violently for or violently against; it ran for forty-two nights and was seen by 27,000 paying spectators. (Five or six performances were an average run.) On the first night old Arouet sat in a corner of the theatre, weeping with pride and ejaculating '*le coquin*', in the time-honoured manner of the goose that has hatched a swan. After this, until his death some three years later, father and son were on good terms. The Regent now forgave Voltaire, allowed him to come and pay his court, presented him with a gold medal and a pension from the King. This was often done for people who were recognized to have been unjustly imprisoned. Voltaire rather cheekily remarked that, while he was all in favour of the King paying for his food he would prefer, in future, to find his own lodging. The Regent laughed heartily. The two men might have been friends had they been on a more equal footing. Voltaire was always at his worst with royalty; besides, the Regent was trying to govern France in the face of great difficulties and Voltaire did not make this task any easier.

During the next few years all went well for Voltaire. His father died without disinheriting him, as he had often threatened to do. A quarrel with his elder brother over the will was no sadness to him as he had never been fond of that sour Jansenist, ten years older than himself. He loved his sister, Mme Mignot, and there was no quarrel with her. He neither made nor lost money through following the famous Scotchman, Law, whose '*système*', introducing paper money, was the sensation of the 1720's. Voltaire kept his capital intact through dangerous years. Finally, when there was a scramble to sell the notes, it was his remark 'they are reducing paper to its intrinsic value' that proved the death knell of the *système*.

A little banishment, of a few weeks only, was spent again at Sully, again with his 'adorable Duke' rather than with the nebulous relations. There was more country-house life in France during the minority of Louis XV than later in his reign, when he attracted the nobles to Versailles. It suited Voltaire to stay in luxurious châteaux where he found the peace and fresh air that his nervous system required, combined with agreeable company. When he had had enough and began to be bored, or wanted a pretext to go back to Paris, his wretched health would be called into play; he would make his excuses and go home for treatment. There was no question of his ever outstaying his welcome; his hosts only allowed him to leave their houses with the greatest reluctance. He was a constant guest at Vaux-le-Vicomte, or Villars as it was then called, belonging to the Duc de Villars, Marshal of France, whose Duchess was, for a time, Voltaire's mistress. Richelieu was another château where he went regularly; he thought it the most beautiful of all. It had been built, together with a little town in the same style, by the Duke's great-uncle the Cardinal.

He stayed at La Source, where Lord Bolingbroke lived
with his French wife, and at La Rivière-Bourdet, near
Rouen, with the Marquis de Bernières. Voltaire made
love to Mme de Bernières, was on very friendly terms
with her husband, and had rooms in their Paris house
(now no. 27 Quai Voltaire) where, by a curious chance,
he was to die. Thieriot was a constant fellow guest at La
Rivière-Bourdet, and Cideville, a member of the Rouen
*parlement*, was a neighbour.

Voltaire, so industrious himself, was for ever trying to
find work for his beloved Thieriot—the last thing that
lazy fellow wanted. He basked in the fame of his friend
and led a parasitical existence with various rich, vulgar
financiers who were ready to put him up for the pleasure
of his company. Very occasionally he did some little job;
he edited the Grande Mademoiselle's memoirs when they
appeared in 1729, and became the greatest living expert
on Voltairiana.

All this time Voltaire was busy with the *Henriade*. It
might have been supposed, and no doubt he hoped, that
a poem in praise of that King of France from whom the
reigning King was five times descended would have been
well-received at Court. Had Voltaire been an obscure
scribbler living in some garret his work might have been
taken at its face value. But his iconoclastic point of view
was well known and prejudiced the authorities against his
books. Everything that he wrote was regarded with the
deepest suspicion, every phrase examined for a subversive
meaning. The *Henriade*, subjected to this treatment, was
supposed to smell of Jansenism; Coligny, the Protestant
Admiral, was over-rated while the King was presented
as a mere human being and not a demi-god. The first
set-back was when Voltaire was refused leave to dedicate
the poem to Louis XV. Worse still, he was also refused a
*privilège*, the guarantee of royal permission to print. So
it seemed wiser to have it published at Rouen and not at

Paris; an edition of 4,000 copies was then secretly brought to Paris and circulated from hand to hand. Another startling triumph. Every woman of fashion displayed the *Henriade* on her dressing-table when she received her friends during the 'toilette', while the literary pundits could not praise it enough. Henri IV who, in the course of years, had been forgotten by the French, now sprang to the position of Best and Favourite King from which he has never since been ousted. The poem was frowned on but not formally forbidden by the police. In this case Voltaire made the best of both worlds; he benefited from the publicity caused by any sort of official disapproval and at the same time was free to arrange for new editions to be printed. But the whole affair had been nervous work. On the other hand his *Marianne* was given at the Comédie-française without let or hindrance; it was a failure and Voltaire realized when he saw it on the boards that this had been inevitable.

His star continued to rise. At the age of thirty young Arouet had become the famous M. de Voltaire, France's greatest living writer. His little love affairs prospered. Except for that with Mme de Bernières they were quite unimportant; in all of them it was he who called the tune and the women who made the jealous scenes. After the Regent's death in 1723 France was ruled by the Duc de Bourbon whose mistress, Mme de Prie, was very much attached to Voltaire. She took him to Versailles where he was made welcome. The young Queen, Marie-Leczinska, told him that she had wept at *Marianne* and laughed at his *L'Indiscret*; she called him 'mon pauvre Voltaire' and settled a pension on him. His influence seemed unlimited, and in 1725 he put it to the proof.

A literary acquaintance, the Abbé Desfontaines, was arrested and sent to the criminal prison at Bicêtre for corrupting little chimney-sweeps. Voltaire said he must have mistaken them for Cupids, with their bandaged

eyes and iron rods. The current, rather excessive punish-
ment for sodomy was burning at the stake in the Place de
la Grève outside the Hôtel de Ville; Desfontaines
trembled in his shoes and wrote frantic letters to all his
friends, begging them to help him. Nobody lifted a finger
except Voltaire. Although he was ill, he got up and went
to Fontainebleau where the Court was in residence. He
saw people, pulled strings and rescued Desfontaines from
an unpleasant death. The trial was stopped and the Abbé
set free. Thieriot, who had introduced the two men in the
first place, now took it upon himself to make mischief between them. It seemed that no sooner was Desfontaines
out of Bicêtre than he had written a disgusting pamphlet
against Voltaire. He showed it to Thieriot who very
properly threw it in the fire, but then could not resist
telling Voltaire about it, thus laying up misery for all
concerned. Voltaire brooded over the Abbé's ingratitude
and hated him.

Voltaire's health was a good deal better than when he
had been younger. The nervous indigestion which was
his chief complaint was cured by happiness and success.
He began to understand his own body, an unfailing
source of interest to him; he knew that it needed rest,
regular exercise and a careful diet. He had sensible ideas
about health, greatly in advance of his time. Most illness,
in his view, came from overeating. 'Good cooks are
poisoners, they ruin whole families with *ragoûts* and *hors-
d'œuvre.*' When he was ill he went to bed and starved himself. He was never at war with the doctors and said the
advice of a sensible one was by no means to be despised,
but he mocked at all medical superstitions. He thought it
ridiculous to pretend that animals enjoy better health
than human beings. Stags and crows were supposed to
have exceptional longevity—he would like to see the stag
or the crow which had lived as long as the Marquis
de Saint-Aulaire (nearly a hundred). In 1723 Voltaire

recovered from a virulent form of smallpox, which carried off one-third of the population of Paris; he attributed his cure to eight emetics and two hundred pints of lemonade. Probably he loved life too much to die. But his happy, industrious existence was soon to suffer a very disagreeable interruption.

In December 1725, Voltaire was at the Opera with Adrienne Lecouvreur, one of the most famous actresses in the history of French drama. The Chevalier de Rohan-Chabot came into her box, evidently anxious to pick a quarrel with him. Rohan-Chabot was a stupid, peppery soldier and man-about-town, ten years older than Voltaire. He was a member of a powerful clan.

As Mlle Lecouvreur had not only been, but possibly still was, Voltaire's mistress, there may have been jealousy between the two men; Voltaire may have been giving himself airs or perhaps Rohan-Chabot was one of those people who could not endure him. During the evening the Chevalier said, insultingly and several times: 'M. de Voltaire, M. Arouet or whatever you call yourself.' In the end, Voltaire lost his temper and said that he was the first of his name while the Chevalier was the last* of his. This stung Rohan-Chabot on the raw. His grandmother had been the only child of the Duc de Rohan, an ancient family descended from Kings of Brittany. She had married a Chabot; the family was no longer Rohan at all. The Chevalier, furious, lifted his cane and said that such an insult could only be wiped out by a good hiding. Voltaire put his hand to his sword; Mlle Lecouvreur tactfully fainted away and the Chevalier left the box.

Two or three days later Voltaire was dining at the Hôtel de Sully, with his adorable duke, when he received a message asking him to go outside as somebody wished to see him. He went out; there was a hired car-

* *le dernier*, which also means the lowest.

riage drawn up in the street and Voltaire, supposing
that whoever had sent for him was sitting in it, put his
foot on the step. At this moment several ruffians fell upon
him from behind and roundly whacked him with sticks.
The Chevalier de Rohan-Chabot, watching the scene
from his own coach, called out, 'Don't hit him on the
head, something might come out of that one day,' at
which the bystanders are supposed to have said, 'Oh!
the gracious Lord!' Describing the scene later to his
friends, Rohan-Chabot said, 'I commanded the labour-
corps* in person.'

When Voltaire had finally struggled away from his
tormentors he rushed back into the house and told his
host and fellow guests what had happened. He was received with cold embarrassment. Nobody took his side,
sympathized with him or even agreed that he had been
vilely treated. The Duke behaved outrageously. He had
been like a father to Voltaire for years, yet he would not
raise a finger to obtain justice for his guest. The police,
whom Voltaire bombarded with complaints, did nothing
whatever, nor did his friends at Court. Mme de Prie was
on his side, but the Duc de Bourbon's position was weak
and he could not afford to alienate any supporters.

Like a herd of cows, one of which has got into a shindy
with a small, furious dog, the French aristocracy now
drew together, staring sadly but inertly at the fray.
Nearly all Voltaire's friends would have been glad to
help him to justice, but nobody cared to make the first
move. Unluckily for him, Richelieu, who had nothing
bovine in his make-up and who might have rallied to his
friend, was now French Ambassador at Vienna. He was
kept informed of the affair by Mme de Prie, entirely
sympathetic to Voltaire.

Voltaire's nerves began to give way under the strain
of so much humiliation. He wandered about Paris, fre-

* *Travailleurs*, a military term for the men who dig trenches.

quenting low haunts and curious company, continually changed his lodging and presently went to stay in
the house of a fencing master. The police, hitherto so
torpid over this affair, now began to take notice; he was
obviously learning to fence in order to fight with Rohan-
Chabot. They informed the Chevalier and his family
who immediately caused Voltaire to be arrested and put
into protective custody. It was his second Bastille. The
Governor again treated his prisoner very well, entertained him at his own table and allowed him as many
visitors as he wanted, until the crowd became unman-
ageable and had to be cut down. The Comte de Maurepas, Minister of the Interior, who never got on with
Voltaire, had the decency to write to the Governor sug-
gesting special treatment for him, adding that his character called for a good deal of tact. Voltaire's imprisonment
lasted less than a fortnight. He asked permission to go to
England, and this was granted.

# Chapter Three

## Voltaire in England

IN THE month of May 1726, Voltaire sailed up the Thames. It was one of those perfect days of early summer which make our island seem like fairyland. The aspect of London as he saw it from his ship is familiar to us in the pictures of Canaletto: a low skyline of brick houses, overshadowed by the huge white dome of St Paul's Cathedral and punctuated by the white spires of innumerable churches. The Thames was crowded with boats; flags were flying in honour of the King and Queen,* who presently came down the river in a gilded barge. Voltaire said it was easy to see by their faces that the boatmen were not slaves and furthermore that they lived on the fat of the land. They held their heads high, knowing that not a hair could be touched. When he landed, it seemed that the streets were full of lords and ladies who, he soon discovered, were merely the honest burghers going about their ordinary occasions. Voltaire's whole view of England was for ever coloured by this smiling first impression. But a shock awaited him when he presented himself at the house of a Jew to whom he had a letter of credit.

'My damned Jew,' he wrote, in English, to Thieriot, 'was broken. I was without a penny, sick to death of a violent ague, a stranger, alone, helpless, in the midst of a city wherein I was known to nobody. My lord and my

* This Queen only existed in Voltaire's imagination. George I was still on the throne.

lady Bolingbroke were in the country. I could not make
bold to see our Ambassador in so wretched a condition.
I had never undergone such distress; but I am born to
run through all the misfortunes of life. In these circumstances, my star, that among all its direful influences
pours allways on me some kind refreshment, sent to me
an English gentleman unknown to me, who forced me
to receive some money that I wanted. Another London
citizen that I had seen but once at Paris carried me to his
own country house, where I lead an obscure and charming life since that time, without going to London and
quite given over to the pleasures of indolence and friendship. The true and generous affection of this man, who
soothes the bitterness of my life, brings me to love you
more and more. All the instances of friendshipp endear
my friend Tiriot to me. . . .'

The 'other London citizen' of whom Voltaire speaks
was Everard Fawkener, a merchant. While Voltaire was
in England he met Pope, Gay, Swift, Congreve, Wilkes,
Lord Hervey, Lord Oxford, the Duchess of Marlborough,
Lord Peterborough (with whom he stayed for three
months) and many other prominent and charming
people, but far the best he loved Everard Fawkener.
Fawkener was ten years older than he and came from the
same class; his father was a mercer, as Voltaire's grandfather had been, and his grandfather a druggist. Like
Voltaire, but more mysteriously, as it is not recorded
that he was particularly brilliant in any way, he cut a
figure in society. He was knighted in 1735, became
English Ambassador to the Porte, then secretary to the
Duke of Cumberland. Later in life he married a natural
daughter of General Charles Churchill and, although he
died poor, their children made good marriages. His
daughter, Mrs Bouverie, was both fast and fashionable,
the bosom friend of Mrs Crewe.

'Hypochondriacs,' said Voltaire, 'are very well received here.' So were exiled French poets; the English were not at all averse from showing their old enemies across the Channel how a famous man of letters ought to be treated. King George II sent him 100 guineas and Queen Caroline a gold medal. England, then, was regarded by writers rather as France is now; the only country in the world where there was a real respect for literature, where it was encouraged and where anything, however outspoken, could be printed without fear of the police.

Voltaire noted the 'difference between their liberty and our slavery, their sensible toughness and our mad superstition, the encouragement that all the arts receive at London and the shameful oppression under which they languish at Paris'. He really loved and admired England, no doubt, but he also made the most of this love and admiration in order to tease his fellow countrymen. He laid it on very thick, writing to his French friends in English and referring to France as 'your nation'. 'I write and think as a free Englishman.' He arrived knowing English like a dead language, able to read and write but not to speak it. An interview with Pope, who had no French, was so frustrating that Voltaire retired to Mr Fawkener's house at Wandsworth for three months, and only reappeared in London society when he could speak fluently.

'You are so witty, profligate and thin
At once we think you Milton, Death and Sin.'

So wrote Edward Young after a discussion in which Voltaire had held forth about Milton's dialogue between Sin and Death. His English must have become very good as it is not easy to be witty in a foreign language.

A meeting with Congreve is on record. Voltaire, rather

gushingly, no doubt, said that he had long wished to meet one whom he put on a par with Molière and regarded as the greatest living playwright. Congreve: 'I had rather you wished to meet me because I am an English gentleman.' Voltaire: 'But there are so many of them!'

Voltaire could not live without working and as soon as he was settled in England he took up his *Henriade* once more. He re-wrote the part already published, eliminated all references to the great Duc de Sully, ancestor of the ex-adorable, and added to the poem. When it was ready he applied for, and received, permission to dedicate it to Queen Caroline. A limited edition was very soon subscribed by English bibliophiles, while the popular edition on sale in London had to be reprinted three times in the first three weeks. In France Voltaire's agent for the new *Henriade* was Thieriot. Eighty copies of the limited edition there, all subscribed, were stolen while Thieriot was at Mass or in other words by the wretched fellow himself. This was a financial blow to Voltaire, but the *Henriade* earned large sums in England, which he invested cleverly, laying the foundation of his riches. His love for his friend was not affected. 'I always forgive the weak and am only inflexible towards wickedness. . . . Men, in general, are so treacherous, so envious and so cruel that it is a comfort to find one who is only weak.' A few months later he was writing, in English, to Thieriot: 'We fall out for ever if you do not take 500 French livres from the arrears which the Queen owes me. You must have an hundred crowns beside from Bernard . . . that must be so or we are no friends'. Later, when Thieriot went to England, he lived entirely on Voltaire's royalties there.

In March 1729 Voltaire was allowed to go back to France. In spite of his love for England, he had become homesick; like many a Frenchman, he could not stand the austerity. In well-to-do houses, according to him, there was no silver on the table; tallow candles were burnt by all but the very rich; the food everywhere was uneatable. The arts of society, the art of pleasing were hardly cultivated and social life very dull compared with that in France. Furthermore, the weather did not suit his 'unhappy machine'. He often said that his unhappy machine demanded a Southern climate but that between the countries where one sweats and those where one thinks, he was obliged to choose the latter. The climate of Paris was bad enough but that of London was killing him. So, all in all, he was glad to go home. He never crossed the Channel again.

Warned that it would be better, for the present, if he did not go to Paris itself, Voltaire took lodgings at Saint-Germain-en-Laye, appearing from time to time 'like a hobgoblin' at the town houses of such faithful friends as the Duc de Richelieu. Soon, however, he was allowed 'to drag my chain in Paris', that is to say full liberty to resume his old life of work and pleasure. Richelieu took him down to Fontainebleau and arranged that he should pay his court to the Queen; this put him on the same social footing as before the exile. The Duc de Bourbon had been overthrown while Voltaire was in England. He had been banished to Chantilly, and Mme de Prie to her husband's château, where she very soon committed suicide. The boredom of country life was more than she could endure. The young King made his tutor, Cardinal Fleury, chief Minister. The Cardinal had been Bishop of Fréjus, an obscure diocese in Provence, most of his life; at seventy-three he found himself dictator of France. He ruled for seventeen years.

Everything Voltaire touched now turned to gold. He won an enormous state lottery, his investments prospered and his books were selling better than ever. *Zaïre*, the best of his tragedies, was published. It is about a Christian-

born slave in Turkey who reverts to the faith and dies:
the censor could find no objection to it. But of course
Voltaire provided one. He dedicated it to Mr Fawkener
('I like to dedicate my works to foreigners because it gives
me the opportunity to speak of the follies of my fellow-
countrymen'). He used the opportunity, in this case, to
compare French intolerance with English freedom; the
preface was seized by the police. Voltaire, however,
made the necessary cuts and they withdrew their ob-
jections. Another play, *Brutus*, received a *privilège*; the
*Histoire de Charles XII*, one of the most readable of
all Voltaire's books, appeared without the formal consent of the authorities but without any unpleasant consequences. He then settled down to write his next two
works, *Le Temple du Goût* and *Lettres Philosophiques*, for
both of which unpleasant consequences were in store.

In spite of his prosperity, however, Voltaire was unhappy. 'My misery embitters me and makes me shy.'
He told Thieriot that he had more friends in Constantinople than in Paris, since there he had two and in
Paris only Thieriot—who, however, was well worth two
Turks. He wandered from lodging to lodging; he needed
an anchor. His affair with Mme de Bernières did not
begin again; hardly had he left for England than she
was seen at the Opera with the Chevalier de Rohan-
Chabot. Voltaire had forgiven her, but she belonged to
the past. His sister, whom he was so fond of, had died
while he was away. Matters were made worse for him by
two more deaths, those of Adrienne Lecouvreur and of
the Marquis de Maisons who, having nursed Voltaire
through the smallpox in 1723, was himself carried off
by that disease in 1731. Both these dear friends 'died in
my arms'. As always when he was unhappy his health
began to suffer and sometimes he wondered whether he
would be able to go on working at all.

In the winter of 1731–2 Voltaire took up with an old

Baronne de Fontaine-Martel. He went to live in her house in the rue des Bons-Enfants, looking over the gardens of the Palais-Royal, acted as host at her supper parties, conducted rehearsals of his plays in the drawing-room and generally dug himself in. She was most unattractive. She had been obliged to give up having lovers, not because of old age, which is never taken into account in these matters by the French, but because of her eczema. She was rich and miserly, her suppers were nasty, unless a Prince of the Blood happened to announce himself, when they became just eatable. Voltaire said the passport to her favour was impotence; she had a morbid fear that some man would cut her throat in order to give her money to an actress. She put up with Voltaire (according to him) because he was too ill to make love.

'I live very easy at the Baronne's house.' He thought it would be a good idea for Thieriot to live easy there, too, but the Baronne was no fool; she refused to fall in with this plan. She also, quite rightly, refused to harbour a new friend and protégé of Voltaire's, the Abbé Linant. Linant, who came from Rouen where his mother kept a tavern, was an unlucky find of Cideville's. He had literary ambitions and was writing a tragedy of ancient Rome. Cideville sent him to Voltaire, who soon became quite obsessed with him, bothering all his friends to find some agreeable, well-paid job for the Abbé. He admitted to Cideville, however, that it was not easy to place Linant, who was neither attractive nor well-read, whose writing was too illegible for secretarial work, who stammered too much to be a reader and who possessed the amiable virtue of idleness. Never mind, this excellent fruit would no doubt ripen.

In January 1733 Mme de Fontaine-Martel was taken ill, and Voltaire had to tell her that she was dying. She had no desire to see a priest, but he insisted that she should, fearing that if she did not people would say that he had prevented her from doing so. He went out himself and found one. He had never become fond of her and was jocular about the way in which she received the Sacrament. She did not die in his arms. His only regret was for the excellent house of which he had been master and the 40,000 livres a year which had been spent on his pleasures.

Mme de Fontaine-Martel's last words were very strange: 'What time is it?' 'Two o'clock, Madame.' 'Ah,' said she, 'how consoling to think that whatever time it may be there is somebody preventing the extinction of our race.'

# Chapter Four

## Emilie Inherits Voltaire

THE GREAT question now was not who would inherit Mme de Fontaine-Martel's fortune and furniture but who would inherit Voltaire? Her house had been a centre of merriment for the whole of Paris while he lived there; what lucky person would now carry off this fascinator? The answer was not long in coming. Voltaire took a lodging in a wretched neighbourhood and a hideous house, behind the Hôtel de Ville. Here, one summer evening, 1733, he received a surprise visit: the three angels appearing to Abraham, he said. Two of the angels were lovers, the Duchesse de Saint-Pierre and M. de Fourqualquiers; they were chaperoning Voltaire's new friend, the Marquise du Châtelet. The occasion was very cheerful. Whereas the three angels had supped with Abraham, Voltaire's angels, fearing perhaps that the food in his bachelor establishment would not be up to much, preferred to take him to an inn where they ate fricassée of chicken. Just as well: 'Marianne, my cook, would have screamed at the idea of such a supper-party in this slum.' Voltaire probably showed his visitors the view, from his window, of the façade of Saint-Gervais saying that it was the only friend his *Temple du Goût* had made him. It was a joke he was very fond of and had a certain truth.

*Le Temple du Goût* had just appeared and hardly had a single supporter. Most people nowadays would agree with the choice of writers, artists and monuments which

46

Voltaire allowed into the temple. They include Mme de Lafayette, Mme de Sévigné, Pascal (with reservations), the inimitable Molière, Racine who was Voltaire's favourite poet, La Fontaine; Poussin, Lebrun, Le Sueur, Le Vau, Perrault and his *cour carrée* at the Louvre, the fountains of Jean Goujon and Bouchardon, the Porte Saint-Denis and the façade of Saint-Gervais. 'All these monuments are neglected by the barbarous masses as well as by frivolous society people.' His exclusions are more questionable. Notre Dame, 'cluttered up with rubbishy old ornament', is one. (The hatred of Gothic art in France during the eighteenth century was extravagant: one wonders that any was allowed to survive.) The chapel at Versailles and 'that monument of bad taste' which was being built by Servandoni, the church of Saint-Sulpice, were also excluded from the temple. Perhaps nothing arouses such strong feelings in the breasts of civilized human beings as questions of taste and Voltaire laid down the law in a very provocative manner. Even Cideville said that his feelings were hurt by some of the statements. The Comte de Caylus, a great collector and connoisseur but a disagreeable man, who was praised in the poem, asked that his name should be removed from it.

Voltaire had rashly attacked the whole body of literary critics, 'cowardly persecutors . . . who used to pretend that Scudéry was greater than Racine,' as well as various contemporary writers, including Jean-Baptiste Rousseau and the Abbé Desfontaines. This stirred up a hornets' nest and the hornets began to buzz. At the Marionettes there was a skit on *Le Temple du Goût* which was both coarse and cruel. Polichinelle is ill—comes the doctor— orders a good beating and a purge—after which the *Temple du Goût* is carried on to the stage, in the shape of an object that can be imagined. Voltaire, by bothering all his powerful friends, had this parody taken off. Another one then appeared at the Comédie-italienne in which Voltaire, dressed as an Englishman in checks, made idiotic remarks on the subject of taste. Voltaire never could bear parodies of his works; he was now so furious that he became ill with inflammation of the bowels.

In the middle of this fuss about his *Temple*, Voltaire was courting Emilie. The day after the angels' visit he wrote a letter to the Duchesse de Saint-Pierre which was clearly meant to be read, over her shoulder, by another angel. 'The charming letters that you write, Madame, and those sent you by somebody else turn the head of the people who see them. . . . I no longer venture to write in prose since I have read yours and that of your friend.' It was natural that he and Mme du Châtelet should be attracted to each other. He had come back from England imbued with the scientific discoveries of Newton and the philosophical teaching of Locke. There were few people in Paris with whom he could discuss such matters, certainly no woman except Emilie. The French academic scientists were still Cartesians and looked with the greatest suspicion at the new ideas from England. Emilie, however, young, ardent, with a brilliant scientific mind, not only understood what he was talking about but was quite ready to be convinced by his arguments. She loved to learn; the tutor-pupil aspect of their relationship was not the least of its charms in the eyes of both. Voltaire was gratified, too, by her rank and the enormous privileges which she enjoyed at Court. He was never insensible to such trivia, least of all now. It was soothing to his pride that a woman of genuine social importance should become his mistress. His love-affairs had hitherto been rather insignificant, but he had never been without one until his exile had put an end to that with Mme de Bernières. In England we hear of whores and Laura Harley, who, most likely, only provided him with an exercise in English verse:

'Laura, would you know the passion
You have kindled in my breast?'

After that, for four years nothing at all (unless, indeed,
he had a little fancy for the Abbé Linant? His preoccupation with the chubby fellow is so difficult to account
for otherwise.) Voltaire could not live without feminine
company: 'the only difference between men and women
is that women are more amiable'. But he was never a
very ardent lover, even in his youth. He met Emilie only
a few weeks after having announced that he was too ill to
make love, and he once said: 'I feel that it is ridiculous
for me to be in love.' A man who has had this feeling is
incapable of passion such as Emilie would have liked to
inspire. However, the compensations were great. Voltaire may never quite have satisfied her physical nature
or her romantic cravings, but for many years she was con-
tented with what he did give. The most famous, most
amusing man in the world was pulling out his conjuring-
tricks for her and her alone. It was not nothing.

Falling in love inspired both of them to hard work.
Emilie was learning English conversation from Voltaire;
in three weeks she spoke fluently and thereafter they
often talked together in English. She was also learning
algebra from Maupertuis. Typical society woman, she
had no compunction about eating up his time and pick-
ing his brains; she complained if he was not always at
her disposal. Soon she wanted much more than lessons
from him; she fell in love with him, too. Maupertuis was
then about thirty-five, handsome, hard-hearted, attractive to women. He does not seem to have responded to
Emilie's amorous advances very warmly, but we have
only her letters, not his. 'I shall be at home all day; come
and see if you can teach me to elevate a nomos to a given
force.' 'I have no more work unless you set me a task; I
desire one extremely.' 'Come today at 6.00.' 'It is not

surprising that when one leaves you one should think of nothing but the pleasure of seeing you again.' 'My life, at present, is very disorganized; I am dying; my soul needs you as my body needs repose.' 'I love you as much as if you had been here this evening.'

Emilie was not only engaged in absorbing the lessons of two famous masters. She led an energetic social life, with her bosom friend the Duchesse de Saint-Pierre. They went together to the Opera, the Jardin du Roi (the Zoo), to various cafés and to the meetings of the Académie des Sciences. At all these places Mme du Châtelet gave a rendezvous to Maupertuis. She also took him to see her mother, now a widow living at Creteil, near Paris. Emilie was always able to cram more into a single day than most women into a week; she was as strong as an ox and required very little sleep. If necessary she could work all night; indeed she liked to do so because then she knew she would be left in peace.

Unfortunately, except for two or three little notes, the entire correspondence between Voltaire and Mme du Châtelet has disappeared. They were both enormous letter writers: even when living in the same house they wrote to each other. She was disconcertingly frank when she put pen to paper, saying all that came into her head. If we could see her letters to Voltaire at this time we should know more about her feeling for him. Those she wrote to Maupertuis make it hard for a twentieth-century reader to believe that she could have been engaged in an absorbing love affair with somebody else. But Emilie's view of human relationships had not been muddled by the romantic movement. Voltaire had much to give, but he was ill, more than usually just then. Maupertuis gave something else. Emilie took what she wanted from both of them.

Voltaire had many another reason for being jealous of Maupertuis, who shadowed his footsteps. They had been in England at the same time and Maupertuis had been made a Fellow of the Royal Society. He, too, was an enthusiastic disciple of Newton and no doubt understood his scientific teaching better than Voltaire did. He, too, was trying to convert the French from Descartes to Newton; he had already written several papers on the subject. He, too, was a favourite in society, though of bourgeois origins. Later on, when Voltaire went to Germany, there was Maupertuis, President of the Berlin Academy with a high-born Prussian wife. In the end the accumulated bile of some twenty years turned Voltaire against him and he literally killed the poor man with ridicule. But, in 1733, they were on friendly terms.

Voltaire, surrounded by workmen in his new lodging, was finishing his *Lettres Philosophiques*. He was also rehearsing *Adélaïde du Guesclin*; writing an opera for Rameau; writing a piece against Pascal, which he truly predicted would annoy everybody (even though he was good enough to pass over Pascal's silly views on miracles); finding a lodging for Linant and sitting him down to write a tragedy on the subject of *Rameses*. He also showered poems on Emilie: 'I write no verses now, except to her.' No wonder he said that the days were too short and that writers ought to be given a double ration of them.

His interest was centred in what he called his "*Lettres philosophiques, politiques, critiques, hérétiques, diaboliques*"; letters supposed to have been written to Thieriot while Voltaire was in England. Thieriot himself was now there with Voltaire's authority to publish the *Lettres* in London and use the money which they earned. In August 1733 they appeared under the title of *Letters Concerning the English Nation* and were soon selling like hot cakes. Naturally enough, the English did not object to them. In Voltaire's own words, they were heretics who did not care a fig for the Pope and who were quite ready to acclaim the works of the devil himself. Besides, the

*Lettres* were nothing if not flattering to their race and
nation. Voltaire knew that in France they would make
a greater scandal than anything he had ever written. He
half dreaded their appearance and half longed for it; he
had unwisely given the manuscript to a publisher at
Rouen called Jore, whom he then bombarded with
letters, begging him in no circumstances to allow anybody to see it. In July he told Jore that a police spy
had been sent to Rouen by the *Garde des Sceaux** to find
out what he could about the book. Jore must hide the
manuscript and the copies already printed and above
all not let a single copy out of his own hands. Public
opinion must be prepared to receive the *Lettres*, the
storm over *Le Temple du Goût* given time to subside, a
suitable patron must be found and above all a suitable
moment chosen before they could appear in print. Voltaire repeated these arguments over and over again, to
Jore himself and to Cideville, at Rouen, who was to im-
press them on the publisher. He also sent Jore quite a
large sum of money so that he should not be out of
pocket by the delay.

Voltaire was ill all that winter, in bed off and on, for
months. He had not recovered from the intestinal
troubles caused by the parodies of his *Temple*; he was
worried about the *Lettres Philosophiques*; *Adélaïde du Guesclin* came on in January and failed; there is no proof that
Emilie was much of a comfort to him at this time, and the
Abbé Linant, who was living with him, was thoroughly
on his nerves. The wretched little fellow went to bed
every evening at seven only to rise again after midday;
he was eating his head off and constantly demanded
more pocket-money. Voltaire got him a pass for the
Comédie-française so that he could study the art of
writing plays; he would go off there, dressed and pow-

* Keeper of the Seals; but often, as in this case, possessing also
the powers and pecuniary rewards of the Chancellor.

dered like the son of a prince, and gossip for hours with the actors and actresses at the Café Procope, opposite the theatre. Yet he made no headway at all with *Rameses*. Voltaire, to whom time was so precious, hated above everything to see it wasted.

# Chapter Five

## The Richelieu Wedding

THE LOVE affair, after its flourishing start, really seemed in danger of being submerged by the various distractions which beset the lovers. However, in April 1734, Voltaire rose from his sick-bed, which at one moment had looked like becoming his death-bed, and the two of them went jaunting off to a country wedding in Burgundy. The Duc de Richelieu was marrying Mlle de Guise. The bride was a relation of the Marquis du Châtelet; the bridegroom an old love of the Marquise and the marriage was made by Voltaire. The bride's father, the Prince de Guise, was one of his debtors. As soon as Voltaire had any spare cash he hastened to invest it, and a favourite security was loans to noblemen; he used to say that he was never let down by '*les grands*', and that even if they were not punctual about paying the interest they always did so in the end. Guise was a proper scoundrel; both he and his wife, who had died in 1732, were so well known for the irregularity of their conduct as to be almost *déclassés*, if such a thing were possible in that irregular century. These immoral people had produced a virtuous daughter with intellectual tastes and Voltaire had conceived the idea of marrying her to his friend Richelieu. He undertook all the negotiations, which were not easy. Richelieu was of mediocre origins, his dukedom having come from merit and not from ancient lineage; to make matters worse he was not even a Du Plessis (a noble but obscure county

54

family) like the Cardinal himself, but a Vignerot, descended from the Cardinal's sister. He minded; all his life it tormented him to feel that he was not as other dukes. He very much wanted this marriage which would improve his coat of arms. The family of Lorraine, however, to which Guise belonged and who considered themselves almost royal, refused to think of such an alliance. At last Voltaire, knowing that the Prince was in financial difficulties, made the magic suggestion that Richelieu should take the lady without a dowry. Guise allowed himself to be persuaded, the more readily because his daughter, to everybody's astonishment, declared herself well suited by the Duke. He seemed the last man in the world who would attract her, but like many another she had fallen in love with him.

Richelieu was one of the charmers of his age. Almost illiterate, though he knew a little astronomy, he was sharp and funny. He made both the Regent and Louis XV laugh so much that they forgave him everything; and there was a good deal to forgive, including treachery. He loved to invent mischievous anecdotes. It was he who put it about that Mme de Grignan hated her mother Mme de Sévigné; he also said he knew for a fact that Bossuet had secretly married a niece of Bussy-Rabutin, a story that was eagerly taken up by the Protestants. He swaggered through life like some hero of *opéra bouffe*, talking in a French equivalent of a cockney accent, which had been fashionable among the bloods of the Regency, killing his enemies in duels and carrying off fair ladies under their husband's noses. More than one royal princess had been in love with him. No woman of fashion felt that she was in the swim unless she had been his mistress, even if only for a few days. He was a dashing and successful, though unscientific, soldier; not for him the drudgery of reading maps, organizing supplies or planning campaigns. Above all things he adored battles and afterwards he loved to pillage, rape and loot with his soldiers. Unfaithful in most of his other dealings, he was a faithful friend to Voltaire from the days of Louis-le-Grand; their friendship survived everything, even the huge sums of money which Voltaire lent him. 'A great betrayer of women but essential for men.' Voltaire's advice to the couple not to love each other too much, since that is the surest way of loving for ever, was intended no doubt for the bride. If Richelieu, however, were capable of loving one woman, rather than the whole female sex, that woman was his own dowdy wife. He went to a great deal of trouble to conceal his amorous escapades from her; and she was happy with him.

The wedding took place at the Château of Montjeu, the Prince de Guise's country seat. Two cousins of the bride, the Princes de Lixin and de Pons, refused to attend it, professing themselves disgusted by the misalliance. Otherwise everything went off well and the Richelieus were duly put to bed by the assembled company. Voltaire, who was delighted to have been a prime mover in the business, wrote to various friends: 'So I have come 240 miles to see a man in bed with a woman', as if it had all been rather tiresome. Three days later the bridegroom went back to the army which, commanded by the Duke of Berwick, was besieging Philippsburg in Germany.

The wedding guests stayed on to keep Mme de Richelieu company and all was merry as a wedding bell when a startling piece of news arrived from Paris. The *Lettres Philosophiques*, including the *Pensées sur Pascal*, most dangerous of all the letters, were being sold there under the counter. Voltaire's name was on the title page, but even had it not been he could hardly have denied having written the book which had been out for months in England. He now flew into a state of acute alarm, seized his pen and wrote to everybody he knew who could possibly help him. He told Cideville and Mme du Deffand that when he first wrote the letters he had decided to make his home in England, but that he found he missed his friends too much. Now, of course, he had a new reason for not wishing to live abroad.

He had been betrayed, he said to Cideville, by 'your protégé, Jore'. (Cideville was always being scolded for having produced Linant. He never answered back, or pointed out that Voltaire was old enough to choose his own publishers and friends.) Probably Jore was to blame, but it is impossible to know the truth of the matter for certain. Voltaire had moved in a maze of double-dealings and lies over these letters ever since they first appeared in England. He had not written them to see them moulder indefinitely in a Rouen warehouse, and may well have taken the opportunity of his absence from Paris to have them put on the market. This was pointed out by Jore in no uncertain terms. However, the evidence is on the side of Voltaire, who seems to have done all he could to stop Jore from publishing, given the silly indiscretion of letting him have the manuscript in the first place. Jore stood to make enormous sums with the book, of which 1,500 copies at ten livres apiece had been sold in a few days. Furthermore, such illicit publishing was in the tradition of his family; his father had had several Bastilles during the reign of Louis XIV. It must have been worth their while, in terms of cash.

The party at Montjeu waited breathlessly for the post from Paris. The news got worse and worse. Jore was in the Bastille, Voltaire's house had been searched and there was a *lettre de cachet* out against him. As the authorities had no real desire to imprison this eminent man, they allowed him to be warned in time to get away from Montjeu, which he did with all possible speed. Two days after his departure the *lettre de cachet*, ordering him to report at once to the prison-fortress of Auxonne, was delivered to Mme du Châtelet. But the bird had flown. 'I have a mortal aversion to gaol.'

Mme du Châtelet's letters now breathe despair, and no wonder. She had been envisaging a long, peaceful life with her lover, and now their happiness seemed to be destroyed for ever. She was afraid he would be caught and put in a dungeon which, delicate as he was, might easily kill him, or where he might languish for years. At best he would have to live in exile where she would not be able to follow him. For a while she felt sure he had been arrested on leaving Montjeu; the lack of news added to her misery. She wrote to Richelieu: 'What is the use of being young? I wish I were fifty, living in some country place with my unfortunate friend, Mme de Richelieu and you. Alas! We spend our lives making plans to be happy and we never suceed!' Her great consolation was her friendship with Mme de Richelieu, whom she truly loved. She implanted Newton's ideas in the mind of the young woman so thoroughly that a few months later Mme de Richelieu confounded a Cartesian Jesuit, to the admiration of some English tourists who were present. The fact that she was hardly grown up, and a Duchess, added to the interest they felt in this performance. Voltaire said of her that she really did seem to understand the rudiments of philosophy.

Soon the time came when Mme du Châtelet must leave Montjeu and go back to Paris. Here she began to agitate on Voltaire's behalf with such energy and disregard of appearances that even he cried caution. It was too much, he said, people would begin to talk in a disagreeable way about their friendship. The whole affair was worse for Mme du Châtelet than for Voltaire. He was so well hidden, probably in Lorraine, that to this day nobody knows for certain where he went. The innumerable letters he wrote were posted in towns as far apart as Dijon and Basle, no doubt by travellers to whom he gave them. He had no intention of going to prison: he felt sure that he would wriggle out of the mess and meanwhile had the satisfaction of knowing that everybody in Paris was reading his book. He pretended to be indignant at the thought of society women and loungers in cafés discussing the rival merits of Newton and Descartes: in fact that was the object of his work. He never, himself, had an original philosophical idea, but he had a genius for simplifying the ideas of others so that society women and loungers in cafés could grasp them. 'If I had not cheered up the subject (*égayé la matière*) nobody would have been scandalized; but then nobody would have read me.'

It was not only Voltaire's philosophical ideas and the attack on Pascal that were provoking anger in Paris, anger which this time was by no means confined to the Church and State. The theme of the *Lettres*, repeated over and over again, was that everything English was true and orderly, everything French rotten with frivolity and reaction. The English are free men, the French are enslaved by superstition, tyranny, and unreasonable laws. They have forgotten how to think. The serious English give their Kings a fair trial and then execute them. The capricious French assassinate theirs. English clergymen are old and married; when they get drunk they do it earnestly without causing a scandal. There are no gay young *Abbés de Cour*, no boy bishops in England. Which is the more valuable citizen, a French nobleman who can tell you exactly what time the King gets up and goes to bed, or an English merchant who gives orders to Surat and Cairo from his office, contributes to the happiness of the world and enriches his country? The English had a theatre long before the French. It was created by Shakespeare, a genius of force and fecundity though without a ray of taste or any knowledge of the rules of drama. No people in the world love a public hanging so much as the English and this partly accounts for the success of his plays, in which he loads the stage with corpses. Literature is more honoured in England than in France, and if there were an English Academy of Letters it would be vastly superior to that ridiculous institution the Académie-française. English doctors are stamping out the dreaded smallpox with the simple process of inoculation. The French medical profession, of course, is far too hidebound to allow its patients to benefit by this discovery. As for philosophy, a Frenchman arriving in London finds everything upside-down. In Paris the universe is composed of whirlwinds which do not exist in London. Voltaire then proceeds to demonstrate the superiority of Newton as a thinker over Descartes.

To say that the French were displeased would be putting it mildly. The whole reading public was in a rage. How dared Voltaire set the barbarous English, heretics and regicides, above the civilized French? How dared he compare their primitive literature with that which had produced Racine? Shakespeare indeed! And what of Grévin, who lived at the same time and wrote a splendid play about Julius Caesar? 'The English are very welcome to this deserter from our land,' said Mathieu Marais.

As angry as anybody were the scientists. Nationalism had a strong influence on eighteenth-century thought. The French were prejudiced in favour of Descartes because he was French; it was years before Voltaire, Maupertuis and other philosophers were able to get Newton accepted in academic circles. In the same way, the Germans, in spite of Frederick the Great's efforts to impose Newton on them, could never really be weaned from Leibnitz, because he was German.

On 10 June the *Lettres Philosophiques* were torn to pieces and burnt outside the Palais de Justice. 'Scandalous, against religion, decent behaviour and the respect due to the powers that be.' When he received the news Voltaire merely remarked that another time he would say a great deal more.

Richelieu, back at the siege of Philippsburg, found himself in the same army group as his wife's cousins, the Prince de Lixin and the Prince de Pons. The Prince de Conti, who was commanding a regiment, gave a party to celebrate his own seventeenth birthday. Richelieu was an old friend of the Prince's father; he felt he could go to the party straight from a day in the trenches, without changing his clothes. When the Prince de Lixin saw him he remarked in a loud voice that M. de Richelieu, in spite of his marriage, still seemed to have a good deal of dirt clinging to him. The Duke called him out; they decided to fight at once, because fighting among officers was forbidden and they were afraid of being stopped. So they proceeded, with their friends, to a deserted place behind the trenches and told the servants to light flares. These attracted the enemy's fire, and the duel took place amid falling shells; the Germans soon found the range and one of the servants was killed. The opponents were evenly matched; Lixin almost immediately wounded Richelieu in the thigh. The Duke's seconds, who were liking the situation less and less, urged him to give up. He refused and the fight went on a good long time. In the end Richelieu ran Lixin through the heart. The officers present, thankful to be alive themselves, carried the two principals off the field, one to his grave and the other to the hospital.

News of the duel reached Voltaire, rather exaggerated as Richelieu was said to be dying. Voltaire did not hesitate; he ordered his carriage and set forth for Philippsburg. He truly loved the Duke and felt a certain responsibility since the marriage had been of his making. However, he found his friend already convalescent and very waggish about Voltaire's troubles. Of course, said Richelieu, the scoundrel, up to his tricks as usual, had himself arranged for the *Lettres Philosophiques* to be published while he was safely out of Paris. The noblemen at the Duke of Berwick's headquarters were delighted to see Voltaire and he soon fell into the jolly life of the camp, all the jollier for his own arrival. Three gay young Princes of the Blood, the brothers Clermont and Charolais and the Prince de Conti, gave parties for him and made much of him. However, they very soon got stern messages from Paris telling them to desist; it was considered quite out of order that, while the King's police were looking everywhere for M. de Voltaire, he should be making merry with the King's cousins at the front. Besides, a battle seemed imminent; Voltaire felt that the moment had come to be off. Once more he ordered his carriage.

# Chapter Six

## Cirey

THIS TIME Voltaire went to Cirey, a country house in Champagne belonging to the du Châtelets. Isolated in woodlands full of iron-foundries and forges that had been worked there since Roman times, it was a very suitable hiding place since its inhabitants could arrange to be warned if the police were about to descend upon them. The Lorraine frontier, too, was within easy reach. Cirey's foundations were tenth century; it had twice been razed to the ground, during the wars of the League and after the conspiracy of Gaston d'Orléans. Du Châtelet's great-grandfather had partly rebuilt it, but it had stood empty for many years and Voltaire found it unfurnished and derelict. Here Emilie and Voltaire had decided to pursue their *amours philosophiques*, far from the dangers and distractions of the capital. She told Richelieu that she could not imagine not wanting to live quietly in the country with her loved one. Also, she said, in Paris she would be sure to lose him sooner or later. As for Voltaire, he was tired of trying to keep house on his own; he had reached the age when a man likes to settle down and be looked after by some charming woman.

Emilie stayed on in Paris where she continued her lessons with Maupertuis, her social life and her gambling. She may have been unable to go to Cirey at once owing to the illness of her baby, aged sixteen months. He died in September. The death of a child was seldom regarded then as a great misfortune. Parents saw very little of their children and one or two in a family were rather expected to die. To her own surprise, however, Mme du Châtelet minded. She sent a note the next day to Maupertuis, saying that she must admit to being very sad indeed. If he cares to come and console her, he will find her alone. She has told the servants she does not wish to see anybody, but there is no occasion on which the sight of him would not give her extreme pleasure. She did not, even then, hurry off to Cirey but stayed on in Paris until Maupertuis left for Switzerland several weeks later. Voltaire was alone for nearly three months.

He had put in hand a large scheme of building and decorating at Cirey. He filled the house with masons and plasterers; outside he planned terraces, gateways and alleys. As society was necessary to his happiness, he paid court to two neighbours, the young Comtesse de la Neuville and youngish Mme de Champbonin. When the builders made him too uncomfortable he would go and stay with Mme de la Neuville, and Mme de Champbonin would drive over and play backgammon with him. This jolly, fat creature became, and remained, his slave. (She already knew Mme du Châtelet with whom she had been at school.) When he was at Cirey, both women supplied him with constant gifts of game, poultry and peaches which were acknowledged in prose and in verse, heavily larded with compliments. 'Paris is where you are.' Delicious words, to a provincial lady.

At last, in October, Emilie appears, arriving just as Voltaire is reading a letter from her telling him not to expect her for a while. She has brought hundreds of parcels and more chaos than ever to the house. 'We have now got beds without curtains, rooms without windows, lacquer cabinets and no chairs, charming phaetons and no horses to draw them.' Mme du Châtelet has had a terrible journey, shaken to pieces in an uncomfortable carriage, and has not slept, but she is in tearing spirits. She laughs and jokes and makes nothing of the difficulties of getting into a new house. Voltaire, under the charm, hardly even protests when she changes all his dispositions, puts doors where he had ordered windows and staircases where he had planned to have chimneypieces. Luckily he has not planted a kitchen garden, for if he had she would certainly be turning it into a *parterre*. All this is told to Mme de Champbonin, Voltaire's *aimable Champenoise*, without whom he cannot live. Since there is no bed for her (why, oh why must three people have three beds?) they will send a phaeton light as a feather and drawn by horses the size of elephants so that she can come and spend the day. It is really unthinkable that friends should be kept apart simply for the want of a bed or two. Mme de la Neuville is out of action as she is expecting a baby, but Voltaire will drive Mme du Châtelet over to see her as soon as he has finished being the odd man at Cirey. When the visitors' rooms are ready both these charming neighbours must come and share his happiness. Voltaire wrote as if he were lord of the manor and husband of its lady. Du Châtelet was bravely fighting the Germans, serene in the knowledge that his property was being improved and his wife getting on with her mathematics. Voltaire paid for everything at Cirey, but, practical as always, kept accounts and considered the money as having been lent to du Châtelet.

Emilie went back to Paris for Christmas. Her friends said she led such a dissipated life there that it was impossible to see her. She spent a great deal of time with the Richelieus and resumed her pursuit of Maupertuis. On Christmas Eve: 'I'd sooner be at Cirey and you at Basle than see as little of you as I do. I wish to celebrate the birth of Elohim with you. Why don't you come and drink his health with Clairaut and me? I'll expect you between eight and nine. We'll go to Midnight Mass and hear the Christmas hymns on the organ, and I'll take you home afterwards. I count on this, unless Mlle Delagni opposes it.'

Voltaire once more stayed alone at Cirey. He had plenty to do. Work on the house was still in progress, he was writing *Alzire*, he had begun *La Pucelle*, his health was an occupation in itself and he conducted a correspondence that grew daily larger. To Thieriot, in English: 'You tell me you are ready to leave England and come to me. Is it very true? Can you give me such a token of your heart? . . . Let not be your proposal a transient enthusiasm of a tender soul but the firm resolution of a strong and virtuous mind. Come, my dear, I conjure you to do it. It is most certain I have but few years to live, do not debar me from the pleasure of passing these moments with you . . . Literature is nothing without a friend, and a friend illiterate is but dry company; but a friend like you is a treasure.'

In his post-bag from Paris he received young Crébillon's *Contes Japonais* (full of obscenities and sly digs at such various subjects as the Duchesse du Maine and the Bull *Unigenitus*). He said that if he, himself, had written them he would have been sent to the Bastille. Very soon he heard that young Crébillon had gone to the Bastille. Voltaire observed that the State never minds how much it spends on keeping authors in prison, but if the question arises of some tiny pension for an author, that can never be afforded. This was not quite fair. Voltaire himself was receiving a comfortable little pension from the Queen, who had even continued it while he was in England.

'And how is *Rameses* getting on?' he asked Cideville, who had had Linant with him at Rouen. 'I am sure it must be full of virile lines and brilliant reflections.' He added that the art of keeping up the interest of the public during five acts is a gift sent from God. In addition, each play has a curious destiny of its own, which never can be foretold until the curtain rises.

Voltaire had lent money to a certain Abbé MacCarthy who had gone to the East without repaying him. News now came that the Abbé had been circumcised and impaled, in Constantinople. Voltaire remarked that many people had owed him money but so far none of them had been impaled.

He began to wonder how the public would take to *Alzire*. If it miscarried, 'my enemies will be delighted; the Desfontaines of this world will seize the opportunity of holding me up to ridicule and contempt. For such is human injustice: nothing is punished so viciously as the desire to please, when that desire has failed.'

The Abbé Desfontaines, whom Voltaire had saved from the stake, was now his deadly enemy. Voltaire could not forget the lampoon which (according to Thieriot) the Abbé had written on coming out of Bicêtre. He hated the man and never lost an opportunity of hurting his feelings. For some obscure reason he had given the Abbé his *Essay on Epic Poetry* (written in English) to translate into French. Like all translators, the Abbé made one or two slips. Where Voltaire had written of 'cakes devoured by them', the Abbé's translation read 'the devouring hunger of Cacus (son of Vulcan)'. Voltaire flung himself upon this and other mistakes with eldritch shrieks and made the Abbé look a fool. He could not leave the poor fellow's weakness alone, called him 'il buggerone abbate' and made sly allusions to 'les petits Savoyards'. (Paris sweeps are nearly all Savoyards to this day.) He stressed the fact, in and out of season, that he had snatched Desfontaines from the jaws of death. In short he was exceedingly unkind to the Abbé. Desfontaines was not a noble character; he did not turn the other cheek. He, too, had a talent for annoying and he had a powerful weapon: *Observations sur les écrits modernes,* a literary review of which he was the editor. Voltaire, who so loved teasing, was himself a very satisfactory subject for it; he never failed, as schoolboys say, to rise. Not for him the curled lip and contemptuous silence; nobody has ever been so easily aroused to rage. He enjoyed a battle. He liked all forms of human relationship and in some ways his enemies were more necessary to him than his friends. Literary enmities were never lacking.

He had long been at daggers drawn with Jean-Baptiste Rousseau. This popular poet, twenty-three years older than Voltaire, had once shown him an *Ode à la Postérité*, and Voltaire, unable to resist a joke, said that he feared the Ode would never reach its address. After this no punches were pulled. Rousseau was not so well-placed as Desfontaines to do harm to Voltaire, for he was in exile and disgrace at Brussels. He would really have been quite pleased to come to terms, but used to say, 'What can I do? The war is begun and must be carried on.'

Voltaire seldom liked other middle-class writers and he would go out of his way to pick quarrels with them. Piron, a humble Burgundian, came to Paris filled with admiration for Voltaire whom he longed to meet. Mme de Mimeure, also a Burgundian, Voltaire's mistress at the time, took Piron under her wing. She said to him one day, 'Go into my dining-room and there you will find Voltaire.' Sure enough there he was, huddling over the fire. When he saw Piron he pretended to be asleep. Piron sat and stared at him and in the end Voltaire could not keep it up. He took a bit of bread out of his pocket and began to nibble it, explaining that he had an illness which made it imperative for him to eat all day. Piron then produced a flask and said he had an illness which made it imperative for him to drink all day. The great man was not amused. Piron endured many insults from Voltaire before he became another implacable enemy.

One critic whom Voltaire placed in a different category from 'les Desfontaines' was the Abbé Prévost, author of *Manon Lescaut*, who ran a literary paper called *Le Pour et Contre*. The only things he had against him were his tonsure (a disgrace to humanity) and his lack of fortune. Whereas Desfontaines is a literary hack, Prévost is a man. It is very easy to see the difference between their natures, in what they write. One is clearly only fit to run after little boys; the other made for love. If ever Voltaire can render him a service he will be happy to do so.

If Voltaire, on the whole, detested the critics, 'insects of a single day', he felt differently about the public. It was an axiom with him that a play which does not succeed is a bad play, a book which has been allowed to go out of print a rotten book. 'No interesting play ever fails.' There were, according to his reckoning, about 4,000 educated play-goers in Paris and he was prepared to accept their verdict. It must be said that this attitude was made easier for him by the fact that all his books were best sellers and his plays seldom missed the mark.

Largely through the efforts of Mmes du Châtelet and de Richelieu, Voltaire was allowed to go back to Paris at the end of March 1735. The Chief of Police, who had been at school with him, sent him this leave, and begged him, in future, to behave like a grown-up person. Voltaire hurried off at once, but when he arrived in the capital he did not care for what he found there. Maupertuis was now the darling of the salons. Dukes, Duchesses and pretty women had taken to science and were queueing up to have lessons with the great man; he was constantly at Versailles; Newton as expounded by Maupertuis was the modish topic of conversation; high society protested the advantage of the law of gravity over Cartesian whirlwinds. Much as Voltaire way supposed to love and admire Maupertuis—'tenderls attached to you for life—penetrated by the most tender esteem for you'—he was decidedly put out when he found that his great friend had become such a centre of interest.

He wrote, furiously, to Cideville: 'Now they've taken to reasoning. Sentiment, imagination and the graces are banished. Literature is visibly perishing. Of course, I am not displeased that philosophy should be cultivated, but it must not become a tyrant, to the exclusion of everything else. With the French, one fashion succeeds another, only to pass away in its turn.' Emilie was all in favour of this new trend and said, 'long may it last', but Voltaire was not so sure. However, he had something in his luggage that would stir up all these silly, amateur philosophers; something that would fix attention on him again, if only he dared to publish it; something that could put him in the Bastille for ever and in a dungeon at that, far from the Governor's excellent suppers. This barrel of gun-powder was *La Pucelle*, one of the most unseemly poems, according to Lord Morley, that exist in any tongue. Of all Voltaire's works *La Pucelle* was his own most cherished darling; for years he went on adding to it and polishing it up. It is a satirical poem, farcical in parts, about the Maid of Orléans in which religion, patriotism, virtue, courage, the Maid herself and most of Voltaire's friends are held up to irreverent mockery. Voltaire thought it intensely funny. When he felt low or depressed he would go and read it to himself and it never failed to send him into fits of giggles.

He also tells Cideville that the Abbé Linant has been to see him. He has grown enormously fat, and *Rameses*, which he read out loud, is no good at all. The actors would never consent to put it on and they would be quite right. It seems hardly possible that he could have done so badly when Voltaire himself has taken the trouble to find him such an excellent, interesting, one might almost

say cast-iron subject. Now the question is what can become of Linant? It will be difficult to place him as tutor
on account of his stammer, shortsightedness and lack of
education. However, Voltaire thinks Mme du Châtelet
might engage him for her little boy of nine. 'But Mme du
Châtelet has a husband, this goddess is married to a
mortal and the mortal takes it upon himself to have ideas
of his own.' This is the first time the goddess's lover ever
mentions the poor mortal.

Altogether the Paris visit was not a success, nor did it
last very long. Voltaire was warned that he had better
make himself scarce again. People had begun to talk
about *La Pucelle* which, needless to say, he had not left
quietly lying in his luggage. Eschewing the advice of
the Chief of Police and other friends to behave like a
grown-up person, he had been trotting the poem round
the salons, reading out little samples to whet the appetite of the Parisians and give them a rest from too much
science. He read some of it to Maurepas, a man who
loved to laugh. No doubt he did laugh, but he advised
Voltaire to keep it under lock and key, because it was
enough to get him shut up for life. Mme du Châtelet
told Richelieu that the short time Voltaire had been in
Paris had proved fatal; impossible to describe the agitation and excitement caused by *La Pucelle*. How could such
a clever man be so blind to his own danger? However,
she still loved him enough to give up the world and its
pleasures to go and live quietly with him alone.

Richelieu was still at the front. He had promised to
take du Châtelet in hand and explain the new situation
to him, pointing out that it would be foolish to be jealous
of a wife who suited him so well in every way. He must
get used to the idea of Voltaire living at Cirey. Like
many another woman Mme du Châtelet dreaded the
end of hostilities and the return of the warrior. She had
told Voltaire that everything was going to be all right

and that the three of them would get on famously together, but in her heart she was far from sure of it and
had a feeling that the whole thing might end badly.
Voltaire was also writing to Richelieu and urging him
to live with them at Cirey, on condition that he would
spare 'the beauty whom my heart adores'. Richelieu was
not the man to go back to an old mistress and there was
little danger in that direction. As a matter of fact he and
Mme du Châtelet had settled down to a particularly
comfortable friendship. She said she could not have believed that Richelieu would ever care for somebody who
was not necessary to his pleasure, who could not be useful
to him in any way, and who was not even a friend of his
mistress (at this time the Duchesse de Brancas). But care
he did; he was very fond of her.

Voltaire now went to Lorraine where he lay low, not
even announcing himself at the Court there until Mme
du Châtelet got word from the *Garde des Sceaux* that he
could live unmolested at Cirey. Richelieu also obtained
a guarantee for him. Reassured, he went back to Cirey
where he was joined by Mme du Châtelet; her daughter,
who was to go to a near-by convent, her son, and the new
tutor, M. (no longer l'Abbé) Linant. Voltaire had made
him abandon Holy Orders, saying: 'We'll have no
priests at Emilie's.' He was not much good as a tutor.
Mme du Châtelet was obliged to give him lessons in
Latin which he was supposed to pass on to his charge.
As usual he spent half his life sleeping. In his waking
moments he could find nothing more tactful to do than
make advances to Mme de la Neuville, which were very
badly received. Voltaire had to pacify her with a letter—
'He was quite carried away'—and some verses. At last
Linant pulled himself together and wrote a little poem to
the effect that a traveller coming upon Cirey might well
think it was a palace until he caught sight of Emilie
when he would realize that he was in a temple. This was

extravagantly applauded; Linant had the makings of a poet, after all.

Voltaire was in a calm, happy mood, for once. 'I am tasting, in absolute peace and a fully occupied leisure, the sweets of friendship and study with one who, unique among women, can read Ovid and Euclid and who possesses the imagination of the one allied to the precision of the other.' He had begun his *Siècle de Louis XIV*, which was not to be a history of the reign, still less a life of the King, but a picture of French civilization. It is written in the laconic, witty style which was to be borrowed with such effect by Lytton Strachey. 'The King reproached himself for his attachment to a married woman, and felt the scruple more deeply when he had ceased to be in love.' Voltaire was always asking his acquaintances for anecdotes of that reign: its end he himself could remember (he was nineteen when Louis XIV died) but its beginnings seemed incredibly remote. He loved to illustrate his writings with anecdotes and it is he who preserved for us the story of Newton and the apple. He thought that an historical study should be composed like a play, with a beginning, a middle and an end, not a mere collection of facts: 'If you want to bore the reader, tell him everything.'

Calm and happiness were soon succeeded, as usual, by a storm. On 21 August the boys at the Collège d'Harcourt put on Voltaire's *La Mort de César*. He described this play, written on his return from England, as 'a fairly faithful translation from an English author who lived 150 years ago called Shakespeare, the Corneille of London. He was quite mad, but wrote some admirable things'. *La Mort de César* had been acted once before by amateurs, but Voltaire had never published it. It seemed unlikely to please, since there were no women's parts and it was 'too Roman'. He was delighted to present it to the world in this way. It was, of course, a success. The friends and relations of the boys applauded wildly, two of the actors were said to be good enough for the Comédie-française; the production, in short, was greatly over-praised as amateur theatricals so often are. Voltaire was touched and amused. 'I now only write poetry for schools. I have renounced two theatres where intrigue is rife, the Comédie-française and the world.' He sent his compliments to all concerned. Then trouble began to brew. One of the young gentlemen at the Collège d'Harcourt, or possibly one of the professors, made an incorrect copy of *La Mort de César*, added a few dreadful verses of his own and sent it to a publisher. It came out, as pirated works often did, under an Amsterdam imprint. Voltaire was incensed by all the mistakes in the text: 'He has massacred Caesar more than Brutus and Cassius ever did.' Seeing a move ahead and hoping to forestall the worst, he quickly wrote to Abbé Desfontaines and told him exactly what had happened, 'so that he shall not pour his poisons into this wound'. Forlorn hope, of course. As soon as *il buggerone abbate* got hold of *La Mort de César*, he poured the poison of ridicule upon it, in his paper, *Observations*. He said, among other things, that Voltaire's Brutus was more of a Quaker than a Stoic, that it was contrary to public morals to put the assassination of Caesar on the stage and that though there were some fine verses, others were feeble and stiff, while many of the rhymes were detestable. But, far worse than any criticism, however annoying, he published Voltaire's letter to him, dated from Cirey. The whole world could now see, written in black and white, what was supposed to be a secret whispered among a chosen few: Voltaire was living with Mme du Châtelet in her husband's ancestral home. Richelieu needed all his tact and prestige to calm down du Châtelet; the Marquise's Breteuil relations, too, were very much annoyed.

Voltaire's pen never spluttered when he was in a rage. The letters which now filled his outgoing post were written as usual in his small, neat, legible handwriting; they were none the less furious for that. Words were not minced: 'How I repent of having pulled him out of Bicêtre and saved him from la Grève. Better to burn a priest than bore the public.' (His greatest insult was to call somebody a bore.* 'Oh what a bore you are,' he once wrote to Jean-Baptiste Rousseau, when all other epithets failed him.) Desfontaines, calm, aloof and irritating beyond words, said he was sorry but he could not admit that simply because a man had saved him from prison, he, a well-known critic, must praise that man's work to the end of time. He had his own integrity to consider. He put himself in the right over *César* by publishing a statement that the pirated edition had been defective. After this Voltaire calmed down a little for a while, soon to flare again into fury when Desfontaines printed one of his poems to Emilie after having been expressly told not to. Both the opponents were playing a dangerous game. Desfontaines could not afford to be denounced as a sodomite too often since he still was one and sodomy was still punishable by death. And in view of Voltaire's tricky relationship with 'Keeper', as he called the *Garde des Sceaux*, such criticism as that of Desfontaines might well be his undoing. Desfontaines cunningly pointed out all the revolutionary and free-thinking trends in Voltaire's work. It would have been greatly to the interest of each to leave the other alone. However '*qui plume a guerre a*', as Voltaire used to say; these were but minor skirmishes before the great battle was engaged between them.

In the middle of all this upset, Mme de Breteuil fell ill at her house near Paris and Mme du Châtelet had to hurry to her. She found her mother out of danger and

* *Ennuyeux.*

was only away for a week altogether. Her one idea was
to see Maupertuis. She wrote him a letter to be delivered
to him at once wherever he might be. 'If you still love
me a little, come and see me. You know my mother well
enough for that. If you wish, she need never know that
you are here.' But he neither replied nor came to her.

# Chapter Seven

## 'Les Amours Philosophiques'

LIFE AT Cirey began to take shape. Du Châtelet accepted the presence of Voltaire in his establishment; all was exactly as Emilie had hoped. Indeed the two men became fond of each other. The story that du Châtelet once caught out Voltaire with another woman and furiously reproached him for being 'unfaithful to us' is probably apocryphal, but quite in character. He was very dull but he accepted the fact that he had nothing to say to his wife's intellectual friends and never imposed his presence upon them. He liked large, regular meals, and greatly disliked the hours that Emilie and Voltaire kept. When they were working they had little snacks at any odd moment. So du Châtelet had his meals with Linant and the boy, dinner at midday and supper at eight. He was proud of his wife, but could do very well without too much of her company. In any case he was away with his regiment for months at a time.

The workmen finally packed up and left the house and it became possible to have guests. This was very important. Voltaire loved to see his friends and he needed a troupe of actors. Cut off from the Comédie-française, where he spent much of his time in Paris, he now had no means of seeing his plays on the boards when he wanted to put finishing touches to them. The solution was amateur theatricals. Voltaire contrived a tiny theatre in a loft, which still exists; when that was ready, anybody,

77

however dull, who could learn a part was welcome at Cirey. All the neighbours were roped in, Mme du Châtelet's little girl was often brought from the convent and made to act; du Châtelet, too, was forced on to the stage, putting up a remarkably poor performance.

The life of steady, quiet, regular work, which Voltaire so much wanted to lead, was not without interruptions. He still received occasional danger signals from friends at the Court which drove him into Holland for a few weeks, or he engaged in litigation which took him away from Cirey. A new quarrel with Jore ended in a lawsuit during the course of which it appeared that Voltaire (though he may well have been the injured party) had been telling lies. He was quite discredited; even such friends as the Duc de Richelieu shrugged their shoulders and refused to listen to his explanations. They persuaded him to withdraw. Then the du Châtelets were involved in one of those legal disputes which, in the eighteenth century, used to go on through several generations. Mme du Châtelet acted for her husband; this made it imperative for her to be sometimes at Brussels and Voltaire would go with her. But, from now on, their home was Cirey.

Here they lived, worked and conducted their famous love affair. Famous indeed it soon became. Jealous eyes were turned upon the lovers from all over Europe; not so much with sexual jealousy, as at the thought of their brilliant conversation wasted on the cold winds of Champagne. Their contemporaries could hardly bear it, since, of all forms of entertainment, conversation was rated the highest. Every scrap of news that came from Cirey, every doing and saying were noted with passionate interest. Parisian hostesses were as furious with Emilie for stealing Voltaire as if they had been theatrical managers and he a star. As time went on and they got angrier and angrier, so, according to them, Emilie became more and more unattractive. They hit out at her wildly. Mme du Deffand, supposed to be a friend, wrote and re-wrote her beastly pen-portrait of the great desiccated creature without any curves, covered with diamonds, and wearing cheap underclothes. Emilie's cousin, Mme de Créquy, said, 'We could never hear of the sublime genius and profound knowledge of Mme du Châtelet without bursting out laughing.' Such women have no yard-stick with which to measure an Emilie; when they are puzzled or a little frightened by something they often take refuge in idiotic laughter. None of this worried her while she was alive, nor can it detract from her now that she is dead. She was miles above such creatures—a superior person, as Sainte-Beuve said, '*pas une personne vulgaire*'. She was learned, which is rare enough in her sex. Her scientific and mathematical knowledge surpassed Voltaire's and was respected by those qualified to judge. Maupertuis may never have loved her but he had a real affection for her, 'beautiful as well as pretty, the best natured and most amiable woman in France'. 'Marvellous,' he said on another occasion, 'to find sublime knowledge which seems made for our sex, allied to the most lovable qualities of hers. Clever and witty as she was, there was no cattiness; she never said a horrid thing about anybody.' What sets her apart, of course, is Voltaire's regard for her. He was no fool where human beings were concerned, nor was he a knightly character. He was often, in fact, caddish and his pen easily ran away with him. He lived with Emilie in a deep intimacy and knew her inside out; only once or twice did he ever speak of her in disrespectful terms. These lapses have of course been seized upon and magnified. But nearly every day for sixteen years he wrote about her, in his letters, poems, epistles and dedications with loving praise. If he overdid it, giving rise to unkind remarks ('some wags may say they didn't realize they had slept

with such a great philosopher', wrote a friend of Cideville's), there is no doubt that his feelings were genuine.
It is a judgment that must be accepted. Mme du
Deffand saw that it would be, and she pretended that
Emilie was attached to Voltaire only because he brought
her into the limelight and would give her immortality.
At that time Mme du Deffand knew nothing about love
and its many strange manifestations. Her own poor old
sawdust heart had not yet begun to beat and break.

One of the first people to drop in at Cirey was a certain M. de Villefort, gentleman-in-waiting to the Comte
de Clermont. His account of the visit lost nothing in the
telling. He said that though he arrived in broad daylight
he found the house shuttered and in darkness. The
Marquise was informed of his presence and consented to
receive him, upon which he was led by a servant with a
lantern through several large deserted rooms. At last
they came to the enchanted regions; a door opened upon
a drawing-room lit by twenty candles. The Divinity sat
at a writing table covered with pieces of paper on which
she had scribbled x x, books and scientific instruments
lay all round her. She glittered with diamonds like an
operatic Venus. After a little conversation she suggested
that they should go and see Voltaire who was in his own
part of the house. They went up a secret staircase and
knocked at his door. In vain, the Magician was weaving
spells and the hour had not yet come for him to appear.
However, the rules were broken in favour of M. de
Villefort and he came and joined them. Presently a
bell rang and they all went to the dining-room which
had two hatches, one for the food and the other for the
dirty plates. No servant appeared; they helped themselves. (In France it is considered faintly improper for
rich people to help themselves at meals. Louis XV used
to do so when alone with his mistress or a few intimates
and the table, which came up through the floor with all

the food on it, is still shown at the Petit Trianon with more than a suspicion of a wink.) The food and wine were exquisite and the supper very long. When it was over, another bell rang to announce moral and philosophical readings. The guest was asked his permission and the readings took place. An hour later a bell rang for bedtime; the party broke up. At four in the morning there was another bell. A servant came to ask M. de Villefort if he would care to join a poetry reading which he did out of curiosity. Next day they had a picnic. Venus and Adonis in a chariot, the Stranger on horseback, proceeded to a little wood where they ate cutlets. They were followed by a second carriage full of books. The husband never appeared at all.

When this report came back, as it duly did, to Mme du Châtelet, she was annoyed. She said it was a fairy tale without rhyme or reason. Nevertheless certain elements of it are borne out by other visitors: the incessant work, Emilie's diamonds which she always wore, the curious hours kept at Cirey and the excellence of the fare. The lantern-lit walk through empty rooms was quite likely to have been true as they never did up the whole house but built a little wing for themselves. Their own rooms were luxurious and magnificently furnished.

Voltaire was now very rich. His fortune came neither from his books, which were too often pirated, nor from his plays, whose royalties he always gave to the actors, but from astute business dealings. He would exert himself to any extent, he would rise from a sick bed and travel across France, if he saw a good profit to be made. He had no wish for money troubles in addition to all his others and used to say that a man should live to work but not work to live. On one occasion, by a simple calculation which others had overlooked, he discovered that whoever bought up a certain percentage of a public lottery would win, in prizes, much more than the money

laid out. He raised enough cash to do this. The minister
of finance was furious when he realized what had happened, and tried to bring a law-suit, but he had no case
against Voltaire who was perfectly in order. On another
occasion he went the whole way to Lorraine from Paris
to subscribe to a State loan which seemed very advantageous. When he arrived in Nancy, ill and shaken by the
journey, he discovered that only native Lorrainers were
eligible. He made such a song and dance that the authorities allowed his subscription on the tenuous grounds
that his name, Arouet, was the same as that of the
Prince de Beauvau's castle near Nancy, Haroué. This investment trebled in a few months. Voltaire never kept all
his eggs in one basket and had interests in every sort of
commodity and enterprise: house property, army supplies, the Barbary trade and so on. The Paris brothers,
most powerful of all the financiers, were his friends and
often put him in the way of a good thing. He had a
talent for high finance and, almost as valuable, a devoted man of affairs: the Abbé Moussinot. Now that
Voltaire was living in the country he wrote to Moussinot
for everything he wanted from Paris. Oranges, books,
diamond shoe-buckles, a carpet 10 feet by 10, an enormous pot of face-cream from *Provost au signe des parfums*, a
thermometer that will not burst in boiling water (Fah-
renheit's is better than M. de Réaumur's), a silver
watch—quick, quick, for Mme du Châtelet's little boy,
he's ten years old, he'll certainly break it, but he wants
it—two or three fine sponges, 300 louis well packed up,
no need to declare them; all these things and many more
were put on the bi-weekly coach from Paris to Bar-sur-
Aube, the post town for Cirey. The Abbé distributed the
countless sums of money which Voltaire gave away to
friends, acquaintances and even to people he had never
seen but of whom he had heard some sad story. He collected the interest due to Voltaire from his debtors;

Richelieu and Guise were two very tough nuts and a great deal of persuasion had to be used on them when it was time for payment. Moussinot performed all sorts of other jobs. He was told to find some clever young man who could write all the Paris gossip once a week. He also looked out for pictures to add to Voltaire's collection which included, at this time, works by Teniers, Tiepolo, Watteau, Lancret, Albani, Marot and a pair of Galloches. Voltaire sometimes bought pictures purely as an investment, telling the Abbé that he had a certain sum to place and leaving the choice to him. Moussinot never let Voltaire down. He was much more than an agent, a loving and beloved friend, who could hardly be made to accept suitable remuneration for all the trouble he took.

Mme de Champbonin now had her own room at Cirey, and came and went as it suited her. The first guest from the outside world to stay there for any length of time was a twenty-three-year-old Venetian, Algarotti. He had decided that he wished to live among eminent folk and to this end had wisely acquired a knowledge of science which opened doors to him all over Europe. His attraction for both sexes did the rest. He was now on his way to England, to study philosophy, and was writing a simplification of Newton's theories intended for Italian women. Carlyle sees him as 'not supremely beautiful, though much the gentleman in manners as in ruffles and ingeniously logical; rather yellow, to me, in mind as in skin and with a taint of obsolete Venetian macassar'. Anyhow, he was tenderly loved, almost regarded as a son of the house at Cirey. But Emilie and Voltaire shook their heads in private over his *Newtonianismo per le dame*, which they thought too frivolous, with too many jokes and not enough stuffing. Emilie begged him to come whenever he liked and stay as long as he could. She pointed out that she and Voltaire each had an excellent library, hers being scientific and philosophical, and his literary and historical. Algarotti stayed, this first time, for a month, November 1735. When he left he turned out to be a poor letter-writer, and both the 'Emilians' scolded him constantly; however, he made up for this by returning to Cirey for another long visit the following year.

Like all those who live in the country, Voltaire and Mme du Châtelet greatly depended on the post-bag. They complained loudly if they thought that their friends did not write often enough, though they seldom praised a letter, except from royal personages. Lord Hervey, with whom Voltaire had been intimate in London, would have been a more agreeable acquaintance, they said, were he capable of answering a letter. He did not even acknowledge a book that Voltaire sent him, which was not only unfriendly but rude. Thieriot, lazy and selfish, was, of course, a hopeless correspondent. Cideville was better: he lived in the country and had more time. D'Argental, the guardian angel, was perfection in this as in every other way; but then he lived for Voltaire, his only other interest in life being the Comédie-française. He had been so passionately in love with Adrienne Lecouvreur that he had asked her to marry him in spite of her profession, reputation and illegitimate children. After her death he married a charming person, much loved by Voltaire and Emilie, a second angel. He was a pillar of the theatre, had great influence with the actors, and was particularly useful to Voltaire when he could not be in Paris to rehearse his own plays. Voltaire never minded how much he bothered and teased d'Argental, knowing quite well that all the trouble he took was a joy to him.

Maupertuis wrote sometimes 'from the pole'. He went off, in 1736, to Lapland where he expected to prove that Newton was right and the Cassinis, father and son, were wrong about the shape of the earth. Newton said that it was flatter at the poles, while the Cassinis thought that on the contrary it was elongated. Maupertuis was to measure the length of a degree of the meridian. This expedition, which included another friend of Emilie's, the scientist Clairaut, was financed by Louis XV; La Condamine was sent at the same time to the equator. Emilie told Richelieu that Maupertuis had only gone because he could not bear Paris without her. When Maupertuis duly brought back the measurements proving Newton to have been right he was said to have flattened the earth and the Cassinis; after this Voltaire dated letters to him such-and-such a time since the earth was flattened. Maupertuis also brought back a female Lapp who had enlivened his sojourn at the pole, and her sister. *Les tendres Hyperboréennes* seemed very much less attractive in Paris than in their native land; soon he longed to be rid of them. He opened a subscription to which Voltaire gave 100 livres and Emilie fifty; with the proceeds he placed one sister in a convent. The Duchesse d'Aiguillon's excellent butler found a husband for the other, but she turned out to be a disappointing wife, in fact a whore.

From London they heard that a rich, elderly Mr Bond, great admirer of *Zaïre*, had taken Covent Garden and was putting it on there. He himself was to act the part of Zaïre's Christian, nobly-born old father. On the night, he threw himself into it with such fervour that when the moment came for him to die in her arms, he did, actually, expire. This display of sensibility was very well received, at Cirey.

They also heard from London that Everard Fawkener, now a knight, had been appointed English Ambassador to the Porte. Voltaire begged him to go and stay with them at Cirey on his way there; Fawkener was unable to do this. When he had arrived at Constantinople Voltaire wrote to him, in English:

'Now the honest, the simple and good Philosopher of

Wandsworth represents his King and his country and is equal to the grand signior. Certainly England is the only country where commerce and virtue are to be rewarded with such an honour. If any grief rests still upon me, my dear friend (for friend you are, tho a minister) tis that I am unable to be a witness of your new sort of glory and felicity. Had I not regulated my life after a way that makes me a kind of solitary I would fly to that nation of savage slaves whom I hate, to see the man I love. What would be my entertainment and how full the overflowing of my heart, in contemplating my dear Fawkener amidst so many infidels of all hues, smiling with his humane philosophy on the superstitious follies that reign on the one side at Stamboul and on the other at Galata. I would not admire, as says mylady Mary Wortley:

> The vizier proud distinguished from the rest
> Six slaves in gay attire his bridle hold
> His bridles rich with gems, his stirrups gold

For how the devil should I admire a slave upon a horse? My friend Fawkener I should admire. But I must bid adieu to the great town of Constantin and stay in my little corner of the world, in that very same castle where you was invited to come in your way to Paris, in case you should have taken the road from Calais to Marseilles. Your taking the other way was certainly a great disappointment to me and especially to that lady who makes use of your locks* and more of your books. Upon my word, a french lady who reads Newton, Locke, Adisson and Pope and who retires from the bubbles and stunning noise of Paris to cultivate in the country the great and amiable genius she is born with, is more valuable than your Constantinople and all the turkish empire. You may confidently write to me by Marseilles

* Brought over from England by Thieriot at Voltaire's request.

chez madame la marquise du Chatelet at Cirey en Champagne. Be sure I shall not stir from that spot of ground before the favour of your letter comes to me.

'You will see perhaps a renegado, the bastard off-spring of an Irishman who went at Paris by the name of Makarty, a bold busy stirring and not scrupulous man. He had the honour, by chance, of being known to the Marquise Duchatelet, but expelled from her house for his rogueriness and impudence before he left Paris with two young men in debt whom he seduced to turn musulmen. His story and his character must be known at Constantinople. I would fain know what sort of life he leads now with the followers of Mahomet.

'But what concerns me more, what I long more to be informed of, is whether you are as happy as you seem to be. Have you got a little private Scrraglio or are you married? Are you overstoked with business, does your laziness comply with your affairs? Do you drink much of that good Cyprus wine? For my part I am too happy, tho my health is ever very weak,

excepto quod non simul esses, caetera laetus.

'Addio mio carissimo ambasciadore, adio, le baccio umilmente le mani. L'amo e la riverisco

à Cirey ce 22 Fevrier 1736 N.S.

Voltaire.'

# Chapter Eight

## Frederick Appears on the Scene

IN AUGUST 1736 Voltaire received a letter, in bad French, from a young German admirer. Well over 1,000 words, painfully banal ('One feels that Brutus must either be a Roman or an Englishman'), full of heavy praise and metaphysical reflections, enclosing a book which the master was invited to read and comment upon, demanding a reply, it was the kind of letter all writers receive from time to time and which, if they happen to be busy, they positively dread. However, two things made it remarkable. The book which came with it was a French translation of some essays by Christian Wolff, the follower of Leibnitz, and the letter ended with the words: 'If my destiny refuse me the happiness of being able to possess you may I hope, at least one day, to see the man whom I have so long admired from afar, and to assure you, face to face, that I am, with all the esteem and consideration due to those who, following the torch of truth, consecrate their efforts to the public good, Monsieur, your friend Fédéric, P.R. de Prusse.' The long and famous relationship had begun, and so had the tussle between Frederick and Emilie as to who should 'possess' Voltaire.

Voltaire was enchanted. He replied at once, in well over 1,000 words, praising the Prince for praising him; he cannot thank enough for the little book by Wolff whose metaphysical ideas do honour to the human intellect. (As a matter of fact it was Emilie who fell upon this book and assimilated its ideas, which Voltaire thought great nonsense.) He would consider it a priceless happiness to go and pay his court to H.R.H. One goes to Rome to see the churches, pictures, ruins and bas-reliefs. Such a prince is worth much more than a journey and is a most marvellous rarity. But friendship keeps Voltaire in his present retreat and does not permit of his leaving it. No doubt H.R.H. would agree with Julian who said that friends should always be preferred to kings.

In spite of Emilie's protests Voltaire sent his new friend various philosophical writings of his own which, if they were read in Paris, would be enough to get him exiled for ever. Emilie saw the red light at the first exchange of letters. Knowing that Voltaire dearly loved a royal highness and had a weakness for clever young men, she realized that this heir to a throne, babbling of metaphysics, might easily become a dangerous rival. Voltaire lost no time in telling the world what had happened. Here is an enlightened Prince (buried away, unfortunately, in Germanie) who knows a philosopher when he sees one. If they are not careful at Versailles, Voltaire will be lost to France for ever; this splendid Prince, writing as Julian might have written to Libanius, has invited him to his Court. Frederick's letters were copied and copied again and sent off in every direction, Voltaire enjoining each and all of the recipients to keep them a deadly secret. For the present he intends to stay at Cirey and meet the claims of friendship; for the future, who can tell?

We English can only think of Frederick the Great in the accents of Carlyle, who, anxious to seem 'Teutsch', always spelt the name of his hero Friedrich whereas the hero, anxious to seem French, signed himself Fédéric. On 6th August, two days before writing to Voltaire, Frederick had 'kindled the sacred hearth' with his wife.

Carlyle knew quite well that their marriage was never consummated; he only meant that they now had an establishment of their own at Rheinsberg. 'Here he lives to the Muses, to the spiritual improvements, to the social enjoyments and has . . . a sunny time.' 'Voltaire was the spiritual complement of Friedrich; what little of lasting their poor century produced lies mainly in these two.' 'Admit it, reader,' says Carlyle.

Frederick answered Voltaire's letter with another of enormous length which drew tears of joy from the recipient. He foresees that this Prince will be the beloved of the human race: 'You think like Trajan, you write like Pliny and you speak French like any of our best writers. Under your auspices Berlin will become the Athens of Germany and perhaps of the whole of Europe.' Perhaps he really thought so; who can tell what Voltaire really thought? Later in life, speaking of this correspondence, he said, 'all these epithets cost us nothing. He hadn't much to do so he spent his time writing to French men of letters. The principal burden fell on me.' He certainly did not think that Frederick wrote French 'like any of our best writers'. His French was very poor indeed, full of mistakes which Voltaire called '*fautes de doigts*'. He took good care to correct the letters before boastfully broadcasting them to his friends in Paris. Presents soon began to arrive, portraits of the Prince, bibelots for Emilie and a cane with a golden head of Socrates, who, Frederick said, could be compared with Voltaire except for the calumnies with which Socrates had been blackened.

Voltaire wrote all the developments of this interesting friendship to Thieriot. Knowing everybody in Paris, invited everywhere, Thieriot was an excellent publicity agent since this entailed no work or trouble. Voltaire and his doings were news and Thieriot dined out on them. Voltaire engaged him, on Frederick's behalf, to write a regular letter of literary gossip to Berlin. As this did entail a little work and trouble he did it badly, though he kept it up in a desultory way for years. He never failed to include anything disagreeable that appeared about Voltaire, keenly gathering up all the most damaging libels against his old friend and bene-factor in order to post them off to Frederick. Voltaire was aware of this, and sometimes said how pleased he would be if Thieriot would include the good things that were written about him. They were generally forgotten. It was understood that Frederick would pay Thieriot for his trouble, not at once, but on his accession to the throne. He never did. When Thieriot complained about this, Voltaire would vaguely reply that one day he would hear the words 'well done, thou good and faithful servant'.

Voltaire was becoming more and more interested in natural philosophy. As always when an author turns to something new, his friends thought it a great pity that he should give up writing poetry and plays. Cideville sadly asked him what he gained by knowing the weight of Saturn? D'Argenson said there were plenty of people to instruct the world in physical science, but very soon there would be nothing amusing to read. The actors of the Comédie-française were crying out for a play, and Voltaire said they must cry in vain. His mind was filled with Newton and he had time for little else. He was conducting optical experiments, in a dark room, with the aid of instruments sent him by the Abbé Moussinot and was writing *Les Eléments de la Philosophie de Newton*. At that time hardly anybody outside England understood these elements; Newton's own book was written in Latin and in algebra and was therefore incomprehensible to the common man. Voltaire performed a service to France by forcing himself to understand it so that he could make it clear to others. Very likely he never would have done so but for Emilie. '*Minerve dictait*,' he said himself, '*et j'écrivais.*'

When he had been studying physics for some years, he asked Clairaut to give a candid opinion on his progress. Clairaut, who could be trusted to tell the truth, as he was a good and simple man, jealous of nobody, replied that Voltaire had no gift for science and that the greatest industry would never make a first-class scientist of him. After this, independent search for physical truth was given up. Voltaire's real interest was in the human race, past, present and to come. Emilie thought he was too fond of history, which she regarded as singularly useless. 'What does it matter to me, a Frenchwoman living on my estates, that Egil succeeded Harquin in Sweden? I renounced a study which overwhelms the mind without illuminating it.' His scientific work at Cirey however was by no means such waste of time as his Parisian friends thought it. Nearly all that is still read of Voltaire was influenced by it. Nobody now can wade through his tragedies, which seem to us like bad Racine; nobody acts his comedies, or reads the *Henriade*. Marivaux, whom Voltaire despised from the bottom of his heart, has survived as a playwright; Voltaire has not. But *Candide* and the other tales, the *Dictionnaire Philosophique*, and his letters which increased in number, depth and importance during the Cirey period, will be read as long as our civilization endures.

In the middle of more serious work, Voltaire did find time to scribble a poem, *Le Mondain*, to amuse himself and his friends. Its theme was the superiority of civilized over primitive life. Adam and Eve, said Voltaire, must have been too bored for words, poor things, with nothing to do but eat, drink and make love. No soap, no scissors, their nails and hair must have been in a disgusting state. Their supper, under an oak-tree, consisted of millet and acorns washed down with water. What a contrast is the life of a civilized man, surrounded by the children of his taste: Correggios, Poussins, and Gobelins hang on his walls; his silver is by Germain, his statues by Bouchardon. When he wishes for distraction he sends for his carriage and goes to see Camargo dance at the Opera; there all the senses are catered for. People who cry out against luxury are generally themselves poor and bad-tempered. It is in *Le Mondain* that the classic phrase occurs, '*le superflu, chose si nécessaire*'.

Copies of this little poem were sent off, as usual, to a few friends and, as usual, somebody betrayed Voltaire and delivered it to a publisher. The Bishop of Mirepoix, who was later to be Mme de Pompadour's enemy at the Court, read it and objected violently. Since giving up his See in order to become the little Dauphin's tutor he always signed himself anc: (ancien) de Mirepoix, which Voltaire pretended to read as *âne*. The donkey of Mirepoix now complained to Cardinal Fleury and there was trouble. The clergy said that the poem was blasphemous because Adam and Eve were depicted as making love constantly *in* the Garden of Eden. There were other, equally far-fetched complaints. 'Keeper' (the *Garde des Sceaux*) had given his word to the Duc and Duchesse de Richelieu, and to Mme du Châtelet's influential cousin the Bailli de Froulay, that no proceedings would ever be taken against Voltaire while he was at Cirey, without warning. This promise was kept. On 22 December 1736 Voltaire and Mme du Châtelet received an alarming letter from him.

Snow was thick on the ground; Voltaire felt the cold to an exaggerated degree; yet, so great was their agitation that they left Cirey that very night and went to the inn at Vassy whence Voltaire was to proceed, with post-horses, to Holland. There was no thought of sleep, Voltaire wrote letters and at four in the morning he wrote to d'Argental, '. . . but, my true, tender and respected friend, as I see the moment approaching when I must part for ever from one who has given up Paris, society and everything that makes life pleasant, on my behalf, one whom I adore and whom it is right that I should adore, you will understand what I am feeling. . . . My heart is pierced. Simply because I have enemies in Paris, must she return solitary to a house she has built for me, must I be deprived of my life's consolation?' He says that he could easily go and live in Prussia, or indeed in any foreign land without too many regrets were it not for Emilie. 'I am exhausted, overwhelmed with grief and illness. Adieu.'

Indeed it was horrible for him. He had settled down to a routine of congenial work; he had installed his library, laboratory and dark-room; and he had found a woman with whom he could live happily. All this had to be abandoned, at a moment's notice, in the middle of a bitter winter's night. A sense of unfairness added to his misery. The charming, light-hearted *Mondain* certainly did not deserve such treatment. He realized, however, that Emilie's state was even worse than his. She now had to go back to a sad, deserted Cirey where her husband, two dull little children and Linant would henceforth be her sole companions. Voltaire worried about her, and from Givet, the first stop on the road to Brussels, he sent a line to Mme de Champbonin begging her to go to Emilie at once.

Emilie, for her part, worried about him. She thought his health might give way, in that bitter cold. But as she knew, really, that Voltaire's health became very good in times of crisis and was at its best during long, hard journeys, her chief preoccupation was a more selfish one. She feared that he would go to Prussia. In spite of the poor quality of Frederick's letters, which had so far given no idea of his real personality, the curious magnet had begun to work upon Voltaire. Emilie was frightened of

the Prince. She wrote frantically to d'Argental, who must
have dreaded the post-bag during these days filled as it
was with the wails of the two philosophers: 'I beg you
on my knees to stop him going to Prussia.' As a matter of
fact there was no danger of this for the present. Frederick
did not want him there while his father, the King, was
still alive. He himself went in terror of this absolutely
powerful madman, who would certainly regard his
friendship for Voltaire with no good eye. Voltaire told
everybody in Paris, and published in the gazettes that he
was on his way to Prussia, but this was in order to conceal
his whereabouts: in fact he got no further than Amsterdam.

Meanwhile Emilie, pondering and brooding alone at
Cirey, was having second thoughts which she communicated to d'Argental in long, hysterical letters. It really
seems impossible that the French Court, bigoted though
it may be, could exile such a man as Voltaire, merely for
saying that Adam and Eve never had a bath. The explanation must lie elsewhere. D'Argental tells her that
du Châtelet is to be asked to withdraw his protection
from Voltaire and this gives her a clue. The whole thing
must have been plotted by her cousin, the Marquis de
Breteuil, with whom she has quarrelled; it is his way of
taking his revenge. Fortunately, M. du Châtelet is the
soul of integrity, the best and most reliable man in the
world and there is no question of his lending himself to
such proceedings. If her surmise is correct, Voltaire only
has to lie low for a bit and all will be well. But she is
fearfully unhappy. A fortnight ago she never spent as
much as two hours away from him; even when they
were both working they continually sent each other little
notes. Now she is not even sure where he is, since his
letters are not arriving. Meanwhile, Cirey is nothing but
mountains and she is really too wretched. When Voltaire's letters begin to arrive she reads, to her horror,

that he has sent a manuscript copy of his unpublished *Métaphysique* to Frederick. This work is a thousand times more dangerous and punishable than *La Pucelle*. (She need not have worried about that; it was only later that Frederick betrayed Voltaire to the French government. There was no point in doing so at present.)

All the Paris friends upset her by writing their views and advice. Some say that the *Garde des Sceaux* is angry with Voltaire for leaving the country without informing him. Others that the correspondence with Frederick is regarded as highly suspect at Versailles. Others again that Voltaire has written an indiscreet letter about M. Hérault, the Chief of Police. These hypotheses go round and round in her head and nearly drive her mad. Du Châtelet wants to take her to the Court of Lorraine at Lunéville for a change and a distraction, but she cannot leave the place where she last saw Voltaire. So there she stayed, pining like a faithful dog.

In Paris people were saying that Voltaire had seduced the daughter of the *concierge* at Cirey who had had a child. When the girl was questioned she was supposed to have observed that she had only done with M. de Voltaire what she had seen Madame doing and that she knew Madame never did wrong. After which Emilie sent Voltaire packing. Another story had it that the Chevalier du Châtelet, as stupid as his brother but not so easy-going, had chased Voltaire out of the house for dishonouring the family.

Meanwhile, Voltaire was thoroughly enjoying himself. He assumed an alias, M. Revol, but it took in nobody, nor did the notice in the papers that he had gone to Prussia. He only stayed one night in Brussels, a town he never liked and where he risked a meeting with the hated Jean-Baptiste Rousseau. But on that one night they gave *Alzire* in his honour. In Holland he received most flattering visits. The Prussian Minister to London, who happened to be at The Hague, called to put his house at Voltaire's disposal should he wish to go to England. Twenty Englishmen of King George's Household came to see him. The learned 'sGravesande, professor of philosophy at Leyden and a prominent Newtonian, welcomed him with open arms; Voltaire attended his lectures and they had long, interesting talks. His publisher invited him to stay and soon he was hard at work, correcting proofs, seeing about illustrations and so on. Voltaire liked nothing better than to correct and even to re-write his published works; it was a sort of relaxation for him.

He wrote regularly to the Prince of Prussia. 'Frederick, greater already than Socrates'; 'Socrates is nothing to me, it is Frederick whom I love'; 'The olives, the laurels and the myrtles put out their leaves again and Frederick appears'. 'You are composing, in Berlin, French verse as it was written at Versailles in the golden age of taste and pleasure.' 'Bossuet and Fénelon must have been your tutors, Mme de Sévigné your nurse.' 'Like old Simeon in the Temple I say, Lord, now lettest thou thy servant depart in peace, according to thy word, for mine eyes have seen my salvation.'* However he took the repeated hints in Frederick's letters and did not attempt to go and see his salvation that winter.

Instead he went back to Cirey. Du Châtelet had been absolutely loyal, as his wife had said he would be, and announced that he was prepared to speak to Cardinal Fleury on Voltaire's behalf. Good little Mme de Richelieu flung herself into the fray and matters were arranged with 'Keeper'. Voltaire was allowed to return in February; he had only been away two months.

---

* Voltaire always put 'my salvation' instead of 'thy salvation'.

# Chapter Nine

## Exit Linant, Enter Mme Denis

SO THE happy, laborious life was resumed—not quiet and peaceful though. Voltaire engendered disquiet and strife. The post-bag, which he so eagerly awaited, was a constant anxiety to Mme du Châtelet and, in the case of Frederick's letters, a constant irritation. 'Do come and stay,' she wrote to Maupertuis, '+Clairaut and — a Prince, for I do not like them.' Voltaire read Frederick's effusions aloud over and over again, dissecting them and discussing them at enormous length. This was very tedious for Emilie. Then there was generally bad news of some sort from Paris, a new devilry of Desfontaines or Jean-Baptiste Rousseau to throw Voltaire into a frenzy and set him scribbling indiscretions. Rousseau put it about that Voltaire had gone to the Low Countries to preach atheism. 'sGravesande was called to the rescue; he stated in the *Gazette* that Rousseau's story was quite untrue, and he also wrote to Cardinal Fleury.

Voltaire never admitted to being an atheist, it would have been too dangerous; he had not the stuff of a martyr. Perhaps he really believed in God: 'When I see a clock I believe in a clock-maker.' He was certainly not a very good Catholic. He thought the Quakers had evolved the only logical Christian religion; Catholic priests were denied too many pleasures and this drove them to ambition. But he was not yet the avowed enemy of the Church that he became later in life. His bedroom at Cirey was next door to the Chapel so that he could hear

Mass from his bed when he was ill. He wished to employ
a scientific young chaplain; Abbé Moussinot was to find
one for him, making it quite clear that he would be expected to say Mass, give Voltaire a hand with his experiments and have his meals with du Châtelet, the little
boy and Linant.

Soon after Voltaire's return from Holland Frederick
sent him Count Kaiserling, 'ambassador plenipotentiary
to the Court of Cirey'. Caesarion, as they called him,
was a small, fat, jolly, chattering, homosexual Cour-
lander, whom they liked very much. He spoke all languages, sometimes several at once, and was most agreeable to everybody, including Linant. He was attracted
by Emilie, saying that 'when she spoke I was in love
with her intellect and when she was silent with her
person'. They entertained him with fêtes and fireworks;
Frederick's name was illuminated: 'To the Hope of the
Human Race.' Voltaire and Emilie acted for Kaiserling
in their theatre, where they now had two companies, one
for comedy and one for tragedy. They sent him back to
Rheinsberg with the unfinished *Siècle de Louis XIV* and
various other works, but without *La Pucelle* which was
what Frederick really wanted. Emilie had very sensibly
put it under lock and key and nothing would induce her
to give it up. Kaiserling's account of the sparkling life
at Cirey made Frederick more determined than ever to
possess Voltaire, while Voltaire wrote 'every time we pass
your Royal Highness's portrait we sing the hymn of old
Simeon in the Temple'. Emilie told everybody that as
soon as the Prince succeeded to the throne she and Voltaire would both go and see him. This was not at all
Frederick's intention, the idea of 'Milady de Cireyshire'
wearied him profoundly and he had no wish to possess
Venus-Newton as well as Socrates-Apollo. However, in
all the letters between him and Voltaire he exchanged
loving messages with Mme du Châtelet.

Linant was not being a success at Cirey. He gave himself the most irritating airs, behaving as if *Rameses*, of which he had only finished a few indifferent verses, had put him on a par with Voltaire as a writer. He went to stay with some neighbours without so much as a by-your-leave, forgetting that he was paid to look after the child, and while he was away he wrote a rude letter to Mme du Châtelet ending up 'the boredom of Cirey is the greatest of all boredoms'. He was given to speaking of Cideville as poor Cideville, or dear Cideville, instead of Monsieur de Cideville. Voltaire was a great stickler for proper forms of address and used to say that all the nobodies and hangers-on at the Comédie-française spoke of La Lecouvreur, whereas Cardinal Fleury never called her anything but Mademoiselle Lecouvreur. 'Poor Cideville' maddened him. Mme du Châtelet often spoke of sending Linant away, but Voltaire pointed out that though she did not need him he needed her, and in fact if he left Cirey he would starve to death.

Cideville, urged to do so by Voltaire, wrote and scolded Linant for his uppishness and laziness. He replied very wretchedly. He can't help laughing when he is told that he must never remain seated in the presence of Mme du Châtelet because she is of the House of Lorraine. But Cirey to him is a prison and he is miserable there. They expect him to finish *Rameses*; there is nothing he would like better, but how can he work with a little boy on a string? He must stop the child from falling into wells in summer and into the fire in winter. He must teach him things that he, very naturally and rightly, does not want to learn and Linant is sorry that he is paid to make the boy unhappy, but the boy gives it him back, all right. He is like a man who is tied down and told to run.

However, things went rather better after Cideville had read the riot act. Linant took advantage of a happier atmosphere to ask Mme du Châtelet to do something for his mother and sister who were in distress. The mother was placed, through Emilie's influence, in a convent; the sister was more of a problem. Linant begged and bothered Emilie to find her some employment at Cirey. Emilie said it would be difficult to have her there as a maid since that would lower the status of her son's tutor. So she placed her with Mme de Richelieu, but at the last moment that arrangement fell through and there was nothing for it but to have her at Cirey.

After Kaiserling's departure they discovered he was in communication with Linant, who had made a plan with him to go off and join the Prince of Prussia's establishment. Instead of being delighted to get rid of such an unsatisfactory creature, Emilie flew into a fury and said she had counted on him to bring up her son. She strenuously opposed his departure. No doubt she thought he would tell all sorts of tales, at Rheinsberg, about Cirey, and no doubt he would have. So the poor fellow saw that chance of escape fading away; Frederick could not have taken him without the consent of his employer. Meanwhile the sister was being quite a success. When they told her of her brother's plot with Kaiserling, she seemed to be deeply shocked and said that nothing would induce her to follow him. She loved her mistress too much, she said. The mistress was touched by these words. But only a few days later Mme du Châtelet got hold of Mlle Linant's letters to a certain Abbé at Rouen and found herself treated with scant respect—laughed at, in fact. There was a tremendous blow-up and both the Linants left Cirey for ever.

Voltaire wrote to Cideville: 'Linant was stitching away at that Eyptiatic [sic] intrigue which I made him begin some seven years back. He seemed to have gathered up strength and I flattered myself that in fourteen years he would have finished the fifth act. Joking apart, if only he had worked a little I believe it might have succeeded.

But you know that it was the sister who was possessed by the demon of composition in prose, so that Mme du Châtelet was obliged to send away both of them. They are very foolish; they could have led a charming life and looked forward to an agreeable future. Linant would have stayed on here with a pension and his pupil would have taken care of him. . . . M. du Châtelet's tutor died in the family, quite nicely off. Now it is my duty to forget them, since they have failed in theirs to Mme du Châtelet.' He told Thieriot that he felt like a priest whose penitent has ended up in a brothel. This is not the last occasion on which we shall hear of Emilie's reading other people's letters. She gave Linant a good character, however, to somebody who thought of employing him, blaming the sister for his dismissal.

Perhaps it was the fact of his protégé turning out so badly that made Voltaire remember his own kith and kin. He had never liked his brother who was ten years older than he and different in every respect. Arouet had long been a bigoted Jansenist; he belonged to the most advanced congregation of that sect and had taken part in the convulsions at Saint-Médard. Voltaire speaks of his *mœurs féroces* and says he had affairs with all the prettiest convulsionists. But he loved the sister who had died when he was in England and he began to think about her children and make plans for their future. They had recently lost their father. The eldest daughter Louise, at twenty-six, was a spinster and Voltaire proposed to marry her to Mme de Champbonin's son. She would have a little château, not very pretty but it could be arranged for her, *l'aimable Champenoise* as a mother-in-law, 8,000 livres a year and besides all this, she would live near her uncle, a companion for his old age. As the attractions of Champbonin himself are never stressed, they were probably not overwhelming. In any case the future Mme Denis had a mind of her own. She saw her-

self as an intellectual, a musician, pupil of Rameau; a
real Parisian not at all cut out for country life. Without
having been there she seems to have suspected that the
boredom of Cirey was the greatest of all boredoms. She
refused to hear of marrying young Champbonin. Voltaire had promised to give her a dowry and many an
uncle in his place would have waved aside such a refusal
and insisted on the marriage of his own choice. Voltaire
did not even press the point but said that she must be
happy in her way, not his.

She decided to be happy with Denis, a bourgeois of
about the same age and with the same tastes as herself.
The marriage was a success. Voltaire was generous to
her and as Uncle Arouet also did more than his duty (he,
too, was a rich bachelor), Mme Denis started life very
nicely provided for. Mme du Châtelet said she only
wished her relations had done as well for her. Voltaire
made one reservation, he refused to go to the wedding.
He knew too well what such weddings are like, 'gather-
ings of the clan, facetious nuptial jokes and puns,
dirty stories to make the bride blush and the prudes
pinch their lips, a great deal of noise, interrupted conversations, a lot of nasty food, giggles and no real desire
to laugh, heavy kisses heavily bestowed, and little girls
taking it all in through the corners of their eyes'.

The young people went to Cirey for their honeymoon
and Mme Denis wrote to Thieriot an account of what
they found there. Her uncle is lost to his friends, chains
have been forged which can never now be broken. He
and Mme du Châtelet live in a terrifying solitude,
twelve miles from any human habitation, surrounded
by mountains and moors. Hardly any of their Paris
friends visit them there. They have a pretty theatre, but
can seldom raise enough actors to use it, though the
neighbours within a radius of thirty miles have a standing order to come and perform. While Mme Denis was

there none came, and they had to fall back on marionettes. Not much of a life for the greatest genius of the age.
He was ill during the whole of Mme Denis's visit. Mme
du Châtelet has got rather fat, but she is certainly very
pretty, full of fun and takes all the trouble in the world to
fascinate him. He seems more bewitched than ever. The
young couple could not have been more kindly received;
Voltaire likes M. Denis very much indeed and no
wonder!

Mme Denis must have been thanking her lucky stars
that she had not married young Champbonin and gone
to live in far Champagne surrounded by mountains and
moors.

# Chapter Ten

## The Battle of Desfontaines

IN THE spring of 1738 the two philosophers of Cirey entered for a competition, set by the Académie des Sciences, on the nature of fire. (This affair has been described by Mr E. M. Forster in *Abinger Harvest*. It must be read in his words.) Voltaire and Mme du Châtelet were not placed. The competition was won by Euler, who had something new to say on the rapidity of waves of heat. Two other papers, though inferior to those of Voltaire and Mme du Châtelet, pleased the Academicians more because they were faithful to Descartes. Voltaire's paper has since been recognized to have been in advance of contemporary physics; he came very near to comprehending the phenomenon of oxidization, which was mysterious at that time. The lovers were quite resigned over their failure, putting it down to their adherence to Newton. 'In France one is a good citizen only if one believes in the vortex.' 'We are the heretics of philosophy.'

Owing to the prejudice against Newton, Voltaire was having trouble with the publication of his new book, *Eléments de la Philosophie de Newton* (or Newton for the Common Reader). Not wishing to have any more alarums and excursions he sent it to the censor and asked, in a straightforward way, for permission to publish it. The censor adopted stone-wall tactics. He would say neither yes nor no; he would not return the book or suggest any alterations. Months went by. Voltaire had

given a copy to his Dutch publisher but, anxious to be
in order, he told him that it was not to appear until
he had permission in France. He waited, and waited in
vain for an answer from Versailles. Finally the usual
thing happened. A pirated edition appeared in Holland.
It was full of printers' errors, but, even worse than that, it
contained two or three chapters added by a Dutch physi-
cist, without a word of explanation. Voltaire was in
despair. This last work of his was by far his favourite;
he had been longing for it to come out. The weeks and
months which had dragged by had already affected his
nerves and therefore his health. Emilie said, 'His sensi-
tivity over such matters may be natural but is not reasonable,' but any writer would understand what his feelings
must have been when he saw this garbled version, over
whose manifold mistakes his enemies would surely gloat.
Frederick, who had got hold of a copy, wrote at once
to say that 'sGravesande had spoken to him of the
book in a tone which he, Frederick, had not altogether
liked. No wonder, said poor Voltaire, considering that
the chapters which had been added to it without his
knowledge had contained slighting allusions to 'sGravesande. The Dutch publisher had put on the title-page
*Eléments de la Philosophie de Newton, mis à la portée de tout
le monde* and Abbé Desfontaines could not resist saying
that this should read, *'mis à la porte de tout le monde'*.

Voltaire began to work himself up in a mad and morbid way against the Abbé, who now seemed to personify
his enemies. He sent the following poem to Thieriot,
knowing quite well that it would be all round Paris in a
few days.

> *Par l'amour anti-physique*
> *Desfontaines flagellé*
> *A, dit-on, fort mal parlé*
> *Du système newtonique*
> *Il a pris tout à rebours*

*La vérité la plus pure*
*Et ses erreurs sont toujours*
*Des péchés contre nature.* *

It was neither wise, nor kind. Desfontaines was tired of being told he was a pederast. He riposted, in *Observations*, with the remark that it would clearly be ridiculous for a philosopher, at an advanced age, to give up philosophy and take to writing poetry, but that apparently there is nothing ridiculous in an old poet taking up philosophy. However, it seems a pity that the old poet should give himself over to Newtonianism which all the real philosophers have condemned.

Voltaire's answer was *Le Préservatif contre les Observations*. In this masterly and very unfair production, he picked out every mistake that had ever appeared in *Observations*, whether of the printers, or of the author; all the errors of grammar, of fact, of taste or of judgment. He took sentences out of their context and turned them to ridicule. He also raked up the old story of having saved Desfontaines from the faggots and of the vile, ungrateful creature's pamphlet, shown to Thieriot. Now Desfontaines was quite a good journalist, but, like all of his profession, he was often obliged to write in a hurry. Printers at that time were notoriously slipshod and uneducated. Back numbers of *Observations* could not stand up to Voltaire's treatment, administered by such a master-hand, and he had no difficulty in making the Abbé look foolish. *Le Préservatif* did not appear over Voltaire's signature but was fastened on to one of his dogs' bodies, the Chevalier de Mouhy, a literary hack whom Voltaire sometimes befriended. Mouhy was made to say that, having read in *Observations* various articles against M. de Voltaire, he has taken the liberty to write to M. de Voltaire, with

* He turns everything upside down and his errors are always sins against nature.

whom he is not acquainted, and this is the answer. The so-called answer was Voltaire's account of Desfontaines's ingratitude to him and the pamphlet burnt by Thieriot. It was quite obvious that Voltaire was the author of the whole of *Le Préservatif*, every word of which could only have come from his pen, but he never admitted it. He told Thieriot that no doubt the Abbé deserved to be taught a lesson, but that if he himself had been consulted he would have advised Mouhy to polish up his style before publishing. 'One can't be everywhere at once.'

*Le Préservatif* came out in November 1738. The Abbé did not waste time and on 12 December he published *La Voltairomanie ou Lettre d'un Jeune Avocat*. In it a 'young lawyer', the opposite number of the Chevalier de Mouhy, flies to the defence of his friend Desfontaines and pours abuse upon Voltaire. *La Voltairomanie* is heavy handed and not very subtle, nevertheless every sentence has its sting. The intention is to show that Voltaire is mad, bad and dangerous. Nobody and nothing is safe from this enemy of the human race, of the living and of the dead. The 'young lawyer' goes to work with a will. He begins with Voltaire's writings. The plays, he says, owe such success as they have had to their bold blasphemy. The *Histoire de Charles XII* is a dismal collection of fusty old anecdotes. The *Lettres Philosophiques* have made it impossible for decent people to frequent Voltaire, and so now he has to live away from Paris. The *Eléments de Newton* have turned him into the laughing-stock of all serious scientists. The 'young lawyer' then goes into the affair of the Abbé's imprisonment and alleged rescue by Voltaire, pointing out with some truth, that while Voltaire may have had a hand in his release, he has accused him ever since of a crime for which Desfontaines was never even brought to trial. The Abbé (or rather, the 'young lawyer') now brings up his big gun. Voltaire's only excuse for his pitiless persecution of a fellow-writer has always been the pamphlet, containing libels against himself, written after the Abbé's release from prison and burnt by Thieriot. This pamphlet, in fact, has never existed. M. Thieriot is beginning (and who shall blame him?) to repent of his friendship with such a blackguard as Voltaire; he denies any knowledge of it. What other evidence is there of its existence? None. The whole story is yet another of Voltaire's lies.

*La Voltairomanie* was a best-seller. Voltaire's enemies fell upon it with glee, while his friends could not help chuckling over it, though pronouncing it a gross and horrible libel. Of all the sorrows which assail our loved ones, the easiest for us to bear is an attack on them in print. While the poor victim is scratching the sore place, reading and re-reading an even greater beastliness into each sentence than was originally intended, we skim through the matter, laugh at the jokes, put it by (or put it in an envelope and send it to a mutual friend) and forget about it. In this case most people felt that Voltaire had brought it on himself by publishing *Le Préservatif*.

*La Voltairomanie* reached Circy on Christmas Day. There were two copies in Voltaire's mail; one was extracted by Emilie who always had a nibble at the postbag before anybody else. She missed the other copy; it was probably in the package from Abbé Moussinot which was sacred and which even she never dared to touch. For several days she and Voltaire pored over this horrible document alone, each keeping it from the other. She thought that if he read it, in his present state of health, it might kill him; he knew how much she took to heart anything which concerned him and wanted to spare her feelings. There was, staying with them at Cirey, a garrulous Madame de Grafigny. They neither of them confided in her but perhaps they were quite glad to have a third person there, in the circumstances. They must have made a considerable effort when she was with them, which was only at meal-times, for, in her letters, she describes scintillating conversation and many jokes.

Of course poor d'Argental was at the receiving end for both of them. Emilie wrote frantically. First she said that their 'friend' must never know about *La Voltairomanie*; it must be ignored, passed over in a contemptuous silence. Her second thoughts, however, were that, on the contrary, it must be answered. The public should not be left with the idea that Voltaire was forbidden to go to Paris. Thieriot must be made to speak up about the pamphlet. She enclosed an answer to *La Voltairomanie* in which she went for Desfontaines tooth and nail. It began: 'Naturalists take pains to trace the origins of those monsters which nature used to produce, they do so out of curiosity and cannot guarantee us against their reappearance; but there is another kind of monster whose study is of greater interest to society and whose extirpation is more necessary.' She demolished all Desfontaines's arguments, one by one, referring to him as '*le misérable*', and ended 'Socrates thanked God that he was born a man and not a beast, a Greek and not a barbarian; and M. de Voltaire must thank Him for such a despicable enemy'. Then she wrote to Thieriot pointing out that it was his duty to come to the support of his friend. Thieriot's reply was exceedingly unsatisfactory. He recognizes and is edified by Mme du Châtelet's zeal on behalf of M. de Voltaire. He has been greatly scandalized by *Le Préservatif* and he is appalled to learn that ill-intentioned folk are attributing it to Voltaire. Since it appeared many people have asked him about the allegedly libellous pamphlet, he always gives the same answer, which he now gives to Mme du Châtelet: he does vaguely remember having seen such a manuscript but cannot say for certain whether this was before or after the Abbé's imprisonment. (The date, of course, was exceedingly important as if the Abbé had written the pamphlet before going to prison he could not be accused of ingratitude.)

Emilie sent this letter to d'Argental with her own annotations.

(1) Too good of Thieriot to have been edified by her zeal and to say that he interests himself in M. de Voltaire in order to emulate her.

(2) He was edified a moment ago. Now, all of a sudden he is scandalized, implying that he suspects M. de Voltaire of having written *Le Préservatif*. This suspicion certainly scandalizes Mme du Châtelet.

(3) It has suddenly become convenient for M. Thieriot to forget circumstances which are important for M. de Voltaire.

(4) He seems to be the only person in the world who does not know the identity of the 'young lawyer'.

She also remarks that they have twenty letters from Thieriot written in 1725 in which he speaks of this affair. If his memory continues to play him false, these letters will be printed. On the 3rd of January she tells d'Argental that Voltaire and she have at last had it out together. Greatly to her relief, he minded much less than she had feared, and was more concerned about her feelings than his own. Also she was relieved to find that he did not intend to continue the slanging match in print but merely to bring a lawsuit against the Abbé. He had written to Moussinot telling him to buy the pamphlet in the presence of two witnesses and take it to a magistrate.

Voltaire wrote to Thieriot describing himself as a public figure. He must defend himself against libel and his friend must help him to do so. He has only ever known of Desfontaines's original pamphlet from Thieriot; Desfontaines now alleges that Thieriot denies all knowledge of this pamphlet. Of course the Abbé lies; why only the other day, when Thieriot was at Cirey, they had been talking about it together. Thieriot cannot now say that this is none of his business, he cannot let his old friend down after so many long years. Why, what would the Crown Prince of Prussia think of such behaviour? Friendship and truth must triumph over hatred and perfidy; Voltaire knows that they will—and embraces his friend more lovingly than ever.

Voltaire was evidently not at all sure that his friend would spring to his defence, and he was right. Thieriot was now living, in parasitical luxury, with La Popelinière, one of the richest and most civilized of the Parisian financiers. He enjoyed the easy existence of a man-about-town. Effort, and especially disagreeable effort, was foreign to his nature; live and let live his motto. He was, no doubt, very fond of Voltaire; he knew his works by heart and was the greatest expert on the various editions; he willingly did odd jobs for the inhabitants of Cirey. But all Voltaire's friends were getting tired of his endless, rather ridiculous quarrels. Richelieu once told him so outright, saying 'even Thieriot doesn't stand up for you any more'. It was not the fashion in their light-hearted society to nourish these excessive hatreds. Thieriot had no wish to be involved in a lawsuit which his friend was not at all sure to win and which would certainly give rise to mirth all over Paris. Furthermore the Abbé's paper, *Observations*, was read every week by Thieriot's circle of acquaintances; the Abbé had a nice talent for holding people up to mockery and Thieriot preferred to keep on the right side of him. Voltaire had lied to him about *Le Préservatif*, and if he thought that many another lie was probably being cooked up at Cirey he was not far wrong. The whole of this business was conducted, on both sides, with the maximum of bad faith. It is possible to sympathize with Thieriot's point of view, given his light, unstable character, but nobody can

approve of his sending *La Voltairomanie* to Frederick, as
he now hastened to do. It was the one thing that Voltaire dreaded, though he felt quite sure that it would
happen. This piece of ill-nature was Thieriot's only con-
tribution to the affair: thereafter he sat back and did
nothing.

A new irritant was added to Voltaire's miseries. The
other great enemy, Jean-Baptiste Rousseau, was allowed
back in France after an exile of thirty-two years. Voltaire pretended not to care—'He is to all intents and pur-
poses a dead man, the late Rousseau'—but he felt it as a
slap in the face and knew that Rousseau would make as
much trouble for him in Paris as he could. The sensible
d'Argental wrote and said the best thing that Voltaire
could do now was to forget all these worries and write
some interesting work. He had overlooked the terrifying
energy of his friend; Voltaire wrote *Zulime*, it took him
exactly a week and left him free to go on with his war
against Desfontaines. He wanted total revenge, that is
to say the withdrawal of permission to publish *Observations*. Even that would not be enough unless it were
made quite clear that the paper was suppressed on
account of attacks against Voltaire.

A petition was drawn up. It went over the whole
ground, from the chimney-sweeps onward, letting it be
supposed that Desfontaines's life had been devoted to one-
way persecution of Voltaire. Naturally there was no mention of his many attacks on the Abbé, nor of *Le Préservatif*.
Abbé Moussinot was to present this document to a
magistrate. Voltaire instructed him to hire several
carriages. He was then to go and pick up all Voltaire's
relations, also three people who were mentioned in *La
Voltairomanie*, Pitanal the lawyer, Andy, a fashionable
doctor, Procope, another doctor (son of the Procope who
owned the café frequented by the theatrical world) as
well as Voltaire's various little hangers-on, some of whom

were to receive money for their pains. Money, indeed, was not to be spared. They were all, including Moussinot himself, to pretend to be members of Voltaire's outraged family. It was thought that this display of clannish solidarity would have a good effect on the magistrate. No wriggling out was to be allowed: 'No ifs and ans, no buts, friendship must surmount all obstacles.'

Unfortunately, Thieriot was not guided by this sentiment. In vain did Voltaire write urging him not to listen to those who would advise him to drink a jolly glass of champagne and forget the rest. He should drink but he should also fulfil the sacred and interesting duties of friendship. The tears are pouring down Voltaire's cheeks as he writes: can Thieriot remain deaf to such an appeal? Thieriot remained not only deaf but dumb; after his one letter to Mme du Châtelet he took refuge in silence. Voltaire wrote to him on 2 January, 7, 9, 10, (undated), 15, 17. Mme du Châtelet wrote again. The Marquis wrote. 'M. du Châtelet,' said his wife, 'has behaved like an angel.' Mme de Champbonin (who had suddenly become Voltaire's cousin) wrote a letter soaked in tears. At last, on the 18th January a letter was received from 'this soul of mud' but it did not give much satisfaction at Cirey. Thieriot said he was very sorry for Voltaire, he pitied him from the bottom of his heart. He then went back, irrelevantly, to the old story of the lost, or stolen, copies of the *Henriade*. He answered none of Voltaire's questions, nor did he speak of the petition. He evidently did not intend to appear as a witness. Worst of all, they now learnt from another source that he was going to publish his own letter to Mme du Châtelet in Abbé Prévost's paper *Le Pour et Contre*. More rivers of mingled ink and tears flowed to Paris from Cirey. The good d'Argental managed to stop this publication which would, of course, have been compromising to Emilie. They were all far more furious now with Thieriot than with Desfontaines. His letter replying to M. du Châtelet was opened by Emilie who said that it was neither decent, nor intelligible nor even in good French. They sent it back to Thieriot, telling him to correct it.

Meanwhile Voltaire was writing to everybody he knew to canvass support for his lawsuit. On the whole, his friends responded quite well. Frederick refused, it is true, to break with Thieriot who, he said, had done no more than his duty in sending *La Voltairomanie*. He particularly wished to see all attacks on Voltaire, otherwise how should he understand what was going on? But he instructed his father's Minister in Paris to do what he could for Voltaire. Mme de Champbonin and the Marquis du Châtelet went to Paris to pull strings. The powerful d'Argenson brothers weighed in on Voltaire's side, and so did various old legal friends of his father. Richelieu was at Toulouse, governing Languedoc, and therefore out of action, but he wrote denying a statement, in *La Voltairomanie*, to do with his first wife. Even poor Linant wrote, a pathetic little letter saying that Voltaire had always been like a father to him. Thieriot after many a talking-to from Mme de Champbonin and a letter from Frederick, and seeing, probably, that the wind was now blowing in Voltaire's direction, consented half-heartedly to give the required evidence. He said that he would have acted before if he had understood exactly what was expected of him. In spite of the way he had been treated, however, he would always be fond of his old friend, though he did not think much of his talent as a writer.

The end of this long and increasingly tedious affair might be described as a draw, rather in Voltaire's favour (April 1739). The Abbé was obliged to sign a document stating that he regarded *La Voltairomanie* as a gross libel and that he would have considered himself dishonoured if he had had anything to do with it. Voltaire then disavowed *Le Préservatif*. His friends begged him to stop tormenting Desfontaines, and while of course he gave no such engagement, he did manage to ignore the Abbé thereafter. As for the Abbé himself, he went out of his way to write an eulogistic account, in *Observations*, of Mme du Châtelet's essay on fire. Both the opponents were exhausted by the great battle; a lasting peace ensued. As traitors so often are at the end of hostilities, Thieriot was forgiven. Voltaire said that everybody has a good angel and a bad; in his case one was d'Argental and the other Thieriot. But it is degrading to quarrel with old friends.

# Chapter Eleven

## Mme de Grafigny's Story

'PERHAPS we may look in upon the Cirey household at some future time; and—this editor hopes not,' says Thomas Carlyle. The present editor, however, cannot resist sending the reader on Mme de Grafigny's conducted tour; the reader bearing in mind that she alone is the guide and that there is no corroboration of the scenes which she is about to expose.

While the events described in the last chapter were tormenting the philosophers of Cirey, their guest remained in ignorance of what was going on. She had troubles of her own, including the worst troubles that can assail a middle-aged woman: no home and no money. She was forced to be a country-house parasite, living on a circle of good-natured friends. The type is well known, it has always existed and will, no doubt, continue to do so as long as there are country-houses to harbour it. The parasite sits by the fire in winter, under the cedar tree in summer, ready to perform little jobs for her hosts; she knows every detail of the household, all about the servants, the dogs, the children, the neighbours. It is her special function to be agreeable to whichever member of the family is providing a problem: neglected wife, betrayed husband, cross old uncle, slightly idiotic son. She thus relieves the guilt-feelings of the others and makes everything go more swimmingly. She never has to be entertained; she writes innumerable letters. Her technique has improved since Mme de Grafigny's day and it would be interesting to see one of our modern experts coping with the situation that faced her at Cirey.

Madame de Grafigny was now about forty-four, the same age as Voltaire, whom she had met at Lunéville when the last Duke of Lorraine was ruling there. Since then the Duke had gone to Vienna, to marry Maria-Theresa, the Austrian heiress. Under the Treaty of Vienna, 1738, Lorraine had been given to Stanislas Leczinski, ex-king of Poland and father-in-law of Louis XV, to compensate him for the loss of his own country. Lunéville was about a day's journey from Cirey; du Châtelet often went there, as he had interests in Lorraine. Voltaire and Emilie had not yet paid their court to Stanislas, though both of them had known Lunéville under the former reign and had many friends there. Mme de Grafigny's husband had been Chamberlain at that Court; he was a beastly madman, had nearly killed his wife more than once, and was now shut up. She had obtained a legal separation from him on grounds of cruelty, very unusual in those days. Mme de Richelieu asked Emilie to harbour her for a while, until the Richelieus came back from Toulouse and could have her to live with them. Emilie did not want her in the least but she would have done anything to please this Duchess.

Voltaire and Emilie were divided on the subject of guests. He longed to have his friends to stay and, according to him, Cirey was on the way, wherever they were going. (He told Sir Everard Fawkener that it was on the way from Calais to Paris and once when d'Argenson was supposed to be going to Lisbon, Cirey was said to be on the way there.) But Mme du Châtelet, when she invited somebody, which was unusual, used to say quite firmly, 'You must come for the sake of coming.' Indeed, situated in a remote corner of Champagne, Cirey is on the way nowhere. Emilie very much preferred, for the present,

not to have anybody, unless of course it could be Maupertuis. The work on which she was engaged, an intensive
study of the philosophy of Leibnitz, required con-
centration. Her thought was beginning to run counter
to that of her lover, so unusual in a woman. He never
accepted the ideas of Leibnitz and the two philosophers of Cirey agreed to differ on this subject. 'One
must love one's friends whatever side they take,' he said.
Voltaire too was working hard at several different things,
but he could do so in the midst of a pandemonium
(Frederick used to say he had a hundred arms). Mme du
Châtelet needed quiet and calm. She had no desire to
look after visitors; emotional upsets, which seemed, if
anything, to stimulate Voltaire, were bad for her. Soon
after Mme de Grafigny's arrival at Cirey the atmosphere became heavy with the emotion caused by *La
Voltairomanie*. She could hardly have chosen a more unfortunate time to be there.

Mme de Grafigny had many friends at Lunéville, and
they were agog to hear every detail of the goings-on at
legendary Cirey. It was arranged that she should write
her news to M. Devaux and that he would communicate
it to the others. Devaux, who was never called anything
but Pan-pan, or Panpichon, was the spoilt darling of all
the Lunéville women. He was twenty-seven, had been
destined by his family for the law, but when he grew up
was observed to have a notable aversion to work, although
fond of a little light reading. So his various friends
at the Court asked King Stanislas to take him on as
reader. The good King, who was by no means bookish,
said very well, but that his functions would be those of
Louis XV's confessor, in other words nil. Everybody liked
Pan-pan, and Mme de Grafigny wrote to him as *tu*, then
almost unheard of in France between an unrelated man
and woman. On 4 December 1738 she went to Cirey
from the house of another friend, Mme de Stainville,

which she disloyally called *le château de l'ennui*. From now on every moment of every day was described in her famous letters to Pan-pan.

Cirey, Thursday, 4 December 1738. Pan-pan will jump for joy when he sees where this letter is dated. 'Ah! Mon Dieu, she is at Cirey! But how ever did she get there?' Well, she borrowed horses from a fellow guest and left *le château de l'ennui* before daylight. The day which dawned was perfect, more like June than December except that there was no dust on the roads; she was in a state of euphoria. At Joinville her friend's coachman refused to go on, and she got into a public conveyance which set her down, on a deserted road, two hours after dark. She and Dubois, her maid, trembling with terror, had to feel their way up a mountain; they arrived at Cirey more dead than alive. Mme du Châtelet received her guest kindly and took her to her room, where presently Voltaire appeared, holding a little candle, like a monk. He gave Mme de Grafigny a tremendous welcome and thousands of caresses, he kissed her hand ten times. He asked her news, and took an interest in her replies which touched her to the heart. He spoke of Pan-pan for at least a quarter of an hour before asking about his other friends at Lunéville. Then he left her so that she could dress for supper, which she did, and now here she is, waiting for the bell to ring. She takes up her pen once more. She had said that Mme du Châtelet received her kindly. Yes. But that was all. She wears a printed cotton dress and a huge black taffeta apron, her long black hair is tied to the top of her head, falling in ringlets like a little girl's; this suits her perfectly. She talks like an angel. As for Voltaire, he is dressed and powdered exactly as he would be in Paris. M. du Châtelet is there, but leaving the next day for Brussels so then there will be the three of them. They had already confided in each other that this will not make them cry. Still no bell. Pan-pan's letters are a great joy, he must be sure to go on writing. She misses them all at Lunéville dreadfully. 'So, goodnight, dearest friend.'

*Next day.* Heavens, where to begin! The best plan will be to tell everything that happens, not day by day but hour by hour. So she wrote until supper-time last night, when they came to fetch her and took her to Voltaire's part of the house. No time to look round, they sat down to supper at once. What an enchantment! Delicious food, not too much of it, and so well served—beautiful silver on the table. As Voltaire's study is not ready yet there were globes and various scientific instruments lying about. Impossible to do justice to the conversation which was sparkling in the extreme; it ranged over poetry, science and art and was full of jokes. Voltaire was on her right, so learned, so polite and so sweet; the host on her left, rather dull, but he hardly spoke and went away long before the end of the meal. They were talking of books when somebody mentioned Jean-Baptiste Rousseau upon which Voltaire became less of a hero and more of a human being. It is forbidden to praise Rousseau here. The dame [Mme du Châtelet] says she can't bear odes and the idol [Voltaire] can't understand how any civilized person can read such sad stuff. Then they talked about Abbé Desfontaines's paper, *Observations*. Mme de Grafigny asked if they took it in? Indeed they did, and all of a sudden there was a perfect stream of invective against it. Voltaire pressed into her hands a pamphlet called *Le Préservatif contre les Observations*, written, so he said, by a friend of his. She will send a copy to Pan-pan.

At last they all went to bed and goodness gracious how she slept! She only woke up at twelve, so stiff from yesterday's climb that she could hardly move. The dame visited her in the morning, rather nicer to her than before. Mme de Grafigny has read *Le Préservatif* in order to be able to say so and Voltaire has sent up a copy of Newton to her room. Well, it seems they don't dine in this house, so she read Newton all day in order to have something to talk about at supper. She didn't do too badly, she understood quite a lot. While she was struggling away with it, she had a visitor in the shape of Mme de Champ-bonin, a country neighbour of the du Châtelets who spends most of her time at Cirey. She is exactly like the short fat woman in Marivaux's *Paysan Parvenu*, but really rather a dear; she positively worships Voltaire. Poor woman, they do lead her a dance, they shut her up in her room and make her read all the books in the house, and she is none the wiser for it. She didn't stay long. Then Voltaire came but Mme de Grafigny chased him away as her room is chilly and he has a dreadful cold. Fancy chasing Voltaire! After that the host appeared and bored her for two hours until Voltaire rescued her by sending for her to go and see him. She didn't have to be asked twice!

Voltaire's wing of the house is at the bottom of the main staircase. You go through a tiny antechamber to his bedroom which is small and low and hung with crushed velvet in the winter. Not much tapestry but gilded panelling with pictures set in it; the furniture is chinoiserie. The looking-glasses, lacquer corner-cupboards, china, a clock supported by marabouts, and many, many other valuable things are all in that taste. There is a ring holder with twelve rings of engraved stones and two of diamonds. Everything so clean you could kiss the parquet. A gallery thirty or forty feet long leads out of this room. It has three windows and between them are two very exquisite little statues on lacquer bases; one is the Farnese Venus and the other Hercules. Two cupboards, for books and scientific instruments, have a stove between them which heats the gallery so that it feels like springtime—this will eventually be hidden by a statue of Cupid. The panelling is yellow lacquer, there is a quantity of furniture, clocks, etc., nothing missing unless it be a comfortable chair to sit on. Bodily comfort doesn't seem necessary to Voltaire.

Supper was rather disappointing. There was a tedious fellow called Trichâteau, of whom M. du Châtelet has expectations (he is a cousin) and one had to talk to him. However, she had a little chat with Voltaire afterwards; he spoke of Pan-pan, and said he really ought to do something with his life. 'His father should turn him out, as mine did.' Saint-Lambert,* however, has talent. By the way, Saint-Lambert gave her a message for Voltaire which she has forgotten; can Pan-pan find out what it was?

That was her day, yesterday. This morning she came down at eleven for coffee which they drank in the gallery. Voltaire was in a dressing-gown, his cold is really awful. Then the dame took Mme de Grafigny to see her own rooms. Voltaire's are simply nothing at all compared with these. Her bedroom is panelled in yellow and blue, the alcove for the bed lined with Indian paper, the bed covered with blue moiré—everything, even the dog's basket, is to match. The looking glasses have silver frames, beautifully cleaned. A big glass door, decorated like a snuff-box, leads to the library which is not yet finished, it will have pictures by Paul Veronese. Beside the alcove there is a tiny boudoir; one could fall on one's knees it is so pretty, panelled in blue with a ceiling by a pupil of Martin who has been working here for the last three years. Each panel has a picture by Watteau. There is a chimney-piece with brackets by Martin, which have pretty little things on them, and an amber ink-stand sent with some verses by the Prince of Prussia. A big armchair and two footstools to match are all upholstered

* The Marquis de Saint-Lambert, another Lunéville friend. Mme du Châtelet did not know him as yet.

in white taffeta. This divine boudoir has one window
leading on to a terrace with an admirable view. The
other side of the bed there is a dressing-room paved with
marble, panelled in grey wood and hung with delightful prints. Everything is in perfect taste, including the
curtains which are embroidered muslin. When they had
seen it all, Mme du Châtelet kept her guest in her bedroom and expounded the details of a lawsuit in which
her husband's family had been involved for the last eighty
years. Strange to say she was not boring about it, although
she went on for an hour and a half; she spoke so well that
it was impossible not to be fascinated. She also showed
Mme de Grafigny her jewels which are more beautiful
than Mme de Richelieu's. Funny thing, when she was at
Craon in the old days she didn't possess so much as a
tortoise-shell snuff-box. Now she has at least twenty,
some of gold with precious stones and some in the new
fashion of enamel on gold which is so expensive, as well
as jasper and diamond watches, jewelled *étuis*, rings
with rare stones, in fact no end of trinkets. Mme de
Grafigny was amazed, for the du Châtelets had never
been rich.

The post has arrived—no letter for Mme de Grafigny,
how sad. Back in her own room, she will describe that.
Well, it is absolutely vast and very dark with one
draughty little ill-fitting window which looks on to an
arid mountain you could touch by putting out your
hand, it is so near. [Quite untrue, there is no such mountain at Cirey.] The tapestry is covered with large ugly
people whom she cannot place at all. The bed is upholstered with bits of stuff quite nice in themselves but
which don't match so the effect is hideous. The fireplace is tiny and so deep that you could burn a forest
there without raising the temperature of the room. The
furniture consists of old-fashioned chairs and a chest of
drawers; beside her bed is the only table. She hates this

horrid room, really her maid's is better, though that has
no outside window at all. Except in the part of the house
inhabited by Voltaire and Mme du Châtelet, everything is disgustingly squalid and that's the truth.

Now that Pan-pan knows what the house is like they
will talk about people. It seems the Prince of Prussia sent
an embassy here to bring his portrait and to take away
the *Siècle de Louis XIV*. He must be a handsome prince,
not unlike M. de Richelieu. Voltaire spends his time
looking out books for Mme de Grafigny to read—
manuscripts, too. What a pity she can't copy them and
send them to her Panpichon. By the way, Pan-pan must
be careful how he repeats the things she tells him as it
would never do for her to get into a scrape with these
people. Could he be a dear and go to La Tour for her,
get some of that yellow mouth-wash which is so good for
the horrid little things that come in her mouth and send
it to Cirey? But La Tour mustn't know it's for her, because she owes him money. Good night, good night—she
is off to supper, to stoke up for the morrow.

The letters become more and more enthusiastic, quite
incoherent in fact. Voltaire told funny stories, oh how
she pities Pan-pan for not being here, really they burst
their sides with laughing. Then he read out Algarotti's
book, *Newtonianismo per le dame*, which has just been translated. Only imagine, there was something about physics
being like a town with fields round it; nobody could help
shrieking, though Algarotti is a friend here. Mme de
Grafigny is reading *Louis XIV* now—there's an account
of the Fronde which is simply divine. But the dame won't
let Voltaire finish it, she keeps it under lock and key and
forces him to do geometry. She herself is strangely ignorant of history. They have their tiffs like everybody
else. This evening she had gone to bed, they were sitting
in her bedroom and she told Voltaire to go and change
his coat. It's not a pretty coat, certainly, but he had

beautiful lace and was well powdered. He refused to change it, saying he would catch cold. She went on nagging until he spoke very sharply in English and left the room. She sent after him but no, he was sulking. Then a neighbour arrived and Mme de Grafigny went to find Voltaire who was chatting to the fat lady, as merry as could be. The dame presently sent word to say they were all to come back, but as soon as he saw her Voltaire turned sulky again. Finally they had it out in English and everything was all right after that. This was the first sign that they were lovers because as a rule they behaved with great circumspection together, though the dame leads him rather a dance. By the way, Panpichon can write as often as he likes because the incoming letters are all paid for, is that not gallant? She only wishes it were the same for the ones that go out—oh well!

The dame wanted her to go for a drive, but the horses looked a bit frisky so she went for a walk with fat Mme de Champbonin who then took her to see the bathroom. That is an enchantment! It is entirely lined with tiles, with a marble floor and porcelain baths. The little *cabinet de toilette* has carved and gilded panels of celadon green—so gay, so divine—with a tiny sofa and chairs of the same wood, also carved and gilded. There are prints and pictures, china, a dressing-table, and the ceiling is painted. The other place is to match and here there are looking-glasses and books lying about on lacquer tables. The whole thing is Lilliputian, so pretty, delicious and enchanting that, if it belonged to Mme de Grafigny, she would have herself woken up in the night to go and look at it. All this made a little change because usually she is in her bedroom from midday to supper-time (9 p.m.) without seeing a soul, though not bored for a minute because she has so much to read. Last night Voltaire gave a magic-lantern show, with stories about M. de Richelieu, the Abbé Desfontaines and so on which killed them all with laughing. She is reading some of Voltaire's *Epîtres* at the moment and she likes his notion that pleasure proves the existence of a Creator whom we must love while enjoying ourselves.

Elisabeth de Breteuil has arrived; he is an Abbé and the brother of Mme du Châtelet.* He seems most agreeable and has brought a lot of gossip from Paris. So they will give a performance of Voltaire's comedy, *Boursoufle*, in his honour, they are all busily learning their parts. Mme de Grafigny is coaching the little girl in hers. Panpan really might write more often. No post now till Saturday, it does seem far off. And by the way he must look carefully at his letters to see if anybody has been at them—if he suspects anything he must let her know. Her hosts seem so frightened that she will be indiscreet, she can't quite think why as she never stops saying how perfect everything is. It seems the presence of the brother is a secret however.

She's waiting for the post, it really should have come by now. When it does come, the letters have been written such a long time ago, and then why is Pan-pan not receiving hers? These delays are very odd. The dame always makes up the parcels of letters for the post herself —at night.

Pan-pan says he hasn't quite understood how the day at Cirey is arranged. From eleven until noon there is coffee in Voltaire's gallery, and at noon a meal, which they call the coachmen's dinner, for M. du Châtelet, Mme de Champbonin and the little boy. Voltaire, the dame and Mme de Grafigny look in at it for about half an hour, after which they all go back to their rooms. At four o'clock they sometimes assemble again for a *goûter*, but not every day. Supper at nine o'clock, and they are together until midnight. Oh how she pities her poor friends for not being here to share in this delightful exist-

* Mme du Châtelet's brother, born 1711, was christened Elisabeth.

ence! The dame would like to invite Desmarets,* if he
cared to come and if he could learn two or three parts
beforehand, but Mme de Grafigny thinks he is with his
regiment. She suggests Saint-Lambert, but the dame says
she can only have him if he knows how to stay in his own
room and accommodate himself to their ways. The
dame doesn't really care for visitors, it seems, in fact
she dreads them. Solitude is what she desires. In future
Mme de Grafigny will refer to Voltaire as Nicomède
and the dame as Dorothée, it will be safer. Then she can
say what she thinks, quite comfortably.

Mme de Grafigny now hears that her furniture is going
to be sold, to pay her debts. Pan-pan must try and stop
that, or at any rate send her one of her dresses. One
more or less won't make any difference, it can't be dis-
honourable, but if it is, so much the worse. She wants it.
She has been very low, terrible vapours, she has taken
opium but it did no good at all. Finally the vapours
were cured by Voltaire reading out his *Jeanne* [*La
Pucelle*] which he did in the bathroom. The servant who
went to Lunéville has come back without the mouth-
wash. It is really too bad. Of course Mme de Grafigny
has the satisfaction of thinking how much nicer she is
to her friends than they are to her, but that doesn't cure
her mouth.

To tell the truth she feels sorry for Nicomède because
he and Dorothée don't really get on. Alas! once again we
see that there is no such thing as happiness under the sky.
We think people are quite happy if we only see them
from time to time, but if we insert ourselves into their
lives it is like the Empire of the Moon. Happiness is not
the lot of mankind, Hell is everywhere, since we carry it
inside us.

Now there have been two more readings of *Jeanne*.
Mme de Grafigny gives an account of the latest stanza

* Léopold Desmarets was Mme de Grafigny's lover.

VOLTAIRE IN 1732
by Maurice Quentin de La Tour, engraved by Ficquet

LA MARQUISE DU CHÂTELET 1706-1749
by F.-B. Lépicié
*By courtesy of Mme. Thierry*

ARMAND DU PLESSIS,
DUC DE RICHELIEU
1694-1788
From a painting by an
unknown artist in the
Musée d'Agen

*Photo: Bulloz*

PIERRE-LOUIS MOREAU DE
MAUPERTUIS 1698-1759
Engraving after
R. de Tournières
*By courtesy of the Trustees of the
British Museum*

ABBÉ DESPONTAINES
1685-1745
Engraving by
Desruchers

*Photo: Radio Times Hulton
Picture Library*

LA MARQUISE DE
GRAFIGNY 1695-1758
by F.-B. Lépicié

*Photo: Roger Viollet*

GABRIELLE-ÉMILIE DE BRETEUIL, MARQUISE DU CHÂTELET
From an unidentified painting in the possession of Comte Charles de Breteuil

FREDERICK THE
GREAT, 1712-1786
by Antoine Pesne
*By courtesy of the
Staatliche Museum,
Berlin*

*Photo: Radio Times Hulton
Picture Library*

PRESIDENT
HÉNAULT,
1685-1770
Engraving after
St. Aubin

*By courtesy of the
Trustees of the British
Museum*

LA MARQUISE DE
BOUFFLERS, née
BEAUVAU,
1711-1787
by J.-M. Nattier
*By courtesy of
M. Knoedler & Co.*

LE MARQUIS DE SAINT-
LAMBERT, 1763-1703
by an unknown artist
*By courtesy of the
Vicomte Foy*

*Photo: Radio Times Hulton
Picture Library*

MME. DU CHÂTELET
by Mlle. Loir

BUST OF VOLTAIRE,
1748
after J.-B. Lemoyne, in
the Musée de Chaalis

which is about a certain Agnès. Agnès has an affair with
a page on whose bottom Jeanne had painted a *fleur-de-
lis*. The English appear, there is a battle and Agnès's
horse runs away with her to a convent. Since she is in a
penitent mood she rings the bell and Sister Besogne
opens the door. She takes Agnès to her cell and goes to
bed with her—Sister Besogne, as it happens, is a young
esquire whom the Abbess keeps there to minister to her.
The Abbess, luckily, is away, so Agnès has an exceedingly
diverting time. Mme de Grafigny reminds Pan-pan that
he must be very careful whom he tells this to, as it is a
terrific secret. Also he must be careful how he writes
about Dorothée. If he were at Cirey he would realize
that she is not often as Mme de Grafigny first described
her, but generally cold and hard, it is not very easy to
get on with her. As for Nicodème, he is really a little bit
mad on the subject of Jean-Baptiste Rousseau and Desfontaines. Mme de Grafigny tries to persuade him that
he ought to despise them but he cannot see reason where
they are concerned. He has caricatures made of them and
writes the captions, in verse, himself; he really longs for
everybody to know this but doesn't quite dare admit it.
Pan-pan must be careful how he answers this letter.

After supper the dame asked Mme de Grafigny if she
had ever had any children. Her hosts knew nothing
about her life so she told them the whole story. The
recital had a tremendous effect. The dame was seized
with a fit of giggles which she explained away by saying
she must laugh in order not to cry. [Indeed, the vision of
Mme de Grafigny being flung about in an access of
sadistic passion by her mad husband might well have
been irresistibly funny.] But Voltaire, the human Voltaire, was quite overcome and he wept. He is never
ashamed to show his feelings. 'What, none of your friends
came to the rescue?' In the end they all cried and went
on talking until two in the morning. Good Mme de

Champbonin, who generally goes to bed at eleven, was
in Mme de Grafigny's bedroom when she went upstairs
and stayed there consoling her until three. Pan-pan sees
what charming people she is with.

They are going to give *Boursoufle* and Mme de Grafigny has the part of a wife who loves without return. Oh
how well she will act that! Voltaire suggests, 'Let's
make Pan-pan come here'; she replies, 'But you know
Pan-pan, he is dreadfully shy, he would never open his
mouth in front of this beautiful lady.' Says Voltaire:
'The first day he can look at her through a keyhole, the
second he can stay in the little room next door and the
third day he can sit behind a screen. We shall love him
so much that he'll become quite tame.' 'What nonsense,'
says the dame, 'I shall be charmed to see him and I hope
he won't be frightened of me.' Mme de Grafigny says if
he comes they can give *La Mort de César*; Voltaire is enchanted at the idea as it is his favourite play.

On Christmas Day, it will be remembered, Voltaire
and Mme du Châtelet both read *La Voltairomanie*. Mme
de Grafigny, not knowing that they had had this terrible
shock, rattled on to Pan-pan, saying that Voltaire
seemed very unwell, in bed, with a temperature. They
heard Midnight Mass from his room. He said he had been
having a long talk with the Virgin—he would rather deal
with her than with the others. Next day he was ill again
and very low, though very polite. Mme du Châtelet
began to read aloud a new novel by Moncrif, but it was
too badly written and she had to give it up. Mme de
Grafigny is still struggling with Newton but she would
love to give that up too. Oh! it is dull! Pan-pan's
letters all about the jollities at Lunéville made her cry—
how she loves her friends there. Alas, dear treasures, she
hopes they talk about her sometimes. Desmarets' letter
putting off his visit has cast her down dreadfully.

From now on Mme de Grafigny's outlook changed

entirely. She was no longer the happiest, luckiest person
in the world, she no longer felt sorry for Panpichon and
all who were not living in the same house as the Idol.
Her letters are pathetic. The cold of a Continental
winter has descended upon Cirey and the poor woman
hates her horrid room more and more. The draughts
are so terrible they nearly put out her candle, she sits
with a screen round her but it does no good. She
has no comfortable chair, her body is not at ease.
Then the hours go so slowly, it is now 7 p.m. and
she has seen nobody all day. When she went down for
coffee at eleven, the door was bolted. None of this would
matter if she were a little more comfortable. It's not
that they are mean with wood, there's a fire like the
burning of Troy in her fireplace but the room gets no
warmer. There are thirty-two fires in the house altogether. Then her dog, Lise, is on heat and Mme de
Grafigny is afraid she will be covered by one of those
great mongrels in the farm-yard. Another misfortune:
Dubois has given notice. Well, she has been unbearable
lately, so rude and bad-tempered. And now here
is the post and not a single letter. What does it mean?
She is too sad, her friends alone keep her going and she
begs them to remember it.

It is New Year's Day, she has been ill with colic.
Pan-pan has written to say the stanza of *Jeanne* is charming. Mme de Grafigny tells him to send back whatever
she wrote on the subject. This is terribly important, he
must send it and make no more comments, he has been
indiscreet enough as it is. He asks where she will be in
March. Certainly not at Cirey. She hasn't enough money
to go to Paris so she has sent to Saint-Dizier to know if
there's not a convent where she could retire. He will ask
why Saint-Dizier? Because it seems the posts there are
regular and the only pleasure she has left in the world is
the letters of her friends. Besides it is on the way to

Paris. Once a year somebody might visit her for an hour. Admittedly she wouldn't think of such a thing if there were a better prospect in view, but as there is not she must fulfil her destiny.

A few days later she has received a letter from Pan-pan, but another seems to be lost. He must tell her what was in it, without fail. Her vapours are no better, worse if anything, she seldom goes downstairs now at all. Oh! how divine philosophy would be if it were any help to one!

Pan-pan's next letter had definitely been opened and very badly re-sealed. How disagreeable, really. She is terribly worried about her future, she is sorry to bore Pan-pan with it, but who else is there? Were it not for the fat lady she would have gone mad by now. Of course that ass of a Dubois has allowed Lise to be covered, just as Mme de Grafigny had feared—now they'll have to see about an abortion which may well have fatal results. She has never loved the poor little dog so much. That's it, they can all laugh at her, laugh away, she's only too delighted to make somebody laugh. Two more letters have arrived, obviously opened and Pan-pan seems not to have received hers asking for the stanza from *Jeanne*. She has written to see if her friend Mme de Chatenay can have her for a little while before she goes into a convent. Pan-pan must send her back that letter about *Jeanne*—oh she has already said this, the vapours are making her stupid. If he could see her trembling fits he would be sorry for her. She has been ill for a fortnight. Voltaire has been most good to her and so has Mme de Champbonin. She never goes down for coffee any more, she has some soup with those who dine at midday and the rest of the time she is in her own room. She did, however, sup with M. de Maupertuis when he was there and found him very jolly and learned. As she is neither she never opened her mouth.

She must now tell Pan-pan a dreadful thing. She has

no money at all. If he asks why, the answer is that on her way to Cirey she realized that her old dress would not do and she bought herself a satin one for a louis. Dubois needed a tidy cotton dress, which she also bought and tips to the coachmen finished her few remaining pence. She has written to Mme Badaud to see if she can give her a bed. It seems that Desmarets will be at Cirey in a day or two—Mme du Châtelet has sent up a message to say so, oh what good news!

It is Shrove Tuesday. Desmarets has arrived. He has hardly spoken to her but they have been living in a whirl as an enormous programme of theatricals is on foot. They have learnt and rehearsed thirty-three different acts, have given *Zaïre*, *l'Enfant Prodigue*, and *l'Esprit de Contradiction*. Her vapours are cured, Mme Badaud can have her and she is to leave Cirey in a day or two. Dubois has already gone on, with the luggage. Desmarets is a wonderful actor, nobody can talk of anything else; the wretch has certainly missed his vocation. All day they rehearse and learn their parts and the acting goes on all night, there's no time to breathe, let alone write letters. They have just finished the third act they have given today. It is midnight and they are going to sup, after which Mme du Châtelet will sing a whole opera. This is the last time she will write from Cirey, she can't answer Pan-pan's letter now, she rushes to the delights that beckon to her, though if she had wings she would fly into Pan-pan's arms.

How we wish we could leave Mme de Grafigny on this cheerful if slightly hysterical note. However the moment she was safely away from Cirey, on 12 February, she put into the post a letter she had been cooking up for several weeks, which threw a lurid light on past events and fully explained her change of spirits.

'My dearest friend, I can now tell you a horrible thing that happened to me——'

She told Pan-pan that on 29 December they said there were no letters for her. Supper went off fairly well, nobody spoke much certainly, but there was no indication that a storm was about to break over her head and she went quietly upstairs at bedtime. All of a sudden, to her great surprise, Voltaire burst into her room crying that he was lost, that she held his life in her hands, that copies of the last stanza of *Jeanne* were in full circulation and that he would have to leave for Holland then and there. He said that Mme de Grafigny must write now, this minute, a letter, which M. du Châtelet himself would take, to Pan-pan begging him to call in all the copies. But would Pan-pan do it? Mme de Grafigny said of course Pan-pan would do anything for Voltaire and of course she would write. She was only too sorry that such a thing should have happened while she was at Cirey. 'Don't try wriggling, Madame, you sent it yourself.' She could hardly believe her ears. She assured Voltaire that she had never seen a verse of *Jeanne* in her life, how could she have made a copy? He refused to listen to her. He said that Pan-pan had read it aloud in a friend's house and had been giving it to everybody, saying that it came from Mme de Grafigny. Mme du Châtelet, he added, had the proof in her pocket. Poor Mme de Grafigny was completely at sea but nevertheless very frightened. He sat her down and told her to write for the original and the copies. As she really could not ask Pan-pan for something she had never sent, she told him to try and find out what had happened. Voltaire read the letter and threw it at her with yelps of despair, shrieking that his very life was at stake unless she would act in good faith. As nothing the poor woman could say had any effect she took refuge in silence.

This dreadful scene had gone on for a whole hour when in surged the dame. She howled and raged like a fury repeating what Voltaire had already said, over and over again, Mme de Grafigny keeping the same silence. At last the dame produced a letter which she handed to Mme de Grafigny saying: 'You wretched creature, you beast, I've been sheltering you for weeks, not from friendship God knows but because you'd nowhere to go, and now you have betrayed me—murdered me—stolen a paper from my desk and copied it——' She went on like this, screaming into Mme de Grafigny's face; only the presence of Voltaire seemed to restrain her from physical violence. At last Mme de Grafigny said, 'Madame, I am a poor thing—you have no right to treat me so.' Voltaire then put an arm round Mme du Châtelet and pulled her away, after which she strode up and down the room crying treachery. Dubois, two rooms off, heard every word. Poor Mme de Grafigny was more dead than alive. At last she asked for the proof of her alleged misdeed. It was a letter to her from Pan-pan and merely said, 'the stanza from *Jeanne* is charming'. Then of course Mme de Grafigny saw the whole thing, as she would have seen it sooner if they had given her time to collect her thoughts. She explained that what she had sent Pan-pan was a little account of the stanza and the impression it had made on her. Voltaire believed her at once and begged her pardon. He said that Pan-pan had read her letter to Desmarets, who had told somebody about it. That somebody had told Mme du Châtelet who had then opened Pan-pan's letter which seemed to confirm her worst fears. It was now five in the morning. Mme du Châtelet was still not appeased. Voltaire talked to her for a long time in English and finally obliged her to say that she believed Mme de Grafigny and was sorry she had spoken as she did. They made her write to Pan-pan and ask for her original letter, to prove that she was innocent, and then they left her. An hour after they had gone the fat lady who, hearing all the noise had looked in and quickly fled again, came back. Mme de Grafigny was being sick.

She asked Pan-pan to envisage her situation after this, without a home, without money and unable to leave a house where she had been so insulted. She would rather have slept on straw than stayed there, but had not the wherewithal even to go to the nearest village. 'Oh! Pan-pan!' Next day at noon the good Voltaire came back, almost in tears at the state he found her in; he said over and over again how sorry he was. M. du Châtelet came too and was very kind to her. At eight o'clock the dame came, supported by M. du Châtelet and the fat lady. She curtseyed, said: 'Madame, I am sorry for what happened last night', and then calmly spoke of other things. Ever since then Mme de Grafigny's life had simply been hell. She was shut up in her room all day and every day with nothing to read but the deadliest books. Voltaire and the dame got all the novelties from Paris but nobody else ever saw them. The suppers were an agony with the Shrew giving her furious looks; as soon as they were over she went upstairs again. The fat lady was nice to her but she is their friend and naturally was obliged to take their side. She said the Shrew was being so disagreeable because she felt guilty. All the same, Mme de Grafigny will never forget the fat lady's goodness.

When at last Desmarets came things were not much better. The first thing he did was to tell Mme de Grafigny that all was over between him and her; he neither loved nor wished to love her. Then the dame made up to him quite brazenly, languishing after him like a silly little débutante and they had an affair under the very noses of herself and Voltaire. Voltaire was furious, bitterly sarcastic with both of them.

When Mme du Châtelet knew that Mme de Grafigny had made arrangements to leave Cirey she began begging her to stay on: 'What will Mme de Richelieu say if she hears you are going already?' (It is regrettable to note that as soon as Mme de Grafigny had got away from Cirey, Emilie wrote her a very undignified letter, asking did she love the inhabitants of Cirey a little? She was clearly very much afraid of the stories which her erstwhile guest might put about Paris.)

The rest of Mme de Grafigny's retrospective letter was full of reproaches to Pan-pan for his various indiscretions, not only the things he had repeated at Lunéville from her letters and the silly observations on them which he made in his (all read, of course, by the dame) but for the irresponsible way in which he sent back her letter with the account of *Jeanne*. She had written in it that she was hoping to arrange things so that she could stay on at Cirey. As usual they had opened it before sending it up to her—see how humiliating this was in the circumstances! Really Pan-pan might have cut that bit out. Summing up the character of Nicodème and Dorothée she said they were both eaten with jealousy, he of other writers and she of him. According to Mme de Grafigny Emilie kept a servant who did nothing but report Voltaire's movements to her—if he went to see either of the other women in their rooms a message would immediately come summoning him to Mme du Châtelet. One day he invited Mme de Grafigny to his room and was reading something aloud to her, when suddenly the dame appeared in the doorway, her hair down, her eyes flashing, white with rage and said, 'Madame, I wish to speak with Monsieur if you please!'

Safely on the road to Paris, with Desmarets, Mme de Grafigny wrote more and more cattily about her erstwhile hosts, Desmarets joining in. For his part he has never spent such an agreeable week, Voltaire's jealousy adding greatly to the fun; Mme du Châtelet has invited him to go back and he'll be hanged if he'll refuse. 'The voluptuous disorder which reigns in that house makes me regard it as a terrestrial paradise.'

Mme de Grafigny lived for the next eighteen months in elegant luxury with the Duchesse de Richelieu at Paris and Versailles. But her troubles were not over. In 1740 the Duchess died to the great sorrow of everybody who knew her. She left Mme de Grafigny a little pension, but it was not paid regularly and the unlucky woman found herself too poor even to retire into a convent. The actress Clairon took her as *dame de compagnie* for a while, but Mlle Clairon's men friends were very much against 'l'exécrable Grafigny' and that came to an end. An Irish lover called Drumgold was her next venture; he wrote a satire against Voltaire, and together they kept a lodging house. She published a few little things with no success; at last, in 1747, her undoubted literary talent came into its own, with *Lettres d'une Péruvienne* which had a vogue of sixty years and a host of admirers, including Charles X. This was followed by *Cénie*, a phenomenally successful play seen by 20,000 people. She opened a literary salon and took a niece to live with her. This niece married, for love, the enormously rich Helvétius and became a feature of Parisian society. In 1758 a play by Mme de Grafigny, *La Fille d'Aristide*, was produced, and was a failure. She died a few months later. Abbé de Voisenon said: 'She read me her play, I thought it bad, she thought me unkind. The play was put on, the public died of boredom and she of grief.' She left debts to the tune of 47,000 livres.

# Chapter Twelve

## Various Journeys

VOLTAIRE'S HEALTH had been so much impaired and his nerves so shattered by all the events of that winter, that Emilie thought it imperative for him to have a change of scene. They had been at Cirey over four years; their honeymoon had been long and on the whole successful and now they were both ready to face the world again. For some months Mme du Châtelet had been negotiating the purchase of the Hôtel Lambert or, as she called it, the Palais Lambert, a wonderful house on the Ile Saint-Louis, which has been preserved through all vicissitudes and for over a hundred years now (1957) has belonged to the Czartoryski family. She was buying, Voltaire was paying. The sale went through in the spring of 1739. They gave 200,000 livres for it and thought it a great bargain because it had cost over a million to build. But the district had become unfashionable. Voltaire said they were not buying a palace but a solitude; none but philosophers would visit them there. It was much too far away for society people. When they left Cirey, however, they did not go to Paris but to Brussels. Mme du Châtelet wanted to wind up the family lawsuit. Her husband's cousin, the Marquis de Trichâteau, who would benefit if the case were won, was safely expiring at Cirey. He had no children and had made a will in their favour. The moment seemed to have come when the affair should be settled.

So, on 8 May 1739, the du Châtelets and Voltaire set

out for the Low Countries, to the despair of all the Cirey neighbours. They had tasted the delights of Voltaire's company for so long, it must have been hard for them to return to bucolic dullness. The philosophers took in their train one Koenig, a protégé of Maupertuis, who was to give Mme du Châtelet lessons in algebra. They went by easy stages, much fêted on the way. At the garrison town of Valenciennes there were balls, ballets, comedies and many gallant colonels. They stayed a while in a dilapidated castle belonging to du Châtelet in a land of savages, cut off from all news, impossible to get the gazette, no bathrooms but fine avenues of trees. It could not compare with Cirey. Emilie was doing well with her algebra which would be a comfort all her life, according to Voltaire, and make her very agreeable in society. At last they arrived in Brussels where they took a house in the rue de la Grosse Tour and as there was nothing else to do they both settled down to hard work. Voltaire was writing *Mahomet* (a play), finishing *Louis XIV* and, as usual, rewriting and correcting old publications. Emilie, as well as her algebra, had acquainted herself with every detail of the lawsuit and was on the way to becoming a wise young judge. Voltaire had taken the practical step of getting Frederick to put in a word with the Imperial judiciary (telling them to flap it up a bit, says Carlyle) and the case, though sure to go slowly, was as good as won.

After the Peace of Utrecht in 1713 Belgium had ceased to be the Spanish Netherlands and became the Austrian Netherlands. Its history was sad and deplorable. It had been the cockpit of Europe for generations. Any native of the country who showed signs of being at all bright in the head had had it chopped off by the Regents of Spanish tyranny. It was safer not to think. The Flemings were now entirely occupied with material progress and the rebuilding of their cities; they had neither the time

nor the wish for an intellectual life. It was no place for
Voltaire and he complained bitterly. 'Brussels is the ex-
tinguisher of imagination.' 'It is the home of ignorance
and stupid indifference. There is no decent printer or
engraver, not one single man of letters. . . . This is the
country of obedience.' When he gave a fête for Emilie he
sent out invitations in the name of 'the Envoy from
Utopia', only to find that not one of the guests had ever
heard of Utopia. He and Emilie went to stay at Enghien
with the Duc d'Arenberg, where the only books in the
whole house were those they brought with them. The
host, however, charmed them (he was a powerful duke)
and the gardens were lovely. Frederick said d'Arenberg
was a debauched old fellow and told Voltaire to stop him
writing letters in German. When people wrote to
Frederick they should do so in French. The Prince sympathized with Voltaire's complaints about the Flemings
but said he should see what the Germans were like: fero-
cious as the beasts they pursued. There was, however, a
certain intellectual awakening at Berlin of which he had
hopes; some few roses were blossoming among the
nettles.

Frederick, greatly encouraged by Voltaire and other
hopeful liberals all over Europe, was now engaged upon
his *Anti-Machiavel*. He was going to refute the cynical
maxims of that Italian enemy of the human race, mouth-
piece of Satan, and prove that it was to the interest of a
ruler to be good, honest and above board. He also had a
plan for sponsoring a great *édition-de-luxe* of the *Henriade*,
to be printed and illustrated by the Englishman Pine,
famous for his beautiful *Horace*. Pine's *Henriade*, however, came to nothing; he was busy with the *Aeneid*;
Frederick declared that he ought to abandon it, since
Voltaire was greater than Virgil. Pine may not have
agreed with this verdict.

In August Voltaire and Mme du Châtelet were on the

road again, this time for a short visit to Paris, 'a town of which one used to hear much good'. Voltaire wrote to his 'gros chat', Mme de Champbonin, saying that if she asks why he goes there his answer is because he follows Emilie. But why does Emilie go? He has no idea. She declares that it is necessary and it is his destiny to believe her as well as to follow her. Not a single fête on the way back, they are like a village doctor who is fetched in a carriage and sent home on foot. Voltaire had bought pictures in Brussels for the Palais Lambert at a cost of about 6,000 livres. He declared their value at the customs as 260 livres, was caught out by the excise men and all the pictures were confiscated.

In Paris Emilie stayed with the Richelieus and Voltaire took a furnished room at the Hôtel de Brie, rue Clocheperce, in the Marais. Two pieces of news were very well received by him on arrival. Linant had won an Academy prize for a poem *Le progrès de l'éloquence sous le règne de Louis-le-Grand* and Louis XV had at last taken a mistress, Mme de Mailly. 'Down with hard hearts. God loves a tender soul.' Paris was *en fête*; the King was marrying his eldest daughter to a Spanish Prince. Voltaire thought the various entertainments were inadequate. Under Louis XIV such fêtes were presented by Molière, Corneille, Lulli and Le Brun and works of art were the result. Under the Romans solid stone arches were erected for a day's ceremonies. But now, a scaffolding is put up outside the Hôtel de Ville, where only yesterday a couple of thieves were broken on the wheel, and a few fireworks are attended by a mob of over-dressed bourgeois and poor people. The money would be better spent on a theatre or an opera house, both of which are inadequate in Paris. (Louis XV's contemporaries were always scolding him for not spending enough money.) Frederick, to whom Voltaire wrote all this, replied that he heard of nothing but fêtes and balls on every hand. In Petersburg the niece and heiress of the Empress Anne was marrying the Duke of Brunswick. Frederick had recently seen this Prince with the Duke of Lorraine (Maria-Theresa's husband) and said that he could not imagine why Providence should arrange for these two to govern the greater part of Europe between them. 'I've seen them chattering together in a way which hardly smelt of kingship.' On the other hand he was all in favour of fêtes. 'Pleasure is the greatest reality of our existence.'

Voltaire did not really enjoy his two months in Paris. The wear and tear of the life was destructive to a temperament like his own, and he realized that he would never be able to live there again for very long at a time. Everybody is in too much of a hurry, there is too much noise, haste and confusion, impossible to get hold of one's friends: the whole town seems to be whirling round in Descartes's vortex. One flies between the Opera, the theatre and seeing the sights like a foreigner. There are a hundred people to be embraced in a single day, a hundred protestations to be made and received; not a moment to oneself, no time to write, to think or to sleep. However there is one comfort, Desfontaines never shows his face anywhere now, just as J.-B. Rousseau never shows his in Brussels. These spiders are not to be found in well-kept houses.

Emilie had soared back into the social life which she loved so much. She was at the age for it, and it did not tire her. Her unsatisfactory relationship with Maupertuis was resumed; she still pursued him with little notes, alternately ordering and imploring him to come and see her. He must find her a substitute for Koenig who does not look like staying. At the Court everything seems much more as it should be now that the King has a mistress. Her friends there do not change, they are delightfully frivolous.

As inconsequently as she had dragged Voltaire to

Paris, she dragged him back to Brussels, calling at Cirey on the way. This journey was made disagreeable by a dispute which broke out and raged in the carriage between Emilie and Koenig on the subject of the infinitely little. They were at it hammer and tongs the whole way to Brussels. There had already been quarrels between them; Koenig was supposed to have been ungrateful in some respect. This was the end of their association, though by no means the end of their differences. Maupertuis offended Mme du Châtelet deeply by taking Koenig's side. After this she and Maupertuis were on bad terms for a while until at last Voltaire wrote him a conciliatory letter. He was afflicted, he said, by the coldness between Maupertuis and the only woman in the world capable of understanding him. 'You two are made to love each other.' (In 1752 Koenig got into trouble with the Berlin Academy for publishing a forged letter from Leibnitz. On this occasion Voltaire took his side in order to annoy Maupertuis.)

It was as well that they had returned to Brussels when they did. They had hardly arrived there when they received bad news from Paris. Voltaire had given a few oddments to his new publisher Prault—the first chapters of the *Siècle de Louis XIV*, an *Ode sur le Fanatisme* and various pieces which had already been published—to make up a book called *Recueil de Pièces Fugitives*. Whether because the censor really found something objectionable in this little collection, or because Prault was printing the book without a *privilège*, the police raided his premises and confiscated the sheets. He was fined 500 livres and obliged to shut his bookshop for three months. Had Voltaire been in Paris all this would have been disagreeable; as it was, safely in Brussels and working harder than ever, he did not take it to heart. This time there was no quarrel with the publisher: he was entirely on Prault's side and himself paid the 500 livres. Of course he wrote his usual letters of complaint to d'Argental and protest to the authorities. 'I love the French, but I hate persecution so I shall stay here.'

In the summer of 1740, Prault published a book by Emilie called *Institutions de Physique*, in which she expounded the ideas of Leibnitz as disseminated by Wolff. It was dedicated to her little boy: 'I have always thought it a solemn duty to educate children so that they will have no reason to regret their youth, the only time of life when it is possible to learn. You, my dear son, are at that happy age when the mind begins to think and is not troubled as yet by the passions of the heart. . . . So I want you to take advantage of the awakening of reason and I shall try and protect you from that ignorance which is only too common among people of your rank. . . .' Leibnitz was introduced to the French by Mme du Châtelet as Newton was by Voltaire. Her contemporaries admired this work for its extraordinary clarity. 'Everybody understands the monads,' said La Mettrie, 'since the Leibnitzians made the brilliant acquisition of Mme du Châtelet.' Voltaire disagreed with the argument of the book and was sorry that Venus-Newton should have turned into La Belle Wolffienne. He had nothing but praise for the quality of her work. She surpassed Leibnitz, he thought, in elegance, lucidity and method. But he disapproved of her wasting her time over 'the scientific absurdities that Leibnitz gave to the world from vanity and which Germans study because they are German. It is deplorable that a Frenchwoman such as Mme du Châtelet should use her intelligence to embroider such spiders' webs and make these heresies attractive.'

One of the interminable quarrels which the philosophers of Cirey so often drew upon themselves broke out over this book. The tutor Koenig, who had left them after the disagreeable scene on the high road, told everybody in Paris that *Institutions de Physique* was a rehash of his own lessons to Mme du Châtelet. When Emilie heard this she retorted that he had been engaged to teach her algebra, not metaphysics. True, he said, and he had indeed begun with algebra. But at the end of every lesson Mme du Châtelet would madden him by remarking smugly, 'Cela, c'est évident.' One day he was stung into offering to teach her truths of equally great importance but without one shred of evidence, in other words metaphysics. At this she burst into shrieks of annoying laughter. However, she told him he could try and interest her if he liked and he succeeded so well that her book was a collection of these lessons.

Mme du Châtelet was, naturally, furious. She had acknowledged Koenig's help in the book itself and in a letter to Maupertuis, but it was ridiculous to suggest that it was not her own work. A great deal of it had been written before she had ever set eyes on Koenig. She dragged the Académie des Sciences into the dispute, appealing to Mairan, the secretary-general, to tell the world that she had expounded her Leibnitzian views to him a whole year before Koenig went to Cirey. Mairan's reply was ambiguous. The whole thing was unfair because all the scientists knew that Mme du Châtelet was perfectly competent to write such a book. Perhaps they would have been more ready to take her side, had she not been a woman. Parisian society and the scientific world buzzed over this dispute for months. Voltaire tried to keep out of it as much as possible, he wanted to be on the right side of the Académie des Sciences. He thought metaphysical speculation great waste of time and could not get excited over the controversy; his aim now was to bring Emilie back to Newton.

Voltaire to M. Fawkener, 2 March 1740, received 1 August (in English):

'Dear Sir, I take the liberty to send you my old follies

having no new things to present you with. I am now at Brussels with the same lady Duchastelet, who hindered me some years ago from paying you a visit at Constantinople and whom I shall live with in all probability the greatest part of my life, since for these ten years I have not departed from her. She is now at the trouble of a damned suit in law that she pursues at Bruxelles. We have abandoned the most agreeable retirement in the country to bawl here in the grotto of the Flemish chicane. The high dutch baron who takes upon himself to present you with this packet of french reveries is one of the noble players whom the Emperor sends into Turkey to represent the majesty of the Roman empire before the Highness of Musulman power.

'I am persuaded that you are become, nowadays, a perfect Turk; you speak, no doubt, their language very well and you keep, to be sure, a pretty harem. Yet I am afraid you want two provisions or ingredients which I think necessary to make that nauseous draught of life go down, I mean books and friends. Should you be happy enough to have met at Pera with men whose conversation agrees with your way of thinking? If so you want for nothing for you enjoy health honours and fortune. Health and places I have not; I regret the former I am satisfied without the other. As to fortune I enjoy a very competent one, and I have a friend besides. Thus I reckon myself happy though I am sickly as you saw me at Wandsworth.

'I hope I shall return to Paris with my lady Duchastelet in two years' time. If, about that season, you return to dear England by way of Paris, I hope I shall have the pleasure to see your dear Excellency at her house which is without doubt one of the finest in Paris and situated in a position worthy of Constantinople for it looks upon the river and a long tract of land, interspersed with pretty houses, is to be seen from every window. Upon my word,

I would with all that prefer the vista of the Sea of Marmora before that of the Seine and I would pass some months with you at Constantinople if I could live without that lady whom I look upon as a great man and as a most solid and respectable friend. She understands Newton; she despises superstition and in short she makes me happy.

'I have received this week two summons from a French man who intends to travel to Constantinople. He would fain entice me to that pleasant journey. But since you could not, nobody can. Farewell my dear friend whom I will love and honour all my life time farewell. Tell me how you fare; tell me you are happy; I am so if you continue to be so. Yours for ever. V.'

# Chapter Thirteen

## Frederick comes to the Throne

IN VOLTAIRE'S New Year letter to Frederick, 1740, he asks what can be wished for a Prince who not only has everything which, as a Prince, he could desire, but also has talents that would make the fortune of any commoner. He therefore wishes nothing for Frederick. For himself, he repeats *ut videam salutare meum.** For the public, that it will be allowed to see the refutation by a Prince of Machiavelli, corrupter of Princes. Voltaire and Mme du Châtelet have been devouring this precious monument of literature. Their only criticism is that, in one or two places, the author's zeal against the tutor of tyrants has carried him almost too far; a fault, however, on the right side. Certain branches of the splendid tree might be pruned and Voltaire is going to submit a plan for the pruning to his Prince. He also begs to be allowed to write the preface. He has had an enthusiastic account from Algarotti of his visit to Rheinsberg, where he went with Lord Baltimore on their way back from Russia. Ah! Why is Voltaire not Algarotti and M. du Châtelet not Lord Baltimore?

Voltaire often hinted that du Châtelet should be given a post of some sort in Prussia, so that the three of them could go and live with their Prince. In that case he would see the model for all Kings. Meanwhile he remains with the model for all women. But Frederick was good at

* The correct quotation is: *Quia viderunt oculi mei salutare tuum.* (St. Luke, Chapter II.)

turning a deaf ear to suggestions that did not appeal to
him, another of which was that he should buy the du
Châtelet estate under litigation. He passionately wanted
Voltaire, but was determined to possess him without all
these encumbrances, while Voltaire was equally determined not to abandon Emilie. The correspondence between the philosopher and the Prince, or, as Frederick
would have it, the two philosophers, flourished more
than ever. Voltaire corrected the *Anti-Machiavel* while
Frederick corrected *Mérope*; each privately thought that
the other's observations on his work were idiotic, but
their letters were none the less loving for that. Voltaire
continued to compare him, favourably, with Aescula-
pius, Trajan, Prometheus, Marcus Aurelius, Horace,
Hercules, the Infant Christ and other respected figures.

Frederick wished the *Anti-Machiavel* to be published
anonymously; he left the business side of the transaction
to Voltaire. As soon as he had received all the sheets,
Voltaire got in touch with Van Duren, a publisher at
The Hague. He described the book to him as a refutation, chapter by chapter, of Machiavelli's *Prince*, written
by one of the most important men in Europe. *The Prince*
itself, either in French or Italian, must be incorporated
in the book, which should be beautifully printed, with
big margins. Van Duren can keep all the profits, but
must send two dozen copies finely bound in morocco, to
a German court to be specified later, and another two
dozen, in calf, to Voltaire himself. He asks for an immediate, and very precise, reply. If Van Duren could know
who the author of this work really is, he would see what
a favour Voltaire is doing him. Should he not wish to
take advantage of this piece of luck, Voltaire will put it
in the way of somebody else.

On 31 May 1740, Frederick's Most All-Gracious
Father, a beastly old man of fifty-two who had been
quite senile for many months, was gathered to the

primeval sons of Thor. Nobody outside Prussia knew
that this had happened; the post was stopped at Berlin
and the gates closed for several days, until Frederick felt
himself securely in the saddle. Rarely had the accession
to a third-class throne provoked so much interest. It
seemed, to liberal-minded people everywhere, that kingship might at last become respectable. Algarotti and
other visitors to Rheinsberg had broadcast descriptions of
the Crown Prince, extolling his high principles, his love
of philosophy and of the arts. Frederick's letters to Voltaire had been copied out and circulated in the Paris
salons; the contents of the *Anti-Machiavel* were also
pretty well known. The sentiment which ran through the
correspondence, the whole theme of the *Anti-Machiavel*,
was the wickedness of those rulers who seek self-aggran-
dizement at the expense of other men's lives, the useless-
ness of territorial conquest, the importance of learning
and above all of pleasure.

Unfortunately the Germans have a way of turning
their rulers into war lords with a taste for popular philosophy. Voltaire must be given some credit for the fact
that Frederick was so much the most enlightened of
them all. He began his reign with many a liberal
measure. He spoke of reducing the Prussian army to
45,000 men (but never did so). He disbanded his father's
regiment of giants, so that Germany was filled with huge,
weak nitwits, sadly lurching along the roads looking for
work. The year 1740 was one of those when summer
never comes to the north of Europe: the harvest failed
completely. Frederick opened the state granaries and
sold the corn at a reasonable price to his hungry subjects. He put a thousand destitute old women into well-
warmed rooms and set them spinning. He abolished
torture which was not used again in Prussia for nearly
two hundred years, and did away with censorship;
all through his reign his subjects were at liberty to write

as they chose about him, though foreign rulers were protected. He brought the philosopher Wolff back from the
exile to which the late King had condemned him, and he
summoned 'sGravesande and Maupertuis to found a
Berlin Academy. 'sGravesande refused, but Maupertuis
could not resist the honour and publicity of such an
appointment.

On 6 June Frederick wrote his first letter, as King, to
Voltaire whom he would see, he hoped, this very year.
It was a short, affectionate note and contained the pro-
phetic sentence, 'The whirlwind of events carries us
away and we must let ourselves be carried.' 'Love me
always and always be sincere with your friend, Fédéric.'
Voltaire's instant reaction was to send the *Anti-Machiavel*
to Van Duren, saying he had better get on with it as
quickly as possible. Then he wrote to Frederick, addressing the new monarch as 'Votre Humanité'. He is overwhelmed by one word in H.M.'s letter which gives him
the hope of a blessed vision this very year. He would re-
mind His Majesty that the Queen of Sheba, too, longs to
see Solomon in his glory. (The husband, of course, would
accompany her.) Frederick countered this by saying that
two divinities at once would blind him with their dazzle
and he would have to borrow the veil of Moses to protect him from the rays. Meanwhile he and the Marquise
wrote to each other in terms of exquisite politeness, saying how greatly they wished to meet.

Now that Frederick was himself a ruling Prince he
found that there were certain things in the *Anti-Machiavel*
which would better have been left unsaid. This had been
foreseen by Voltaire, whose flair for knowing what
people would do must have made the fortune of a for-
tune-teller. He had been jostling Van Duren to rush the
book into print ever since the death of the old King. In
July Frederick, as Voltaire had expected, told him that
he must get hold of it at all costs and prevent its publica-

tion. After some high words with Emilie, who thought this journey quite unnecessary, Voltaire dashed off to The Hague to see what could be done. He regarded publishers as his natural enemies and was always glad of an excuse to cross swords with a member of the hated profession. 'All publishers are fools or knaves; they misunderstand their own interests as much as they cling to them.' In Van Duren he found a worthy antagonist; he came to grips with him at once. 'I had to do with a Dutchman who abused both the freedom of his country and his own right to persecute authors.' In other words, the publisher, realizing that he had got a gold-mine, refused to part with it at any price. Voltaire asked for the proofs, saying he wished to correct them. Van Duren said very well, but he must do so in the office, surrounded by members of the firm. Voltaire agreed. He carefully corrected a few pages, and having thus gained Van Duren's confidence, went back the next day to finish the work. This time he was left alone in the room. He scribbled rubbish over so much of the text that he thought he had quite got the better of Van Duren. He went gleefully back to Brussels. But he had underestimated his opponent. Van Duren engaged a literary hack to rewrite the mutilated passages and then published the book. No result could have been more annoying to an author. Frederick was obliged, in self-defence, to allow Voltaire to publish the original edition, but with Voltaire's own cuts and corrections, which Frederick disliked. He no longer recognized the *Anti-Machiavel* as his own work. He intended to re-cast it himself and have it printed at Berlin. However, this particular Prince was soon too busy following the maxims of Machiavelli to bother much more about his own refutation of them.

Voltaire could now think of nothing but his meeting with Frederick. The Prussian King was on the move, inspecting his dominions, and rumours about his future prospects filled the gazettes. His father had never allowed him to make the Grand Tour, which was considered to be part of a German Prince's education and included Rome, Holland, Brussels and Paris. It was thought that he now intended to do so. Voltaire and Emilie were determined that if he went to Brussels and Paris he should stay with them; they began to make preparations for receiving him. Voltaire wrote to the Abbé Moussinot instructing him to get the Hôtel Lambert ready without delay. Mme du Châtelet had left some of her possessions, notably a bed without a mattress, in the house of her midwife. Moussinot and the midwife were to go and buy whatever else was needed. (Oh happy age, when everything made by man was beautiful, when the furnishing of an Hôtel Lambert could as safely be left to a clergyman and a district-nurse as, nowadays, to a Ramsay or a Jansen!)

In Brussels there was a nasty scene between Emilie and Princess Thurn and Taxis. The Princess announced that the King would be staying with her; not at all, said Emilie, the King belonged to Voltaire and would certainly not be allowed to stay anywhere but with him. Excitement mounted. Frederick, accompanied by Maupertuis, Algarotti and Kaiserling, was on his way to Brussels. Voltaire and Emilie were to meet him at Antwerp and he would then go and stay for a few days, strictly incognito, in the rue de la Grosse Tour. But, when he was only 150 miles from Brussels, he suddenly fell ill. He sent for Voltaire to go to him at once but said that greatly to his sorrow, deeply to his disappointment, he was too unwell to receive a woman. Mme du Châtelet was very much offended, but agreed to lend him Voltaire for a few days. As nothing could have stopped him, she was obliged to put a good face on his departure. Of course she thought the King's illness was a ruse to get

Voltaire to himself, but it was quite genuine. He told his friend Jordan that at his first sight of Voltaire his mind was as unstrung as his body was feeble.

Voltaire posted off under a harvest moon, and in two days (11 September 1740) he arrived at the derelict Castle of Moyland, near Cleves. Here he found his King, here his eyes finally beheld, across a huge, dark, empty room, a little fellow, wrapped in a blue duffle dressing-gown, shivering and shaking with the four-day ague. Voltaire, like all chronic invalids, was perfect in a sick-room; he broke the ice by sitting on the King's bed and taking his pulse. He prescribed the Jesuits' remedy (quinine) saying that the King of Sweden had been cured of the ague by it, and though the minds and souls of the two Monarchs had nothing in common, their bodies probably worked in the same way. Frederick declared that if the sight of Voltaire did not cure him he might as well seek absolution. Accordingly he rose from his bed, dressed and dined with his friends. For three days they all enjoyed each other's society to the full, talking of this and that, the immortality of the soul, fate, free-will and the men-women of Plato. It was no doubt more amusing for Voltaire than if the du Châtelets had been there. He read out his new play *Mahomet* which delighted them all. He helped Frederick to write a manifesto to the Bishop of Liége, against whom the King had certain claims. Voltaire was so over-excited that he forgot his pacifist principles and cheered when he heard that 2,000 soldiers would carry it to the Bishop. He had brought Mme du Châtelet's new book for Frederick, who lavished compliments on it to Voltaire though he told other friends that it was sad stuff and anyhow written by Koenig, embellished with a few of Voltaire's brilliant remarks. But, oh what a lucky woman, to possess him! Why, anybody with a good memory could write a classic simply by making notes while he talked.

As for Voltaire himself, his emotions on this occasion could only be expressed in platitudes. The King was such a charmer that, whoever he was, he would be an ornament to any society. A second Cideville in fact (Piron used to call Frederick '*le Thieriot du Nord*'). Voltaire had to keep reminding himself that the man who came and chatted with him, perching on the end of his bed, was the master of 100,000 soldiers. What a miracle that this son of a crowned ogre, brought up among animals, should have such a great love of French civilization. On this occasion there was no disillusionment and Frederick was more than ever determined to get Voltaire away from his Emilie. When the time came for the King to return to Berlin he prevailed upon Voltaire to go to The Hague on Anti-Machiavellian business, instead of immediately rejoining her in Brussels.

At The Hague Voltaire was grandly if uncomfortably lodged in La Vieille Cour, a palace belonging to Frederick, which served as Prussian embassy. It was 200 years old and Voltaire described its crumbling magnificence in a poem—rotting floor-boards, leaking roof, gilded rooms minus doors and windows, attics full of rusty armour. There were books but they were read only by rats and the thickest cobwebs in Europe veiled them from a profane eye.\* Voltaire was not displeased with the address, and wrote to all his humbler friends in Paris : A la Haye, au palais du roi de Prusse. The first round of the fight between Frederick and Emilie went to the King.

Mme du Châtelet, however, was by no means defenceless. She now had the clever idea of patching up Voltaire's quarrel with the French authorities and getting him invited to his own Court. She knew that, if ever he

---

\* This sixteenth-century house, which then seemed to be on its last legs, survived until it was burnt down in 1948. It had become a royal palace and the present Queen of the Netherlands was married from its walls.

found himself welcome there, no German in the world would be able to entice him away. So she left Brussels and went off bag, baggage and husband to join the Court at Fontainebleau, where she began a campaign on Voltaire's behalf. One kind protectress was lost to them: the Duchesse de Richelieu had died, after a long illness following a difficult pregnancy, on 2 August. The Duke was extremely sad. 'Are you satisfied with your confessor?' he asked her. 'Yes, since he has not forbidden me to love you.' She said her only wish was to die in her husband's arms; she did so. Voltaire, Maupertuis and many others regretted her deeply. She was one of the few women who really liked Mme du Châtelet.

But Emilie never lacked powerful men-friends, and never minded bothering people. By a cunning move she made Frederick instruct his ambassador to speak up for Voltaire; Frederick knew that this was playing the enemy's game, but could not very well do otherwise. She brought a letter from Voltaire for Cardinal Fleury with a handsome copy of the *Anti-Machiavel*. Voltaire reminded His Eminence of old times at Villars. He said he had just left the author of this book and would be visiting him again soon. Had the Cardinal any message for him? Voltaire, who always liked to see himself in some new role, thought he might become an unofficial envoy between the French and the Prussian Courts. Frederick had taken a great dislike to the Marquis de Valory, the new French Ambassador at Berlin. Valory had a bumptious manner and was fond of laying down the law; he talked to Frederick in the tones of an experienced soldier to a young man who had never been at the front and Frederick complained to Voltaire: 'I am always afraid that he will mistake me for a fortification and launch an attack on me.' Voltaire, too, had reasons to be displeased with the Ambassador, whom he did not know but who had spread a rumour that he lived in Brussels because he had been exiled from Paris. In the end both men became very fond of 'my fat Valory' as Frederick called him (perhaps they were both seduced by the Ambassador's excellent cook with whom Voltaire used to say he was in love). But at present he was 'not a man one could ask to dinner'. So Voltaire planted the idea of a different sort of mission in the mind of Cardinal Fleury and the Cardinal was thinking it over when events in Europe began to move.

The year 1740 was fatal to three crowned heads. Frederick William of Prussia's death was followed, within a week of each other at the end of October, by those of the Emperor Charles VI and the Empress Anne of Russia. Charles VI had no male heir; he left his possessions to his twenty-three-year-old daughter, Maria-Theresa, having made an agreement with the sovereigns of Europe (the Pragmatic Sanction 1713) by which they were to respect her rights. No sooner was he dead, however, than they all remembered that they had wives or female ancestresses through whom they themselves might have a claim to the Empire. Europe was thrown into confusion. Frederick wrote to Voltaire, 'this death has disturbed my pacific ideas' and then, bursting, as he loved to do, into French verse:

> *'Déjà j'entends l'orage du tambour*
> *De cent heros je vois briller la rage*
> *Déjà je vois envahir cent états*
> *Et tant d'humains moissonnés avant l'age.'*

This may not have been very elegant but was perfectly clear.

Fleury wrote to Voltaire, who was still at The Hague. He knows Voltaire through and through, a good, honest man. But he was once young and has been too long in growing up. When young he kept what mistaken people

called good company, that of the greatest in the land.
These high and mighty lords had spoilt Voltaire, they
praised him and were right to do so, but they gave way
to him in everything and went too far. Now Voltaire
himself has become aware of all this and in his letter to
the Cardinal, which has given great pleasure, he speaks
respectfully of religion. A civilized man owes two main
duties—to his King and to his creator—even barbarians
know that. It is time that Voltaire should return to his
native land with these thoughts in mind. His talents do
honour to his country, now he should put them to a
patriotic use which will bring him lasting fame.

This letter expressed, with affectionate moderation,
the official view of Voltaire. He was an *enfant terrible*, and
it was time he grew up. The clever old priest was now
going to give him a chance of serving his country instead
of sitting on its frontiers flouting and annoying the authorities. He told him to go to Berlin and see what Frederick
intended to do in the new international situation. Fleury
himself, old (he was eighty-seven), wise and ruler of a
land that had all the territory it wanted, was in favour of
the *status quo*, but if others were going to snatch and grab
he might have to reconsider his position. Why had
Frederick suddenly sent troops to Silesia? Fleury waded
through the *Anti-Machiavel* and found no answer there.
He now had two official envoys in Berlin, Valory and the
Marquis de Beauvau; they were both at sea. Perhaps
Frederick would open his heart to his great new friend.

Pleased as Punch, without having seen Emilie between
the two visits, Voltaire started off for Berlin. There were
one or two little matters he wanted to settle on his own
account, apart from his important mission. Frederick
must be made to pay Voltaire's out-of-pocket expenses
for the *Anti-Machiavel*, he must also pay Thieriot for his
news-letters and the books and pamphlets he had been
sending Frederick, for four years now, from Paris. Vol-

taire was accompanied on his journey by one Dumolard, an orientalist, protégé of Thieriot, who was to take up the post of librarian to the King.

The second meeting of Voltaire and Frederick was not such an enchantment as the first. Frederick complained of Voltaire's bill on which he had put, as well as everything else, his accounts for the journey to Berlin. 'As Court Jesters go, this one is expensive.' All through their long friendship Frederick accused him of being a miser. He must have known the symptoms, nobody was more miserly than he. But the correspondence between Voltaire and Moussinot shows Voltaire to have been generosity itself. He certainly disliked being cheated, particularly of small sums. But when he lost, as he sometimes did in the course of his speculations, many thousands of livres, he was always very philosophical about it. He never set up a Shylock wail. He saw no reason why Frederick should not pay what he owed. On this occasion Frederick made the ridiculous observation that as his purse was longer than that of Mme du Châtelet he had every chance of getting Voltaire away from her. Meanwhile, in spite of repeated promises, the King had still not given Thieriot one penny.

At the end of the visit Voltaire, whose rashness when he put pen to paper was inconceivable, sent a note to Maupertuis inviting him to come and sup with Valory and Beauvau. He wishes to embrace his philosopher before taking leave of '*la respectable, singulière et aimable putain qui vient*'. Marcus Aurelius, on further acquaintance, had turned into a respectable prostitute.

These were afterthoughts: while they were together, the miser and the prostitute made merry. Voltaire's health had never been better; Frederick's malaria had been cured by the death of the Emperor. They wrote verses, some of a curious nature, calling each other *coquette*, and *maîtresse*. They gossiped, made music, and gambled in a purely masculine society. The vice which was so disgusting and ignoble when practised by Desfontaines, took on a classical, lyrical aspect when *tendre* Algarotti and *beau* Lugeac* forgot themselves in Valory's drawing-room. Shades of a young, handsome, Venetian Socrates were evoked. Had not Voltaire always said that Frederick's court would be the modern Athens?

Frederick played the flute. He showed Voltaire his collection of pictures which included four little Watteaus declared by Voltaire to be copies. 'Germany is full of sham pictures; the Princes there are easy to cheat and not at all averse from cheating when they get the opportunity.'

Nothing could have been more diverting than the Prussian Court; nothing more mysterious than the Prussian King's intentions. Funnily enough, he never spoke of them. Voltaire was no more successful in finding out what he was up to than Valory, Beauvau, Dickens and all the other ambassadors. On 12 December 1740, however, Frederick gave a bal masqué and on the 13th he invaded Silesia. Voltaire had already left. After a visit of a fortnight he had suddenly torn himself away from his *coquette*, who begged in vain for three more days. 'Tyrannical Emilie, violent in her jealousy,' as Frederick rather smugly put it, had written threatening suicide.

This second journey to Frederick had thrown her into a state of despair. She told d'Argental that it was a cruel reward for her efforts on Voltaire's behalf in France, where she had paved the way for an honourable return, and even for membership of various Academies. He had announced his departure to her dryly, knowing that it would wound her. Very well, now she is ill and will soon be in her grave, like poor Mme de Richelieu, though

* The Marquis de Lugeac, a secretary at the French embassy, later married Mlle de Baschi, niece of Mme de Pompadour.

quicker than she and with fewer regrets. Voltaire may be sorry, in the end. The Prussian Court will lose its attractions and he may well be tormented by the remembrance of Emilie. She only hopes her friends will never reproach him for what he has done to her.

Angry and distracted, but not actually dying, Mme du Châtelet left Paris for Brussels where her presence was again needed for the lawsuit and where she hoped to meet the returning Voltaire. Since he had abandoned her to go to Frederick at the Castle of Moyland everything had gone wrong for her. In Paris they were saying that Koenig had written her book.* They were also saying, though it is to be hoped she did not know this, that her despair at the absence of Voltaire was accounted for by the fact that he did her work for her. This, of course, simply shows up the stupidity of those who believed it. Voltaire could no more have done her work than she could have written *Le Mondain*. Another humiliation; while she was at Fontainebleau, where she stayed, as she always did, with Richelieu, she had tried in vain to renew their old love affair. No doubt the Duke had other fish to fry. Waiting for Voltaire at Brussels she wrote to Richelieu: (24 December 1740.) 'I have suffered the only two misfortunes which could really wound me to the heart; I have cause to complain of him for whom I have left everything and without whom the universe (if you were not part of it) would be nothing to me; and my best friends are suspecting me of unworthy behaviour. Your friendship is my only consolation, but you are 300 leagues away. My heart feels at home in your company, since you alone understand it. What seems to others a pitiable folly is a sentiment not

* It is pleasant to know that in his *Leibnitz in France* (Oxford University Press, 1955), Mr W. H. Barber never suggests for a moment that *Institutions de Physique* might have been written by Koenig. He treats Mme du Châtelet as a philosopher in her own right.

foreign to your own nature, even though it may be un-
natural. I do not know why I made you that confession
at Fontainebleau. Do not ask me, for I cannot explain it.
It was the truth, and I always like you to know the truth
about me. I could not have stopped myself; I might feel
sorry except that I know you so well, so well that I shall
always tell you openly, remorselessly, what my heart
feels about you. This would be incomprehensible to anybody else and it has nothing to do with the frenzied
passion which is killing me at present. Useless to say "all
this is impossible" because I have an unanswerable reply,
"it is so"—even if you don't happen to like it. I hear
from Paris that my book is a success; I now wish its
success to make itself felt.'

At Brussels she waited a whole month for Voltaire. He
was having a dreadful winter journey through 'detestable
Westphalia' and other German states whose inhabitants
were more like beasts than men, so that a traveller
whose arrangements went wrong was in for a rough if
not a dangerous time. At last, early in the New Year,
1741, he arrived safely and there was a touching reunion.
He had a little inflammation of the eyes, and in a letter
to Frederick he blamed Emilie for this, saying that on her
account he had lost his eyesight, his happiness and his
King. But he told all his other correspondents that
Mme du Châtelet had never seemed so far above
monarchs.

But Emilie was not in luck that year. No sooner had
Voltaire returned to her arms than he announced that
he was now too old (forty-six) to make love! 'The heart
does not age, but this immortal is condemned to live in a
ruin.'

> Si vous voulez que j'aime encore
> Rendez-moi l'âge des amours
> Au crépuscule de mes jours
> Rejoignez, s'il se peut, l'aurore.

*On meurt deux fois, je le vois bien*
*Cesser d'aimer et d'être aimable*
*C'est une mort insupportable*
*Cesser de vivre ce n'est rien.*

*Du ciel alors daignant descendre*
*L'amitié vint à mon secours*
*Elle est plus égale, aussi tendre*
*Et moins vive que les amours.*

*Touché de sa beauté nouvelle*
*Et de sa lumière éclairée*
*Je la suivis mais je pleurais*
*De ne plus pouvoir suivre qu'elle.*

Mme du Châtelet said she defied the King of Prussia to hate her more than she hated him.

# Chapter Fourteen

## Voltaire fails for the Académie-française

AFTER ALL these agitations the two philosophers settled down together again. It is probable that their relationship, never dependent on ordinary, physical love, had not changed very much in spite of Voltaire's depressing declaration. There had always been gossip about Emilie's gallantries; she was soon said to be having an affair with her son's new tutor.

Voltaire told his nephew's little boy: 'My child, to get on with men, one must have the women on one's side, and to get on with women one must know what they are. Mark my words all women are faithless and unchaste.' 'All women?' cried Emilie. 'What are you saying, Monsieur?' 'Never misinform a child, it is not right to do so.'

They stayed in Brussels for the next few months. Mme du Châtelet was easier in her mind now about Frederick who, busy 'protecting' Silesia, no longer required the presence of her companion. She said that there could be no greater contradiction to the principles of the *Anti-Machiavel* than this invasion, but that Frederick was welcome to all the provinces he wanted so long as he did not take away what made the charm of her existence.

On the 10th of April 1741, Voltaire put on his *Mahomet* at Lille, where Mme Denis was now living, and where she had a salon for the officers of the garrison and the local intellectuals. Half-way through the first performance, Voltaire received the news of Frederick's victory at Mollwitz. He stopped the play and made an

announcement to the wildly cheering audience. The
Lillois were anti-Austrian to a man. Nobody knew then
that Frederick had lost his nerve and run away when the
battle seemed to be going badly (snatched by Morgante
into fairyland, says Carlyle indulgently) and had not re-
appeared on the field until he heard that it had been won.
Later in life Voltaire was to say that the only living
creature to whom Frederick had ever felt gratitude was
the horse that bore him from Mollwitz.

Maupertuis had become involved in the battle while
on his way to join Frederick and was said to have been
killed. Presently they heard that he had not been killed
at all, but had fallen into the hands of Silesian peasants.
Emilie shuddered at this thought, for the Silesians did
barbarous things to the followers of their Protector whenever they got a chance. However, Maupertuis turned up,
naked but unhurt, at Austrian headquarters. As he had
seen their army by then, and was so good at arithmetic,
the Austrians thought it better not to let him go back to
Prussia for a while. They gave him some clothes and fifty
louis and sent him off to Vienna where people were
delighted to entertain him. Maria-Theresa asked how it
felt to see two Princes fighting for such a small portion of
that earth which he had measured? 'It is not for me to
be more philosophic than Kings,' he replied diplomati-
cally. Maria-Theresa's husband, discovering that Maupertuis had lost, among other possessions, his Graham
watch, took out his own which was also by Graham and
gave it to him. Mme du Châtelet wrote to congratulate
him on being alive and begged him to go and see a cousin
of her own at that Court.

The lawsuit began to take a more favourable turn for
them now, flapped up, no doubt, by Frederick. In October its mysteries led them back to Cirey. (M. de Trichâteau had died and his will must be proved.) They went by
way of Paris. Here they did not stay at the Hôtel Lam-

bert, which, in spite of the efforts of L'Abbé Moussinot and the midwife, was still not ready to receive them, but at the house where Voltaire had lived with Mme de Fontaine-Martel. He invited Thieriot and d'Argenson to go and see him there to cheer up her ghost and remember the old times and all those hilarious if uneatable suppers they used to have.

In the summer of 1742 Voltaire and Mme du Châtelet may have moved into the Hôtel Lambert for a week or so. As they have become a part of its story we like to think of them there, but in fact no letters are dated from it or contain a word about it. In June it went back to its original owner and soon after was sold for twice the amount Voltaire had paid for it, if, indeed, he ever had paid in full. He was badly hit just then by the bankruptcy of one Michel, an important Parisian financier to whom he had lent a large sum of money. Possibly he thought the Hôtel Lambert too expensive for him. Mme du Châtelet took a little house, No. 13 Faubourg Saint-Honoré next door to the Hôtel de Charost (now the British Embassy) and this was their Paris residence until the summer of 1745. It is a great pity that no Mme de Grafigny has described Voltaire's various town houses with their furniture and general arrangement. He was always surrounded by beautiful things.

In June 1742 Voltaire wrote to Sir Everard Fawkener:

'If I had forgot the scraps of english I once had gathered I'll never forget my dear ambassador. I am now at Paris, and with the same she-philosopher I have lived with these twelve [sic] years past. Was I not so constant in my bargains for life, I would certainly come to see you in your kiosk, in your quiet and your glory.

'You will hear of the new victory of my good friend the King of Prussia, who wrote so well against Machiavel and acted immediately like the heros of Machiavel. He fiddles and fights as well as any man in Christendom. He routs the Austrian forces and loves but very little your king, his dear neighbour of Hanover. I have seen him twice since he is free from his father's tyranny. He would retain me at his court and live with me in one of his country houses, just with the same freedom and the same goodness of manners you did at Wandsworth. But he could not prevail against the Marquise du Châtelet. My only reason for being in France is that I am her friend. You must know my Prussian king, when he was but a man he loved passionately your english government. But the king has altered the man and now he relishes despotic power as much as a Mustapha, a Selim or a Soliman.

'News came yesterday at our court that the king of Sardinia will not at all harken to the Borbonian propositions. This shrub will not suffer the french tree to extend its branches all over Italy. I should be afraid of an universal war; but I hope much from the white hoary pate of our good cardinal, who desires peace and quiet and will give it to Christendom if he can.

'I have seen here our Ottoman minister, Sayd Bacha. I have drunk wine with his chaplain and reasoned with Laria his interpreter, a man of sense who knows much and speaks well. He had told me he is very much attached to you and loves you as all the world does. I have charged him to pay my respects to you and I hope the bearer of this will tell you with what tenderness I will be for ever your humble and faithful servant.

Voltaire.'

Voltaire was preparing his *Mahomet* for the Comédie-française. Its enthusiastic reception in Lille, where nobody, even the clergy, had found anything to object to, had greatly encouraged him. Cardinal Fleury read it, liked it and made one or two corrections of a literary nature which Voltaire accepted. But there were various obstacles to its production; for one thing it was not an easy play to cast. The delegation of delightful Turks, friends of Fawkener, was still in Paris. The Ambassador was a most seductive man; he charmed everybody and knocked down French wives like ninepins. Voltaire had no desire to hurt his feelings: better wait until he had gone. So he went on polishing and correcting and biding his time with all the impatience of a writer longing to give his work to the public.

Unfortunately he remained in Paris where of course he soon got into a scrape. Voltaire was a consistent pacifist. Warring Princes, to him, were, 'hateful spiders, tearing each other to pieces instead of spinning silk.' Ever since Frederick had invaded Silesia he had been scolding him for breaking the peace of Europe. 'I am so afraid that you will come to despise human beings.' 'I only put my foot on the banks of the Styx, but I was grieved, Sire, at the number of poor wretches I saw passing by.' 'Will you and your fellow Kings never stop ravaging this earth to which you say you want to bring happiness?' Frederick took all this quite good-naturedly: 'It's the fashion now to make war, and presumably it will last a good long while.' 'I can remember the time when, if you had had an army, it would have marched against Desfontaines, Rousseau and Van Duren.'

Cardinal Fleury agreed with Voltaire on the subject of peace but most of their compatriots did not. French public opinion was strongly in favour of joining Frederick in his war with Austria. If rich pickings were to be had, at nearly no cost to France, it seemed foolish, almost unpatriotic, not to benefit. The Austrians were in a very bad way and Frederick had easily won the two battles which he had fought against them. French general officers were violently belligerent and so were the Ministers. Against the will of the Cardinal and the better judgment of the King, a Prussian alliance was signed. A French army was sent to Prague; whereupon Frederick immediately made peace with Maria-Theresa. He was naturally considered by his new allies to have behaved in a twisting and dishonest way; and he became most unpopular in Paris. Voltaire, always for peace at any price, now wrote an indiscreet effusion, in verse to Frederick. 'Paris—*your* capital—your name on everybody's lips—wherever I go I am mobbed by people asking if I have really seen you.' Some unknown person, a post-office employee at Brussels, according to Frederick, sent copies of this letter to the Ministers, the Ambassadors and to Mme de Mailly, the King's powerful mistress. This trouble-maker was of course Frederick himself; his idea was so to blacken Voltaire in the eyes of his compatriots that he would be obliged to leave France for ever. Then Frederick could be sure of possessing him.

As the Prussian King had foreseen the Parisians were furious with Voltaire. President Hénault described the letter to Mme du Deffand as perfectly mad. Voltaire seems to be one of those people who would get into trouble even in a Trappist monastery. He is now hotly denying that he has said any of the things imputed to him, and has written to Valory to ask for his real letter so that he can prove his innocence. But Hénault, knowing his Voltaire, is sure that, even if he has not written the published letter, the real one is just as bad. Mme de Mailly is taking a highfalutin, patriotic line and demanding that Voltaire should be punished; it looks as if he will have to decamp for Brussels without delay. The President added that *la pauvre du Châtelet* ought to put a clause in the lease of every house she took insuring herself against the follies of her lover.

Voltaire grovelled in denials to the Cardinal and Mme de Mailly; there was no proof against him, and some people thought the letter might have been written by Desfontaines, though others swore that it was in the authentic Voltairean voice. In the end no proceedings were taken. But the whole thing gave him a bad press and the atmosphere was favourable neither to him nor to his work.

Nevertheless, *Mahomet* had a brilliant first night. Magistrates, ministers and the fashionable world received the play with rapturous applause. Unfortunately the enemies, Desfontaines, Piron and many a jealous young writer, were also there, listening to the text, as yet unpublished. They noticed various lines, scenes and verses which could have a tendentious meaning; they did not keep their reflections to themselves. Voltaire's ill-wishers were not the only people to be shocked by *Mahomet*. Lord Chesterfield told young Crébillon that Voltaire had read him a good deal of the play at Brussels. While he had greatly admired some of the verses and various reflections (more brilliant, perhaps, than correct) he had seen at once that *Mahomet* was really meant to be Christ. Lord Chesterfield was surprised that nobody had tumbled to this at Lille. He thought it wrong for a man of letters to mock at the religious beliefs of his country, since to do so could only cause trouble and disorder. Many quite unprejudiced French people came to the same conclusions and saw the play as a veiled attack on all religion. It was certainly a dangerous subject for Voltaire to have chosen. Public opinion, already worked up over the poem to Frederick, became strongly inflamed. The chief of police sent a message that he would like to see Voltaire, who rose from a sick bed and went to him accompanied by Mme du Châtelet. After a long and stormy interview they were persuaded to withdraw *Mahomet*, but without making a scandal. Some excuse was found and another play put on at the Comédie-française. Voltaire, more angry than surprised, declared that he would dedicate *Mahomet* to the Pope himself (which, in due course, he did). 'Then I shall be made a Bishop *in partibus infidelium,* the proper diocese for me.'

Upon this, Voltaire and Mme du Châtelet shook the dust of Paris from their feet and went back to Brussels. They visited Rheims on the way, and here they were so much fêted that they stayed longer than they had meant to. The day they arrived, two five-act plays were given in their honour, one before and one after supper, and then there was an impromptu ball. Everybody was entranced by Emilie, her singing at the supper, her dancing at the ball and the enormous quantities of food she ate. She had never stayed up so late in her life. Voltaire, who was secretly planning another infidelity, was in a loving mood.

The French authorities knew quite well that the letter to Frederick was by Voltaire himself, and he knew that they knew, but the Cardinal kept up the polite fiction that it must have been a forgery because he was more anxious than ever to find out Frederick's intentions. This suited Voltaire who particularly wanted an official excuse to go back to his King. Emilie could not say very much if he went on another diplomatic mission. Frederick was at Aix, 'the capital of Charlemagne and of hypochondriacs', taking the waters, bored to death. He was only too pleased to see Voltaire, who, having had an inflammation that made him hard of hearing, put off his visit until he was better. 'To go, deaf, to Your Majesty would be like going, impotent, to one's mistress.' But when he arrived he did not hear so much as a whisper of Frederick's plans and projects. He sent pompous accounts of their conversations to Fleury and d'Argenson; they signified nothing. He put the blame for Frederick's dereliction upon England and hinted, rather unconvincingly, at information too secret to write. The King had been more charming and brilliant than ever. In fact, of course, Frederick had gossiped away about everything under the sun except politics. Voltaire still could not persuade him to settle his debt to Thieriot or to pay for some pictures by Lancret that Voltaire had helped him to acquire. His Humanity was adorable, but the visit was not a success, and in five days Voltaire was back with Emilie. They stayed at Brussels for Christmas and then went to Paris.

Cardinal Fleury died on 29 January 1743. His death was a misfortune which could not have been long postponed; he was eighty-nine. Voltaire had always respected him, and had seen of late how superior to the other ministers he was. A good and clever man, he had made one grave mistake. During the years when he had ruled both his pupil, the King, and France he had failed to cure and had probably encouraged a feeling of inferiority in Louis XV which prevented him from asserting himself at the Conseil des Ministres. The ministers were there only to advise him, he was in no way bound to take their advice, and yet he always did. He had sound political instincts and Fleury ought to have taught him to rely on them, but the Cardinal was too fond of power to want to share it with his pupil.

The death of Fleury left not only the place of first minister vacant, but also a seat in the Académie-française. Voltaire longed to be of the Academy, though he continually made fun of it. As old Fontenelle used to say:

> *Quand nous sommes quarante on se moque de nous,*
> *Quand nous sommes trente-neuf on est à genoux.*

Although the general public thought it quite absurd that the first writer in France should not be a member, the other Academicians were not so very anxious to elect one who would put them all in the shade. Much depended on Versailles. The King had softened lately in his attitude towards Voltaire. He had sent away Mme de

Mailly and taken, as his new mistress, her sister Mme de Châteauroux; she was on Voltaire's side. She was much more intelligent than Mme de Mailly and very friendly with their uncle, M. de Richelieu. Voltaire began to be fancied for the vacant seat, and rumour had it that the King had declared at supper that he would be the next Academician. But Maurepas, now the most powerful of the ministers, was entirely opposed to his election, while the Church party, headed by the Bishop of Mirepoix (the donkey) thought that for Voltaire to succeed to a Cardinal would almost amount to sacrilege. While the matter was still under discussion, *Mérope* came on at the Comédie-française.

*Mérope* was a tragedy which Voltaire had adapted from an Italian play of that name by Scipione Maffei. He had been working at it, off and on, for years and had altered it so much that it had really become his own. The actors had hesitated to produce it because it treated of maternal love, a subject which they thought would send a French audience to sleep. (The French were not such adorers of their progeny as they have since become.) They decided to use it only when *Mahomet* was interrupted in the middle of what ought to have been a record run and they were anxious to have another play by Voltaire at once. He rehearsed *Mérope* himself and inspired the actors with something of his own genius. He reproached Mlle Dumesnil, in the part of an outraged mother, with not putting enough fire and fury into the line: '*Barbare, c'est mon fils!*' He bullied her until she cried: 'But one would have to be possessed of the devil to say it as you want me to.' 'Exactly, Mademoiselle, one must be possessed of the devil to succeed in any of the arts.' *Mérope* was a perfect production and one of the greatest successes ever known on the French stage. The audience wept and sobbed unrestrainedly during the last three acts, and when the play was over let itself go in a torrent of wild enthusiasm. For the first time in history the author was called to take a curtain. Voltaire, of course, was in a box with two duchesses, Mesdames de Boufflers and de Luxembourg. He kissed their hands and vanished, not however to appear on the stage. He was seen entering the box of two more duchesses, the Maréchale de Villars, his old love, and her beautiful, clever daughter-in-law, born a Noailles. The audience cried out that the Duchesse de Villars must kiss him. A graceful gesture, as though asking permission of the Maréchale, having received assent, she flung herself into Voltaire's arms. The cheering went on for another quarter of an hour. Perhaps not the least satisfactory feature of the whole evening was the aspect of his enemies. They were seen to have the wild, livid faces and staggering gait of dying men. The box-office takings for this play were a record at the Comédie-française. Voltaire said, generously, that *Mérope* was not worth printing and that it owed its success to the wonderful performance of Mlle Dumesnil.

And now for the Academy. After such a rousing success, with the King's mistress on his side and the King not, apparently, opposed to him, Voltaire felt that the moment had come to present himself openly as a candidate for Cardinal Fleury's seat. He wrote a letter to one of the Academicians and circulated it in Paris and Versailles: Voltaire is a follower of Newton, and of all philosophers Newton is the most convinced that there is a God. His works are to the learned what the catechism is to a child. Voltaire is the enemy of faction, enthusiasm and rebellion; he adores the religion which has made one great family of the human race. In fact, religion alone has supported him during the thirty years of sorrow and calumny which have rewarded his toil. Inspired by patriotism he has lived like a hermit and given himself over to the study of physics. Now he has been encouraged by various members of the Academy to ask for admission to that body, the glory of a reign on whose history he is engaged. He is particularly anxious to be the one to praise (in the inaugural speech always delivered by a new member) the father of Church and State so that he can make it quite clear, for evermore, how much he loves Cardinal Fleury's religion and how great is his zeal for the Cardinal's pupil, King Louis. It will be the final answer to cruel accusations which have maligned him and will provide a guarantee of his submission to those who are bringing up the Dauphin to be worthy of such a father.

What followed was even more abject. He wrote to the Bishop of Mirepoix, denying authorship of the *Lettres Philosophiques*. He has sometimes written letters to friends, but he would never have given them such a pretentious name. As a matter of fact most of those particular letters are forgeries. Ah! Well! He has been greatly persecuted but he knows how to forgive!

Unfortunately he ate all this humble pie in vain. An old, dull Bishop, brother of the Duc de Luynes, and a member of the Queen's little circle at Versailles, was unanimously elected to the vacant place. Frederick was delighted. Voltaire's friends in Paris were furious; Voltaire took to his bed. Frederick crowed and jeered and sneered and inflamed the wound by all the means in his power. He is astounded at Voltaire's letter to the mitred Midas, and outraged to see a philosopher bending the knee to the idol of superstition. Surely, after this insult, Voltaire will come and live with a King who recognizes his merit and will give him his due?

The Comédie-française had put *La Mort de César* into rehearsal. The night before the first performance the police ordered its withdrawal.

It was no surprise to anybody that Voltaire should now

turn savagely on his fellow countrymen. He has had enough of persecution and ridicule. Luckily there is in Europe a monarch, a real man who loves and cultivates the arts. Nobody now can prevent Voltaire from going to this Tacitus, this Xenophon—nobody, not even Mme du Châtelet. He will leave Minerva for Apollo: 'You, Sire, are my greatest passion.' Suspiciously gleeful, in high spirits and a hurry to be off, he began ostentatiously preparing his departure.

The whole thing had been carefully contrived and plotted by Voltaire himself, Richelieu and the d'Argenson brothers. The ban on *La Mort de César* had been arranged by the four of them to give colour to his indignation and make his flight seem natural. His journey was to be paid for by the French Court; he was granted a year's extra pension and he and two of his cousins received the monopoly of providing clothes for the French army and hay for its horses. In other words he was taking enormous sums to go and spy on his adorable monarch, and do what he could to get him back into the war.

The French were beginning to realize that their hasty and ill-considered move against Austria might turn out to be a poor gamble. A loan from England to Maria-Theresa was beginning to bear fruit. The French army, rushed off to Bohemia with bad generals and insufficient preparation, was suffering a series of defeats. Voltaire was always boasting about his influence with the King of Prussia; the government decided that he had better use it on this recalcitrant ally, to the benefit of his own King.

Nothing could have exceeded the merriment with which the old school friends laid their plans. The mitred donkey and the hero of Mollwitz were the butt of equally hilarious jokes. The shrieks of laughter which rang through Versailles finally reached the ears of the Bishop who went and complained to Louis XV. He got small change. The King told him that everything was in order, that he himself knew exactly what was going on and that Monseigneur de Mirepoix had better forget all about it. Boyer (Mirepoix) was not Fleury and his influence was with the Queen, not the King.

Frederick was triumphant. 'This time I think Voltaire will leave France for good.' '*La belle Emilie* and Paris are in the wrong at last.' Paris was not very much cast down by the poet's defection, but poor Emilie was. Before he left she made scene upon scene, begging him to stick it out in France, to go anywhere but to Berlin: she maddened him as only a woman in her situation can. 'Don't look at me with those haggard, troubled eyes (*ces yeux hagards et louches*),' he is supposed to have said to her, during a quarrel. Finally, but only in order to shut her up, he let her into his secret and promised that she should play at spies with him. All his dispatches would pass through her hands. It might have pacified a politically ambitious woman or one who was only suffering from wounded pride. But Emilie's strange heart beat for Voltaire: by leaving her for an indefinite length of time to go to this man who hated and despised her, by his hurry to be off and his unkind cheerfulness, he trampled on it. The Parisians thought her transports of despair exceedingly funny. 'This woman spent the whole of Saturday and part of today crying because she has not had a letter from this Adonis,' wrote a police spy, soon after Voltaire's departure.

## Chapter Fifteen

## Voltaire and Frederick

AS so often happens in life, Voltaire's fourth visit to Frederick, so much dreaded by Mme du Châtelet, turned out to be less terrible for her than she had feared. He had been well received at his own Court; Versailles had begun to cast its spell; any other palace, any other King, must now come a bad second. Voltaire, with his sense of the theatre and his passion for history, loved grandeur and resounding titles. There could be, for him, no comparison between his own tall, handsome, dignified King, surrounded by fashionable Dukes whose names were part of the French epic, in the most splendid palace ever built by man, and a shivering, waspish little fellow in a duffle dressing-gown, still called the Marquis of Brandenburg by other monarchs, whose Court consisted of middle-class intellectuals, cosmopolitan Sodomites and Prussian soldiers. Frederick's greatness (though Voltaire, in his heart, was always aware of it) was not enough to turn the scales. Nor did the openly homosexual atmosphere of Potsdam attract him, although he rather loved to think how furious the idea of it must be making all the women of Europe.

The only letter that exists from Voltaire to Emilie was written the day after his departure, in June 1743. Some of it is in a secret language, not unlike the wireless messages which the Free French used to send to the Resistance during the War. '*Que dites-vous de St Jean qui ne*

*revient pas? Que dirons-nous de Martin?'* He feels foolish here
without her. He has a greater desire to see her than she
thinks. He is not well. They both thought, yesterday,
that he was all right; he has paid for that illusion. *'Point
de nouvelles de Bretagne, point de lettres, cela veut dire que les
nouvelles ne sont pas bonnes.* I love you [*sic*] V.'

He went first to The Hague, where he again lodged at
La Vieille Cour. He did some useful preliminary spying
there. The young Prussian Minister, Podewils, was in
love with a Dutch politician's wife who kept him informed of many interesting facts. They were an attractive couple and Voltaire became fond of them both. As
he was supposed to be in disgrace with his own people,
the Minister saw no harm in talking to him freely; and
many secrets, highly inaccurate when it came to figures,
found their way home via Emilie. He stayed so long at
The Hague that she began to hope he would not, after
all, go on to Berlin. But at the end of August, to her inex-
pressible affliction, she heard that he and Podewils were
on the road to Prussia.

The visit started very well. When the two men arrived
at Berlin they were immediately received by the King
in the garden of his palace, Charlottenburg. He carried
Voltaire off for a walk and then showed him the late
Cardinal de Polignac's collection of antique statues
which he had just bought. Supper was extremely merry:
as usual, there were nothing but men. Voltaire was given
a room near the King's; there was much coming and
going, chat and banter.

Voltaire has left an account of Frederick's daily life.
The King got up at five in summer and at six in winter.
There were no ceremonies, no *grandes et petites entrées*; a
footman came and lit his fire, dressed him and shaved
him. His bedroom was rather beautiful, there was a silver
balustrade round the alcove. But the bed-curtains hid a
book-case and the King slept on a thin mattress placed

behind a screen. No stoic had ever lain so uncomfortably. When His Majesty was dressed and booted the stoic consecrated a little while to the sect of Epicurus. A few of the current favourites, young lieutenants, pages or cadets, drank coffee with him and one of them would stay on alone. These schoolboy amusements over, the serious business of the day began. The prime minister, an old soldier who had become Frederick's valet, arrived with a bundle of papers under his arm, sent by the other ministers for the King's inspection. As Prussia was a total dictatorship there was no argument about anything: the affairs of state were regulated in an hour. At about eleven the King reviewed his Guards regiments; then he dined, as well as one can dine in a country where there is neither game nor poultry nor eatable butcher's meat. After dinner he retired to his study and wrote poetry until five or six o'clock, when a young Frenchman came and read to him. At seven there was a concert at which the King played the flute as well as any professional. His own compositions were often played. Supper was in a little room whose principal ornament was a picture, designed by the King, of an orgy in which a crowd of humans and animals were all making love. The conversation generally turned on philosophy and the atmosphere was as though the seven sages of Greece were in a brothel. There were no limits to what could be said; God was respected but those who had deceived humanity in His name were not spared. Neither women nor priests ever set foot in that palace. In a word, Frederick lived without a court, without a council and without religion.

If one person in the world was more malicious than Voltaire, it was Frederick. When he tumbled to the object of this visit, which he did almost at once, he began to rag his poor philosopher, pulling his leg unmercifully. Talking politics to Voltaire, he said, would be like offering a glass of medicine to one's mistress. Much better for them to discuss poetry. Whenever Voltaire tried to bring the conversation round to serious matters, Frederick either made silly jokes and puns or became violently insulting about France, her army, her King and her lack of soul. The French are amiable poltroons, who, having lived too much with women, have taken on all their defects. They are made for the theatre and should leave manly occupations, like warfare, to others. He repeated such gibes over and over again to Voltaire in front of everybody. Voltaire kept his temper and whenever he could he changed the subject or made a joke. Frederick said the French general, Broglie, ought to have his head cut off for doing so badly in Bohemia. Voltaire agreed but said, 'We never cut off the head of a person who hasn't got one'. Naturally none of these conversations were sent to Versailles, but long colourless accounts of Frederick's views and possible future intentions went there regularly. Voltaire wanted to show that he was doing his best: he cannot have thought such stuff would be useful to the ministers. He presented a written questionnaire to Frederick, whose answers were so flippant that most people would have thrown the whole thing into the fire instead of preserving it to amuse posterity.

*Voltaire:* 'Your Majesty knows that the Sieur Basse-cour, 1st Burgomaster at Amsterdam, came to the French Minister with proposals for peace?'

*Frederick:* 'Old Bassecour (Poultry Yard) presumably fattens up the capons and guinea-fowls for these gentlemen.'

*Voltaire:* 'Is it not obvious that if Bassecour, one of the Dutch war-party, declares for peace, Holland will soon be out of the war? Is France not showing both vigour and wisdom?'

*Frederick:* 'I admire French wisdom but heaven forbid that I should ever copy it.'

*Voltaire:* 'The Austrians and their allies burn to reopen the Silesian campaign. In this case, Sire, what other ally have you than France?'

*Frederick :* '*On les recevra biribiri*
*De la façon de Barbari, mes amis.*'

And so on.

Voltaire also asked if he could go with Frederick on his forthcoming visit to his sister the Margravine of Bayreuth. Frederick said yes, but not if he was going to be ill. It depended on himself.

As a matter of fact, Frederick had made up his mind to resume his alliance with France but was determined that Voltaire should not have any credit for this change of front. His aim was, on the contrary, to discredit him as much as possible with the French government, for he knew that he would never possess him if Versailles provided an alternative. One of Frederick's agents in Paris was, at this very time, supplying the mitred donkey with letters containing insults to his person in prose and verse, which Voltaire had written to Frederick. Voltaire found this out and told Amelot, the Foreign Minister, that it was all part of Frederick's scheme for possessing him. However, he would rather live in a Swiss village than be in the power of a man who could behave so badly. His explanation was accepted. The Bishop was not pleased, but nobody else minded very much, and that little plot of Frederick's came to nothing.

The atmosphere at Berlin was not one of trustful affection. The two men still chatted together for hours on end but each knew that the other had betrayed him. Voltaire, disappointed and cross, took his revenge on Emilie, who complained that he hardly ever wrote, and when he did it was only a few cold lines. Another woman might have seen that this was a good sign. but she had no feminine intuition. She suffered, and did not keep her feelings to herself.

Voltaire could generally manage to be well when it

suited him, and the visit to Bayreuth duly took place. Frederick, off on a tour of the German states, left him with the Margravine. Voltaire was much happier there than at Charlottenburg where the only woman was La Barbarini, an Italian dancer with the limbs of a young man. (The poor Queen of Prussia had kindled the sacred hearth alone ever since her husband's accession and was said to have become most disagreeable.) At Bayreuth he found a little Court like a French country house, an easy, natural, happy atmosphere and women with the usual contours. The charming Margravine soon coaxed back his good temper. *'Princesse philosophe,'* he called her, *'modèle de la politesse et de l'affabilité.'* She loved him as he had once thought Frederick would; she was, in fact, her brother in petticoats without the spiky, the uncomfortable, greatness. Voltaire's relationship with her and her sisters was the best result, for him, of his visits to Germany. He now wrote long letters to Emilie, drunk and mad, she said, with the pleasures he found in the silly little German Courts (*courettes*). She was beginning to think she would never see him again, and jealousy of Frederick gave way to jealousy of his sister. What was Voltaire doing in Bayreuth, alone, without the King?

He was only there a fortnight, and when the two men got back to Berlin their tempers were much better. Voltaire was preparing to leave and Frederick was putting on charm. There was the usual talk of Voltaire going to live there, *without others* of course. Indeed the du Châtelets would have been fish out of water in that homosexual society; and even Voltaire, much as he liked having his cake and eating it, saw that he must choose between Frederick and Emilie. He still chose Emilie. Valory asked Voltaire to take advantage of the King's better mood to do something for a French gentleman who had been tortured and had his nose and ears cut off by the late King Frederick-William and who now languished in the fortress of Spandau. His crime was that, having been kidnapped and pressed into the regiment of giants he had tried to escape from it. Frederick consented to act, as he said, *La Clemenza di Tito*. He also agreed, at last, to settle with Thieriot. But Frederick was never as good as his word, in big things or in small. The Frenchman was only released in 1749, and Thieriot, after nine years of empty promises, received nothing.

Maupertuis had still not returned to Berlin after his adventures at Mollwitz; Voltaire wrote to his dear earth-flattener, painting his visit in the sunniest colours and giving a lively account of all their mutual acquaintances; Jordan (Frederick's great friend) is still like Ragotin the comic hunchback in one of Scarron's novels, but a genial, discreet Ragotin now, with a good pension regularly paid; the Marquis d'Argens is Chamberlain with a huge gold key. The Academy, where Maupertuis is loved and regretted, is occupied with the experiments of Eller who thinks he can change water into elastic air. At Bayreuth, Her Royal Highness spoke much of Maupertuis; it is a delicious retreat, an agreeable Court without any tedious etiquette. Brunswick (whose Duchess was another of Frederick's sisters) has a different charm. Voltaire flies from planet to planet, to end up at tumultuous Paris where he will be sad indeed if he does not find unique Maupertuis whom he admires and loves for the rest of his life.

Voltaire left Berlin on 13 October and went back to The Hague by comfortable stages, visiting Brunswick on the way. The du Châtelets were waiting for him at Brussels. Emilie was in a morbidly self-pitying mood, and d'Argental, as usual, was the recipient of her whines. Twelve days from Berlin to The Hague when it had only taken him nine to go in the other direction. The absence, which was to have been of six weeks, has been prolonged to five months. Three whole weeks without a letter. For two months she has had to learn of his plans from Ambassadors or the gazettes. Any other woman would have detached herself long ago, but Emilie's sensibilities cannot be extinguished and she will never be reasonable. Voltaire must, however, be made to feel how greatly she has suffered, and d'Argental must let him know what a state she has been in. Her health is sadly deranged, she coughs continually, has a pain between her shoulders and another in what she thinks must be her liver. Anybody else would be dead and it might really be all for the best if she were.

D'Argental duly passed on these remarks to Voltaire, who had the usual male reaction of guilty annoyance, and thought it all a great fuss about nothing. It is not his fault if the posts are bad. He, too, was a long time without letters; he minded, of course, but he did not fly into a rage, or think himself betrayed, or stir up the whole of Germany. D'Argental's friend has made things very tiresome for Voltaire, with all the steps she has been taking. But Voltaire does not have to justify himself to his old comrade who knows quite well what he is. D'Argental must tell his correspondent not to cover a sky, as serene as theirs, with clouds. Voltaire adds a postscript two days later (6 November 1743) to say that he has now arrived at Brussels and has had the joy of finding their female friend in much better health than himself.

# Chapter Sixteen

## A Happy Summer at Cirey

THE TWO philosophers, reunited, were happy to be together again. 'He loves me,' said Emilie, while Voltaire, for his part, said he had never found her so adorable. Emilie, of course, could not help recapitulating her wrongs, and said this must be his very last visit to that horrid Germany where the heart learns to be hard. She is delighted that d'Argental has taken him to task; she can see that Voltaire has received his letter though of course they don't mention it. They only stayed a couple of days in Brussels, then back to the Faubourg Saint-Honoré by way of Lille and Mme Denis. Du Châtelet went to Cirey and plans were made for spending the next summer there.

In Paris, Voltaire worked and Mme du Châtelet gambled. There is a letter (perhaps the only one in existence) from her to Voltaire: it begins 'Dear Lover' (in English) and asks for fifty louis to pay a card debt. She got into further difficulties and had to borrow money from Helvétius. This led to unpleasantness, because she could not pay him back when the time came. Voltaire said of her that the people she gambled with had no idea that she was so learned, though sometimes they were astonished at the speed and accuracy with which she added up the score. He himself once saw her divide nine figures by nine others in her head. It might have been supposed that somebody so quick at figures would have had a good card sense but she hardly ever won, or if she did we do not hear of it. Her losses were often enormous.

In her *Réflections sur le Bonheur*, an essay written at about this time, Mme du Châtelet says that the only pleasures left to a woman when she is old are gambling, study and greed, if she has the health for it. She considers that gambling, by which she means playing for high enough stakes to affect one's fortune, is instrumental to happiness. The soul needs to be shaken up by hope and by fear. Gambling brings it within range of these two passions and keeps it in a healthy state. She herself has often been reconciled to her lack of fortune by the thought that she gets more excitement from playing cards than she would if she were rich.

These *Réflections*, she explains, are not written for humanity in general, but for *les gens du monde*, people with an assured position in life. Unfortunately we only see how to achieve happiness when age and the fetters we have forged for ourselves are beginning to make it difficult. In order to be happy we must be virtuous, get rid of our prejudices, enjoy good health, have strong tastes and passions and keep our illusions. Most pleasure comes from illusions, and he who has lost them is seldom happy. Those moralists who think that we should rid ourselves of passions and desires know nothing about happiness, which chiefly comes from their satisfaction. Le Nôtre was quite right when he asked the Pope to give him temptations rather than indulgences. But, she will be asked, do not passions make more people unhappy than happy? Impossible to say, because it is the unhappy people who talk about themselves, the happy ones remain anonymous. Nobody writes plays about happy lovers. But even if it is true that strong passions make many people unhappy, she still asserts that they are desirable since really great pleasure is impossible without them.

In order to have passions and to be able to satisfy them good health is essential and this depends on ourselves. We are all born healthy and made to last a certain length of time. If we do not destroy our constitution by over-eating, late hours and other excesses, we shall live the ordinary length of human life. She does not speak of sudden death which is out of our control. What about people whose chief pleasure is food? Greed is a wonderful source of regular happiness and it is quite possible to indulge in it without affecting our health, though this entails a certain amount of eating at home. Mme du Châtelet herself has had to renounce alcohol. She often feels so much too hot that she spends her mornings swallowing all sorts of liquid. She gives way to her greed, but as soon as she is uncomfortable she goes on a strict diet.

It is very important in life to know what we want. Too many people have no idea, and yet without an aim there can be no happiness. We destroy in the morning what we did the night before; we commit blunders; we repent. This repentance is one of the most disagreeable of all the feelings that assail us, and we must be careful to protect ourselves from it. As nothing in life happens twice in the same way it is useless to dwell on past faults. We must go on from where we are without looking back, and always substitute agreeable reflections for disagreeable ones. It is foolish, for instance, to dwell upon death, whether our own or that of other people, a sad and humiliating thought which does us no good at all.

For a woman, debarred as she is from political and military ambitions, study is the greatest of resources. Other forms of pleasure extolled by Mme du Châtelet in this sensible analysis are the acquisition of new pieces of furniture, snuff-boxes and so on, which she says give her intense happiness, regular visits to the privy and keeping warm in very cold weather.

Voltaire was ill in bed most of that winter. The gossips said that he was having an affair with the actress Mlle Gaussin and that she visited him at Mme du Châtelet's house when he could not go to hers. Du Châtelet was tired of living alone at Cirey and wanted Emilie to keep him company there, but Voltaire had no wish to leave Paris. He was most disagreeable to Emilie, made scenes and often made her cry. However, he was about to begin a piece of work to which he attached the greatest importance and for which he needed a country solitude. So at last she persuaded him to go with her to Cirey, and in very bad tempers they set off at the beginning of April 1744.

Hardly had they arrived than they got word that M. Denis was ill. Two or three days later he died. His wife and Voltaire both seem to have been sincerely fond of him; Voltaire wrote her a heartfelt letter of sympathy on hearing the news. To Thieriot he wrote that it was for Mme Denis a dreadful loss by day and by night of fortune and a man who adored her.

After an unpromising start, the philosophers spent one of the happiest summers they had ever had together. Cirey had never seemed so enchanting—'a jewel,' said Voltaire, dating his letter '*à Cirey en félicité*', 'my kingdom and my academy'. He wrote over the door of his gallery:

> *Asile des beaux arts, solitude où mon cœur*
> *Est toujours occupé dans une paix profonde*
> *C'est vous qui donnez le bonheur*
> *Que promettait en vain le monde.*

Mme de Châtelet, he said, was in the gallery with him most of the time and that was why it had such a happy atmosphere. Voltaire, who generally had many different works in progress, was now concentrated on one. He

had come away from the distractions of Paris in order to
bestow all his time and attention on it, so wholehearted
in his application that anybody might have supposed his
literary career to be at stake. A young man writing his
first book could not have taken it more seriously.

The Duc de Richelieu, as First Gentleman of the Bed-
chamber, was this year in charge of all the fêtes at Versailles. The King and the courtiers were always nagging
at him about the poor quality of the entertainments he
provided. These generally consisted of elaborate fireworks; people complained that they provided food for
the eye but not for the intellect. At last the Duke, tired of
hearing these complaints every time a gala was in preparation, said that when the Dauphin married the Infanta of Spain he would get Voltaire and Rameau to
write the *divertissement*. The wedding was to take place in
February 1745; poet and composer were given a year in
which to prepare their work. Voltaire had already written
an opera, *Samson*, with Rameau, and knew his difficult
character. Rameau attached no importance whatever to
the libretto, and thought that nothing mattered but the
music.

'Sing faster!'

'But, Maître, if I do the words will be lost.'

'Who cares?'

Voltaire was an easy person to work with, owing, no
doubt, to years spent in the theatre. He was always
ready to alter, shorten or lengthen his verses and would
even give way about the words he used: 'If you like I will
remove the word *d'outrageuse*, though I would point out
that both Boileau and Corneille use it.' He never minded
how much trouble he took, it was a pleasure to go over
and over what he had written; he knew that a fresh eye
often perceives small inadequacies which the author by
himself might never notice.

The *divertissement* which he now planned, opera, ballet,

fêtes within fêtes, and *tableaux vivants*, was to be called *La Princesse de Navarre* and its hero, the Duc de Foix, was to be modelled on Richelieu. The whole long summer Voltaire thought of nothing else at all. He hardly wrote any letters, most unusual for him, and none to Frederick. He constantly sent rough drafts of the *Princesse* to Richelieu, asking for his advice and approval, but was rather annoyed when he found that all Versailles was reading them. 'Very few people can see the quality of the gold when it is still in a mine, covered with earth.' Also, though Richelieu is a great connoisseur, he writes like a cat, impossible to read his letters. Never mind, on with the work. Mme du Châtelet is watching over it and she is the severest of all critics, absolutely reliable in her judgments. Voltaire had never been so anxious to have a success. He hardly hoped to amuse the Dauphin and Dauphine, whose thoughts presumably would be elsewhere at this important juncture in their lives (anyhow they were unamusable) but he longed for the approbation of the King.

Voltaire's feeling for Louis XV was much more straightforward than his love-hatred for Frederick. It was simply that of a subject, anxious to please. There never could have been any question of his sitting on the end of the King of France's bed or assisting with him at homosexual orgies. Such goings-on were unknown at Versailles. The King, apart from the etiquette upon which he thought it right to insist, was a shy man who only felt at his ease with a few old friends. He hardly ever threw Voltaire a word. In spite of this and of the petty persecutions he endured from various officers of the crown, Voltaire often paid tribute to the charm of Louis XV and praised his character. In the *Eloge Funèbre*, written when he no longer had anything to hope or to fear from the King, he warned posterity against listening to 'those secret legends which are spread

about a Prince in his lifetime out of spite, or a mere love
of gossip, which a mistaken public believes to be true and
which, in a few more years, are adopted by the historians
who thus deceive themselves and the generations to
come'. He could not have foreseen more clearly what
would happen.

He laboured at his *Princesse de Navarre*, hoping to entertain the Monarch, taking more trouble than he ever had
for the Comédie-française and the 4,000 educated Parisian playgoers. Emilie too was working hard. She had a
new tutor, Père Jacquier, who was to wean her from the
ideas of Leibnitz and put her back on the wholesome diet
of Newton. In July 1744 President Hénault, the Queen's
great friend and the lover since all time of Mme du
Deffand, spent a day at Cirey on his way to the watering-
place, Plombières. Voltaire and Emilie were delighted
by his admiration of their house and perhaps even more
by his undisguised amazement at the beauty and luxury
in which they lived. He was quite unprepared for what
he found. He wrote various accounts of his visit. To the
Comte d'Argenson: 'I have never seen anything like it.
They are there, the two of them, alone, leading a most
agreeable life. One makes verses, and the other, triangles.
The architecture of the house is romantic and surpris-
ingly magnificent. Voltaire has an apartment ending in a
gallery which looks like that picture, *The School of Athens*,
where there is a collection of all sorts of instruments for
mathematics, physics, astronomy and so on, and with all
this there are old lacquer, looking-glasses, pictures,
Dresden china—really I assure you one thinks one is
dreaming. Voltaire read me his play and I liked it very
much. He manages to be both comic and touching. He
has taken all my advice and accepted all my corrections.
But what do you think of Rameau's behaviour, turning
into a literary critic and correcting Voltaire's verses? I've
written to Richelieu about it.'

In his memoirs he wrote: 'I found them alone with a Franciscan Father, a great geometrician and professor of philosophy at Rome. If one wanted to paint a delicious retreat, a peaceful refuge, a calm communion of souls, amenities, talents, reciprocity of admiration, the attraction of philosophy allied to the charm of poetry, one would paint Cirey. A simple, elegant one-storied building contains cabinets full of instruments both mechanical and chemical, and Voltaire in his bed, beginning, continuing and finishing work of every description.' He wrote to Voltaire from Plombières saying that he was greatly edified by 'your happiness together'.

The President was wholeheartedly on Voltaire's side against Rameau who was, as usual, being extremely awkward. Richelieu, too, wrote to him sharply. They thought he should be reminded that Voltaire was not just any librettist. Voltaire himself took the whole thing light-heartedly. Rameau wanted him to expand four verses into eight and shorten eight verses into four. Oh well, Rameau is a genius and has the right to be a little mad. In spite of his madness and tiresomeness, Voltaire made over to him all the royalties on their joint work. At last his anxiety to finish in time and his efforts to please everybody made Voltaire ill. Emilie became seriously worried about him; he had a high fever, which always frightened her, especially in the country; he could neither sleep nor eat. She said that he was not to be sent any more suggestions, until he arrived in Paris for the rehearsals.

They left Cirey sooner than they had meant to, for various reasons. The farm animals had a disease (foot and mouth?). They thought they would like to be in Paris for the rejoicings at Louis XV's recovery from his illness at Metz. Voltaire wanted to see Richelieu before he went to Spain to fetch the Infanta. He must be made to have a few words with Rameau who was beginning to trade on his genius a little too much; if he went on being so difficult the *divertissement* might never take place at all. So by the end of August 1744 they were back in the Faubourg Saint-Honoré. For the next year they divided their time between Paris and Champs, the country house of the Duc de La Vallière. He and his wife were friends both of Voltaire and Mme du Châtelet; he was an extremely civilized person, one of the great bibliophiles of the eighteenth century. Champs is just outside Paris in Seine-et-Marne. The two philosophers kept bedrooms there and came and went whenever they liked.

The thanksgiving festivities for the King's recovery lasted several days. Paris was in a state of delirium and the traffic became disorganized. Voltaire and Mme du Châtelet went to an open-air concert in the Place Dauphine and on their way home their carriage was held up by a gigantic traffic-block in the rue Saint-Honoré. The street was impassable, 2,000 carriages were said to have been immobilized, while to make matters worse the Duc d'Orléans and his retinue of coaches complete with outriders, guards and pages were trying to get through to the Palais-Royal. Emilie's coachman had never been in Paris before. At last Voltaire and Emilie decided to brave the crowd which surged, drunk and disorderly, round them and walk to President Hénault's house, 219 rue Saint-Honoré. (It still exists.) Emilie was covered with diamonds and screaming like a peacock, but nobody molested her and they arrived safely. The President was away; they made themselves at home, sent out for a roast chicken and drank the health of their absent host. Voltaire wrote and told him all this, adding that they had been lucky to find this friendly shelter so near, because nobody could move until 3 a.m. Emilie's house in the Faubourg Saint-Honoré was only a few hundred yards away, but it would have been impossible for them to have walked home even had there been no crowd; people of quality never set foot in the streets, they were much too dirty. The first person to build a pavement on which it was possible to walk was the Duc d'Antin, outside his own house. This street is known as the Chaussée d'Antin.

# Chapter Seventeen

## Voltaire at Court

EMILIE HAD seen at once that Frederick was likely to become a dangerous rival but she never saw a greater danger, nearer home. Mme Denis, the widow-woman, now came to live in Paris where she set up house in the rue Pavée (a street hardly changed to this day). A cheerful, ugly little thing aged thirty-two, she established a salon for Voltaire's bourgeois friends. When Mme du Châtelet went out gambling, or to suppers where he was not invited, Voltaire would go to his niece for a good laugh with her and the various men who frequented her house. Very soon he found that he was not too old to make love after all and that she had given him back '*l'âge des amours*'. His love was most passionate and a deadly secret. None of his contemporaries knew of it, not even Voltaire's man-servant, and we only do from his letters, recently come to light. When his thoughts became very much inflamed, not to say pornographic, he would often express them in Italian. '*Mia Cara,*' he calls her, '*ma chère Italienne.*' 'A few moments in your company and I forget all my past sorrows.' 'I shall never be happy until I can live with you. I cover your adorable body with kisses.' (*J'embrasse votre gentil cul et toute votre adorable personne.*) 'My soul is yours for ever.' 'Mme Duch dines today with the Duchesse de Modène and I with my dearest Muse whom I love more than life itself.'

It must be borne in mind that an affair with a niece is not regarded as incestuous in a Latin country. To this day Frenchmen of the very best society marry their nieces with a Papal dispensation; at least one of Voltaire's friends, Paris-Montmartel, had done so. If the affair was deplorable it was because of Mme Denis's own character. She was to become an odious figure, eaten up with the love of money. But when she was young her faults were not so apparent. She was extremely attractive to men. Cideville wanted to marry her; Voltaire was enslaved by her. 'You will always be my mistress.' 'I should like to live at your feet and die in your arms.'

During the autumn and winter of 1744 Voltaire had two preoccupations, Mme Denis and the *Princesse de Navarre*. He fussed over this play, writing and rewriting it, asking everybody's advice on little details, in such a torment of creation as even he had hardly ever known. If he livens up this scene, will the next one fall a trifle flat? How would d'Argental cope with it? What does Cideville think? Richelieu wants more ballets, but will they not stifle interest in the plot? He could have saved himself all this wear and tear; interest in his plot was still-born.

On 23 February 1745, the spectacle which had eaten up a whole year of Voltaire's life, causing him a severe nervous breakdown, was performed in front of the newly-married Dauphin and Dauphine, the King and Queen, the Court and a little group of Voltaire's own special friends, including, of course, Mme Denis. This audience was so beautiful that it quite outshone the actors, there was no comparison between the two sides of the curtain. It was like a swarm of golden bees, glittering round the King and buzzing so loud that verses and music could hardly be heard. Voltaire said afterwards that the play had been a firework which went off leaving no trace behind it, but the few members of the audience who paid him the compliment of attending to his script did not see it as a firework at all. They complained that it was exceedingly long and dull. The Dauphine said the jokes were flat, but she was well known to hate jokes: in spite of a French father and an Italian mother she was impregnated with Spanish gravity. Louis XV, however, who had been happily chatting away throughout the performance, pronounced himself more than satisfied. Voltaire wanted no other reward. He boasted to all his friends, even to the austere Vauvenargues who, himself an aristocrat, was not likely to have been impressed, that he now practically lived at Versailles. He excused himself, when he remembered to do so, for this sudden change of front about a Court which he used to regard as the very pit of corruption, explaining that only by royal favour could he be sheltered from the Mirepoix faction and get on with his work in peace. He was ashamed of becoming the King's clown at the age of fifty-one, he said. He was, at the Court, like an atheist in a church. But in truth he was fascinated by Versailles and only when out of reach did the grapes turn sour for him again.

That spring was one of the periods when all went well with Voltaire. He was appointed official historian and gentleman-in-ordinary to the King, with 2,000 livres a year and an apartment at Versailles. This apartment was really one smelly, shabby room over the public privies and the Prince de Condé's kitchen. However it provided what is known as 'a good address'. Most probably he lodged, as usual, with Richelieu. The Comédie-française revived his *l'Enfant Prodigue*, *Mérope*, *Zaïre*, *Œdipe* and *Alzire*. Best of all the King now acquired a new mistress. Mme de Châteauroux had died suddenly at the age of twenty-seven, just after his own recovery. He mourned her for a few months and fell in love again. Fascinating Mme d'Etioles, soon to be Mme de Pompadour, had been brought up in the world of high finance so well known to Voltaire. 'I saw her born.' He was delighted that the King's choice should have fallen on her. Mme de Pompadour was a woman of taste and learning and the writers of the day hoped that through her influence they would henceforth receive more equitable treatment. For the same reason, her rise to power was distressing to the Bishop of Mirepoix, who had done everything he could to prevent it. The mitred ass was soon to receive an even greater blow.

Various events in the families of Mme du Châtelet and Voltaire must be recorded. Her plump little daughter, who used to be brought from her convent to act at Cirey, reached the age of sixteen and was brought from it again to marry an old Neapolitan Duke of Montenero, with a flat chest and a huge nose. He carried her off to live at Capodimonte and she was never more seen by Mme du Châtelet who took less interest in her than in the puppies of Dear Love, her black dog. Voltaire, more of a human being than most of his contemporaries in such matters, disapproved of the bridegroom and corresponded by fits and starts with the bride.

The du Châtelets' lawsuit was finally settled; they won it, and yet in some miraculous way managed to remain on good terms with their opponent, the Marquis de Hoensbrock, who wrote and thanked Voltaire for the part he had played. Du Châtelet also wrote, saying that he and his family had many reasons to be grateful to Voltaire and that he absolutely relied on him never to leave Mme du Châtelet. In the summer of 1745 Mme du Châtelet moved from the Faubourg Saint-Honoré to a house in the rue Traversière (now rue Molière) where Voltaire occupied the whole of the first floor.

During the rehearsals of the *Princesse de Navarre* Voltaire's brother died, leaving him the sole survivor of the Arouets. He may have wondered if he would not soon follow the others to the grave. His health had never

been so bad, his liver and lights played him up terribly,
and he had hardly been well a single day since leaving
Cirey.

Voltaire was enjoying his new situation at Versailles
when Mme du Châtelet's son, who was now seventeen
and had been at the front with his father, was stricken
down with smallpox at Châlons-sur-Marne. Voltaire and
Emilie hurried to his bedside, where they could do
nothing but observe the ignorant tyranny of the doctors.
The Bishop of Châlons insisted that they should stay with
him, in spite of possible contagion. When the boy was
better they returned to Paris, but Voltaire was now forbidden to go near the Court for forty days. This was an
inviolable rule for anybody who had been in contact with
smallpox, whether they had had it themselves or not.
Stupid prejudice, said he, and not the first time it had
done him harm.

All Voltaire's friends, the King at their head, were off
to the war and he had particularly wanted to say good-
bye. Now, in his capacity of official historian he could
only wait, his pen ready poised, to celebrate their feats
of arms in prose and verse. He did not have to wait for
long. On 12 May 1745 news came to Versailles of the
brilliant French victory over the English and Dutch
armies at Fontenoy. The Marquis d'Argenson (now
Foreign Minister), who was at the front, wrote a preliminary account of the battle to 'Monsieur l'Historien'.
He described the irresistible, rolling fire of the English,
like hell itself, the moment when it seemed as if all were
lost and the French would have to swallow a second
Dettingen (where the English had beaten them earlier
in this war), the imperturbable gaiety of the King, his
refusal to budge and the final triumph of the household
cavalry. 'Your friend Richelieu was a veritable Bayard.'

Voltaire, in spite of his pacific principles, rejoiced at
this victory. The French army had suffered many humi-

liating defeats of late and Voltaire had keenly felt the
force of Frederick's jibes and insults at its expense. He
was also delighted to have such a subject with which to
begin his career as official historian. He wrote his famous
poem: *La Bataille de Fontenoy gagnée par Louis XV sur les
Alliés.* By 26 May it had already gone into five editions,
each bringing in the names and feats of more warriors;
Voltaire was besieged by women of his · acquaintance
who wanted a line or two about some loved one. In the
end the thing became a farce and, the irreverent French
being what they are, a parody of *Fontenoy* soon appeared.
Whereas Voltaire's heroes are all, of course, nobly born,
of the highest rank and most impeccable ancestry, in the
parody they have names like Joli-Cœur, La Tulipe or
l'Espérance, sons of *tailleur de pierre, gros marchand d'eau-de-
vie* and so on. The literary critics were unanimous in their
condemnation of *Fontenoy*. But Voltaire now only heeded
the verdict of one judge. Louis XV was not much of a
reader, and Maréchal de Noailles read the poem to him.
Maréchal de Saxe wrote to Mme du Châtelet: 'The King
is very much pleased with it and even says that the work
is beyond criticism.' Voltaire was delighted, but not surprised. There were little *finesses* in the poem, he said,
which could only be understood by gentlefolk, and which
were far above the heads of mere pen-pushers, sewers
from Bicêtre and the like. As usual he was buoyed up
with enormous sales.

As well as the poem Voltaire had to write an historical
account of Fontenoy in prose. He discovered that the
Duke of Cumberland, the English commander, had one
Fawkener attached to him, so he wrote asking if he were
a relation of the Ambassador. To his surprise and delight
it turned out that it was his own Fawkener. 'How could
I guess, my dear and honourable friend, that your
Mussulman person had . . . passed from the seraglio
to the closet of the Duke of Cumberland?' He supplied

Voltaire with details of the campaign from the English point of view. Lord Chesterfield wrote to a woman friend at Paris greatly praising Voltaire's *Fontenoy* which, he said, as far as he could make out was a perfectly correct report of the battle. He went on to say that nobody wanted peace more than he did but: 'We want an equitable peace, you are for an advantageous one, so I am afraid it is further off than ever. We aim at nothing but the liberty and safety of Europe, you seek nothing but the advancement of your own despotism; how, then, can we agree?' All the same he was planning to send his son to school at Paris the following year to learn 'that ease, those manners, those graces which are certainly nowhere to be found but in France'.

Voltaire spent part of the summer at Etioles where Mme de Pompadour was living quietly with her family until Louis XV should return from the war. A fellow guest was the Abbé de Bernis, an amiable, chubby little young man, who for no particular reason was a member of the Académie-française and who, also for no particular reason, was presently to be Foreign Minister. Everybody liked Bernis. Voltaire teased him, called him Babet la Bouquetière and was not even envious of him. Indeed it was so ridiculous that Babet, in 'her' twenties, should be an Academician while Voltaire, in his fifties, was not, as to be a cause for amusement rather than envy. Voltaire loved Mme de Pompadour as most people did who knew her and she was fond of him and understood him. She bossed him about as only a young and pretty person can boss an old, illustrious man. He told Emilie that here was a beauty who hated gambling, it bored her to death. How strange, when Emilie-Newton wasted such hours at the card-table! Mme du Châtelet may well have been jealous of this other Marquise since she was unaware of the much more sinister reason she now had for jealousy.

She was Emilie-Newton again in good earnest. The Père Jacquier had caused her to realize the errors of her Leibnitzian ways and she had begun her translation of Newton. Even so her abounding energy was not fully engaged; she gambled until four or five every morning and went a great deal to Versailles where she was plaguing the War Minister to make her little boy a colonel. The Marquis du Châtelet was now a general, covering himself with glory in a series of prudent retreats. Emilie was in a particularly tiresome frame of mind just then, overdoing everything and giving herself ridiculous airs at Court. She had certain privileges usually reserved for Duchesses, on account of her husband's position in Lorraine. One of these was to travel in the Queen's retinue. When the Court left Versailles for its autumn visit to Fontainebleau, Emilie told the Mistress of the Robes, the Duchesse de Luynes, that she would be wanting a place in one of the coaches and this was duly arranged. The Queen herself left with Mme de Luynes and three other Duchesses straight from the chapel as soon as Mass was over. Two more coaches were waiting in the Cour d'Honneur to bring Mesdames de Montaubon, Fitzjames, Flavacourt and du Châtelet. Hardly had the Queen driven off than Mme du Châtelet hopped into one of them, settled herself comfortably in the corner and called out something like: 'Come on, plenty of room!' The other women, outraged by this lack of manners, all got into the second coach, leaving Emilie alone in hers. Seeing that she had gone too far, she got down again and went to join them but a footman stopped her, saying that there was no room for her. So she drove in solitary state to Fontainebleau. As soon as she arrived she told Richelieu what had happened and he went off to see Mme de Luynes, one of those rare people who like to make everything easy and pleasant. She presented Mme du Châtelet's apologies to the Queen and all was

forgiven, but as nothing else was talked of at Fontainebleau the atmosphere cannot have been very comfortable for Emilie. Indeed, she and Voltaire went back to
Paris almost at once. The Duc de Luynes, telling the
story in his journal, excuses her on the grounds that she is
not as other women but a scientist who has actually had a
book printed. He charitably puts her behaviour down to
absentmindedness.

Voltaire now disconcerted the French Church by
entering into correspondence with the Pope. He thought
that he could thus cut the ground from under the feet of
Monseigneur de Mirepoix and prepare the way to the
Académie-française. Benedict XIV was a shrewd,
learned man with a sense of humour. At the death of
Clement XII the conclave of Cardinals, shut up in the
Vatican to elect a new Pope, was even longer than usual
in agreeing. At last Cardinal Lambertini said to them:
'If you want a saint you must elect Gotti; if a politician,
Aldobrandi; but if you want an ordinary good sort of
fellow, what about me?' They elected him and he was
Pope from 1740–58. Exceptionally humane, he made
various reforms and issued a bull demanding better
treatment for the American Indians. He was not at all
fond of the French Church; he thought it expended too
much energy in hunting down Jansenists and other non-
conformists. Voltaire could not have fallen upon a better
Pope to make friends with. 'He has the face of a good
devil who knows what the whole thing is worth.' With
his usual energy Voltaire pulled strings in many directions; he wrote to Cardinals; Mlle du Thil, a relation of
Mme du Châtelet, wrote on his behalf to a powerful
Abbé at the Vatican and d'Argenson wrote to the French
envoy there. The Pope, who admired Voltaire's works,
responded to the first advance by sending him a large
medal with his portrait. Not knowing this, the French
envoy asked for a large medal for Voltaire. 'But I

couldn't give him a larger one if he were St Peter himself!' Voltaire sent him his *Mahomet*, which the Pope
very sensibly took at its face value without searching
for hidden blasphemies. He praised it and allowed
Voltaire to dedicate it to him. Needless to say, this
commerce with the Vatican was heavily publicized.

Voltaire's favour at Versailles continued but was never
very firmly established because Louis XV could not get
fond of him. He understood the value of Voltaire. Con-
dorcet says: 'It was not without a feeling of pride that he
saw one of his subjects acknowledged by the whole of
Europe as being among the most illustrious of men. He
respected the glory of France in him.' But when they
came face to face, Voltaire, anxious to make an impression, too often made a gaffe. His cheeky yet subser-
vient manner embarrassed and irritated the King. With
Rameau he wrote another *divertissement*, *Le Temple de la
Gloire*, to celebrate the recent French victories. In it
Voltaire doled out a good deal of heavy flattery to Louis
XV who figured as benign, majestic Trajan. At the
royal performance he said to Richelieu, in the King's
hearing: 'Is Trajan pleased?' Trajan was displeased at
such manners and showed it, and there was as much of a
to-do over this incident as over Emilie's little miscalcu-
lation in the coach. However, Mme de Pompadour and
Richelieu saw to it that the King and his historian
should hardly ever meet, and the royal favour was not
withdrawn for the present. The smaller fry among the
courtiers were in a fury at Voltaire's appointment as
gentleman-in-ordinary, a post hitherto reserved for the
nobility. His new colleagues decided that when he came
to dine with them they would send him to Coventry.
But of course when he did present himself he had the
whole table roaring with laughter in no time. The boot
was on the other foot: these gentlemen bored Voltaire
so much that he never went near them again. Very soon,

with the King's consent, he sold his appointment while keeping all its privileges.

Voltaire, universally admitted to be the greatest living French writer, corresponding with the Pope and a courtier at Versailles, could no longer be kept out of the Académie-française; his election took place quite easily and smoothly in the spring of 1746. He was too ill to pay the customary visits and it seemed unlikely that he would live to enjoy his new honour for very long. He succeeded to the *fauteuil* of Bouhier, a magistrate; of his eight successors in it only two have been interesting, Saint-René Taillandier and Paul Bourget. It need hardly be said that Voltaire's inaugural speech gave rise to controversy. He departed from the traditional practice of praising three people: Cardinal Richelieu, Chancellor Séguier and the previous occupant of the *fauteuil*. He took as his theme the universality of the French language. He named his foreign benefactors who spoke it perfectly: Princess Louisa Ulrica of Prussia (now Crown Princess of Sweden), Benedict XIV and Frederick. From them he went on to various French friends such as Richelieu, Fontenelle, President Hénault and, of course, the father of his people, dear, good Louis XV. Those who were mentioned thought this an excellent innovation; those who were not complained that the speech was too long, too dull and in very poor taste.

From the moment of his election Voltaire's luck began to turn against him. His triumph was poisoned for him by the appalling state of his health and by an affair which, since it upset his nerves, certainly prevented his recovery. Though Voltaire had managed for once in his life to pacify Church and State, he had more enemies than ever. Desfontaines was 'dead and gone to Sodom', but many other little insect scribblers, their hearts black with envy, were out for his blood. His election to the Academy was followed by a perfect storm of pamphlets,

poems and the whole paraphernalia of an eighteenth-
century slander campaign. He was not only criticized by
petty courtiers and jealous writers. Society people were
complaining of his and Emilie's manners. When they
went to stay in country houses their fellow guests said
they made no effort to be agreeable and only spoke to
each other. Finally the Pope received at least one letter
saying that the French Catholics had learnt with sorrow
that His Holiness had given a gold medal to the infamous atheist Arouet de Voltaire.

His friends were becoming seriously worried about his
unpopularity. Vauvenargues, almost the only one of his
many young protégés who behaved well to Voltaire
and who loved him deeply, told him, in May 1746,
that he had never known such feeling against him as
there had been during the past four months. He said
the things he had read about Voltaire set him against
not only men of letters but literature itself. Soon afterwards Cideville wrote: 'I really must scold you.' He begs
him not to be so high and mighty with his fellow Academicians, and not to tell illiterate Abbés that they do not
know how to read. One must be polite to one's inferiors
and not proud with one's equals, anyhow who is the
equal of Voltaire? Charming Cideville, no wonder he
kept the lifelong affection of that touchy friend.

It is a commonplace that no literary exercise is so easy
as the denigration of a writer and his works. While talent
and discernment are needed for constructive criticism, a
clever child can demolish almost any book by a twisted
analysis and a false conclusion. Voltaire's greatest surviving enemy was by no means a child. He was that
poet Roy on whose account, many years before, Voltaire
said, jokingly, that he had changed his name. Like
Desfontaines and Jean-Baptiste Rousseau he was a well-
known literary figure, older than Voltaire. Fontenelle
used to say that he was the dullest wit (*homme d'esprit*) he

had ever known. Roy was disgusted at Voltaire's election to the Academy from which he himself had been excluded. He wrote a parody of *Fontenoy* and several pamphlets against Voltaire and reissued a new, long version of a poem he had once written, reconstructing all the farcical and discreditable episodes in Voltaire's life. Furthermore he called Mme du Châtelet a goat. He then used the well-known Voltairean dodge of furiously denying that these writings were by him. If Voltaire could have pretended not to notice, all would have been forgotten in a few weeks and his enemies deprived of their miserable little immortality. (Desfontaines is mentioned in Larousse as '*connu par ses démêlées avec Voltaire*'.) But he, who so loved to laugh, never could laugh at himself and never could ignore such attacks. He always hit back wildly.

Voltaire's quarrel with Roy, with Travenol, an obscure violinist at the Opera, who was supposed to have distributed anti-Voltairean literature, and with one or two other dim, pathetic figures followed the well-known pattern of such quarrels, except that Voltaire, being more powerful than formerly, was able to take a more effective revenge. He forgot that freedom of speech was the most desirable of all freedoms, he forgot that it is wicked to imprison writers because of what they write: he took out *lettres de cachet* against his various persecutors. He then had the joy of seeing them in a situation which he himself knew too well, though in the last resort he had always been protected by his highly-placed friends. They were hunted by the police, their houses were searched and they themselves imprisoned or exiled. Unluckily, in the case of Travenol, the police made a mistake and dragged his ancient old father, '*vieillard irréprochable*', to gaol. He was released again at once, and Voltaire took him out to dinner and wept with him, but public opinion was inflamed by this incident. The inevitable lawsuit which followed ended in the inevitable draw. Meanwhile we have the curious spectacle of Voltaire, on the side of law and order and of the police, writing to Vauvenargues: 'I am glad to think that this affair will serve to distinguish those who deserve the protection of the government from those who deserve its displeasure and that of the general public.'

Voltaire now regarded himself as a dying man. 'I am coming peacefully to the end of my career.' His only regret was that his works had never been correctly printed. He bequeathed his manuscripts to Frederick, hoping that he would publish a proper edition of them. But Voltaire's career, never peaceful, was not yet ended.

*Chapter Eighteen*

---

## The Philosophers in Bad Odour

NO DOUBT a sweet, domesticated woman entirely devoted to his interests would have bored Voltaire. He needed mental stimulants, not to say mental strife, and these Emilie provided. But she was too selfish to be of much use to him in other ways. She had her own career and ambitions to consider; pleasure too was an absorbing factor. In the autumn of 1746 another woman might have realized that Voltaire was boiling up for a brain-storm. He had been hanging about the Court for nearly two years, during which he had hardly ever felt well. Illness with him always came from nervous strain and at this time it can be partly attributed to his affair with Mme Denis. He had been ill, in the same way, for months, at the beginning of that with Emilie herself. Mme du Châtelet did not know this reason for his illness, but she ought to have realized that he needed a period of peaceful country life. She should have carried him off to Cirey, instead of which she carried him off to Fontainebleau where the Court was in residence. She intended to settle down there to some heavy gambling.

This visit was a disaster from beginning to end. Two days before the philosophers were to leave Paris all their servants walked out of the house in a body. Emilie was a bad housekeeper, and an unpopular employer. A maid, who had been with her four years, said that she was sick to death of science, verses and all the rest of it.

Emilie's men-servants were underpaid and had too much time on their hands. She hardly ever entertained; when she did there was only enough food for the guests and no pickings for the servants' hall. She never laid down a cellar but sent round to the wine merchant for a few cheap bottles as she wanted them. She herself only ate once a day, at supper, and was very seldom at home for this. The servants lived on board wages. When they heard that they were going to Fontainebleau they demanded a rise because the cost of living there was much higher than at Paris. Mme du Châtelet refused, so they left. She had forty-eight hours in which to replace them, and she managed to do so, but only by taking what she could get.

Voltaire, too, was in a predicament. He had a secretary who was always fully employed, not to say overworked, since he had to make copies of Voltaire's manuscripts for the friends to read and comment upon. Certain letters, too, were copied over and over again; indeed the mind boggles at the idea of such endless movement of quill on paper. This secretary was suddenly taken ill and had to leave Voltaire. Unable to lay his hands on another to go to Fontainebleau with him, he remembered a young footman once in Emilie's service who used to do a little copying in his spare time. Unfortunately he had also stolen and sold various manuscripts. Voltaire, who was never very exacting about the honesty of his associates, took him on again. The young man's name was Longchamp and we owe a great deal of information about the lives and loves of the two philosophers to his spicy memoirs.

With this household, scratched together, Voltaire and Mme du Châtelet settled as usual into Richelieu's hotel at Fontainebleau. The Duke was not there. Voltaire worked, he was polishing up *Sémiramis*, and Emilie gambled. She was out of luck. She lost all the money she

and Voltaire had brought with them. Then she began
borrowing to right and to left. Finally one evening at the
Queen's table she lost the enormous sum of 84,000 livres.
Voltaire was standing behind her stool. He hated and
despised gambling as much as Emilie loved it. He thought
it waste of time—to him the most precious thing in the
world—and of money, which, since it represented freedom, was precious too in his eyes. It tortured him to
stand there and see time and money being poured away.
At last he could bear it no more, he burst out, in English,
to Emilie that she was playing with cheats. Only the
highest in the land were allowed at the Queen's table:
it was madness for a bourgeois like Voltaire to utter the
word cheat in their presence. Emilie was certain that he
had been overheard. She got up and left the table and
insisted on leaving Fontainebleau there and then, though
it was past midnight.

None of the servants slept in the house except Longchamp and Emilie's maid. They were roused from their
beds and Longchamp had to run all over the town after
the coachman and stable boys. At last the horses were
harnessed, a couple of bags were packed and they started
off. Voltaire was a most unlucky traveller; his journeys
are one long chronicle of disasters, though strange to say
he hardly ever fell ill on the road. This time they had
only gone a few miles when a breakdown occurred.
They had difficulty in finding people to repair the carriage, and then neither Voltaire nor Emilie had money
to pay them. Luckily an early morning traveller coming
from Paris turned out to be an acquaintance. They
borrowed from him and resumed their journey. But
Voltaire, who was by now appalled at the thought of his
gaffe, decided that he had better not show his face in the
capital. Mme du Châtelet left him in a small village off
the highroad and from there he sent a note to the
Duchesse du Maine, at Sceaux, telling her what had

happened and asking if she would shelter him for a while.

The Duchesse du Maine, the widow of Louis XIV's eldest legitimized bastard, was now seventy. She was a tiny creature like a fairy who had lived in a perpetual masquerade. Everything about her had always seemed unreal—the intellectual and philosophical tastes that she paraded, her political intrigues, even her love-affairs. She could not have been more royal, having been born Condé, yet she gave the impression of a pantomime princess ruling over a tinsel court at her palace of Sceaux. She liked to think that it was a more intellectual Versailles and that she bestowed aid and comfort on writers who were persecuted by her cousin the King. Unfortunately her aid and comfort were too whimsical to be worth very much. However Voltaire, who had known her all his life, guessed that his predicament would appeal to her and that she would take him in, as indeed she did. She loved conspiracy, had an age-old grudge against the Court and relished the society of amusing men. Now, for several weeks, she had the most amusing man in France entirely to herself. By day he was concealed in a room, with its own staircase, in a deserted part of the château; as soon as everybody had retired for the night, Voltaire crept downstairs, a table was laid by the little old Duchess's bed and the two of them made merry until dawn. When she was in a good mood she could be excellent company and had a hundred fascinating stories of her father-in-law's reign. Voltaire spent the days in his hiding-place writing *Zadig*, *Babouc* and other tales for the amusement of his hostess, to whom he read them aloud after supper. These are the *Contes Philosophiques* in which the antics of be-turbaned Eastern potentates, their slaves, their viziers and their odalisques reflect the state of society in eighteenth-century France. They are exceedingly funny, and it may be assumed that they kept the Duchess and her poet in fits of laughter.

The only other people who knew where Voltaire was hiding were Mme du Châtelet, d'Argental and, no doubt, Mme Denis, everybody else thought he had gone abroad. Emilie was not having nearly such a delightful time as Voltaire. She was sadly engaged in raising enough money to pay her gambling debts. Some of her creditors, knowing that she was far from rich, accepted a substantial reduction for cash down. Only when the last penny had been paid did Voltaire feel he could creep back to Paris and his normal life. This episode was really the end of his career as a courtier: never again was he kindly received by Louis XV. In any case his downfall could not have been deferred for much longer as he seemed unable to do right at Versailles. Among his many mistakes was to underestimate the Queen's influence. He paid his court to Mme de Pompadour, spoke to her and wrote about her, exactly as if she had been married to the King. But Louis XV, who respected his wife and tenderly loved their children, disliked allusions, even when presented in classical guise, to the fact that he had a mistress. Voltaire never understood this. There was as yet no open break, he continued to go to Court, but he felt that his short period of favour was at an end. His letters from Versailles lack their usual gusto: 'Kings are nothing to me,' he said, most untruthfully. His other King, Frederick, still invited Voltaire to go and live with him, but for the time being did not press the matter very hard.

Unwelcome at Versailles and bored with Paris, Voltaire and Mme du Châtelet began to spend much of their time with the Duchesse du Maine. 'A whole month away from you!' Voltaire wrote to Mme Denis when about to leave for Anet, the Duchess's country house in Normandy. Nevertheless he tore himself from his 'muse' and followed Emilie, as in the last resort he always did. Mme de Staal de Launay, who had been the Duchesse du Mainc's lady-in-waiting for years, wrote an account of this visit to Mme du Deffand. Knowing that her correspondent was not fond of Emilie, Mme de Staal did not mince her words.

'Anet, August 1747.

'Mme du Châtelet and Voltaire were expected today, but turned up yesterday at midnight with the spectral appearance of two embalmed corpses, smelling of the grave. We were just leaving the table; however, the ghosts, it seemed, were starving. They required not only supper but also beds which had not been prepared. The concierge, who was already in hers, was got out of it again in a hurry. Gaya* had always said that his room could be used in an emergency; he was taken at his word and obliged to give it up. He cleared out as hastily and unwillingly as an army surprised in its encampment leaving part of its baggage to the enemy. Voltaire was delighted with the room but that was no consolation to Gaya. As for the lady, she did not like the way her bed was made and she had to be moved today. Please note that she had made this bed herself having brought no servants. She found something wrong with the mattress and this, I think, tormented her orderly mind rather than her body, which is not exactly delicate. She has got a temporary room and is to have that of the Maréchal de Maillebois when he leaves in a day or two. He came when we did with his daughter and daughter-in-law, the former pretty, the other ugly and sad. Our new guests will be better value, they are already rehearsing a comedy. Voltaire has taken the part of Boursoufle, not very brilliant casting nor is that of Mme du Châtelet as Mlle de la Cochonière who is meant to be short and stout.'

* The Chevalier de Gaya, a hanger-on of the Duchess's court.

*Next day.*

'Our ghosts don't show themselves by daylight, yesterday not before ten in the evening and I doubt if we shall see them any earlier today. One is writing about feats of arms and the other commenting on Newton. They join neither in our games nor in our walks, really they are no addition to a society that is not interested in their learned writings. And worst of all, during this evening's apparition we discovered that Mme du Châtelet has her own ideas about the rules of *cavagnole*.'*

*Four days later.*

'The ebb and flow of fellow guests has removed the families Maillebois and Villeneuve and brought us Mme du Four who has come on purpose to play Mme Barbe, the governess of Mlle de la Cochonière and, I think, to be the slave of M. de la Cochonière.

'Since yesterday Mme du Châtelet is at her fourth lodging. In the end she could not bear the one she had chosen because it is noisy and there is smoke without fire (which might well be her own emblem). She tells me she does not mind noise at night but that when she is working it destroys her train of thought. She is engaged upon a review of her principles, an exercise which she performs once a year; otherwise they might escape and go so far that she would never be able to lay her hands on them again. As I think her head is their prison rather than their birthplace it must be very important to guard them carefully. She prefers this occupation to any form of amusement and only leaves it at night. Voltaire has written some gallant verses which have slightly set off the bad impression they have both made. Now pray don't leave my letters lying about on your chimney-piece.'

* A gambling game.

Finally, the two ghosts had to be off in a hurry. M.
de Richelieu was leaving for Genoa and naturally, says
Mme de Staal, could not do so without consulting them.
*Boursoufle* was given a day sooner than had been arranged.
Mme de Staal admitted that Mme du Châtelet was perfection in her part although, out of vanity, she was too
well dressed for it. Voltaire had argued with her about
this, but she was the sovereign and he the slave. After
their departure Mme du Châtelet was found to have collected tables out of all the neighbouring bedrooms. She
had seven in her room, to hold her papers, gew-gaws and
jewels. Mme de Staal had to confess that when the ghosts
had gone she missed them very much.

As soon as the Duchesse du Maine arrived back at
Sceaux for the winter the ghosts turned up again and
set on foot a season of theatrical performances. Mme du
Châtelet, who had a talent for acting and a very pretty
singing voice, always took the part of the leading lady,
dressed up to kill and covered with diamonds. As usual
Voltaire went too far and it all ended in tears. Determined to have a good audience he sent out circulars to
his friends and acquaintances in Paris: 'A new company
of actors will present a new comedy Friday 15 Dec
(1747) at the theatre of Sceaux. All are welcome, without ceremony, at 6 o'clock precisely. Carriages must be
in the courtyard between 7.30 and 8. The doors will be
shut to the public after 6.00.'

So, one evening, the Duchess found five hundred total
strangers thronging into her house, where Voltaire was
receiving them exactly as if it were his. To make matters
worse she discovered that he had told them they need
not bother about her. After this it is hardly surprising
that the Château de Sceaux closed its doors to Voltaire
for a time.

The love affair was in the doldrums. It had imperceptibly turned into a marriage: Emilie found that she had two husbands on her hands while Voltaire was prevented by a middle-aged wife from establishing himself with his new mistress. Chains had been forged (as Mme Denis had truly observed in her honeymoon letter to Thieriot) which could not be broken. She very much wanted, now, to break them and Voltaire was obliged to explain to her why this was impossible. He owed it to his public, he said, not to make a scandal which would cover him with ridicule and contempt. He thought it right to follow a straight line and to respect what he called, with his usual inaccuracy, a *liaison* of twenty years (really about fifteen). If a man wants to leave a woman, however, he can always find ways and means of doing so. In truth, Voltaire was still very much attached to his Emilie, and when it came to possessing him, she won, as she always had.

Emilie, too, spoke of chains. In the *Réflections sur le Bonheur* she described the course of events since the beginning of her life with Voltaire. Mme du Châtelet has received from God one of those tender, constant souls which can neither disguise nor moderate their passions. There can be no question, for her, of love growing weaker, it will resist everything, even the knowledge that it is not returned. For ten years she was perfectly happy, loving and beloved. She and Voltaire spent these years together without one moment of satiety. When age, illness and perhaps also habit made him less ardent she did not notice it for a long time. She loved enough for both of them, he was always there, she had no suspicions and she was happy. Alas, this ideal state of things had not gone on for ever and she has shed many a tear.

Such chains, she continued, cannot be broken without a terrible upheaval. Her heart was wounded and it bled. She had just grievances but had forgiven everything. She was objective enough to realize that her heart was perhaps the only one in the world to be endowed with such constancy, while as for Voltaire, had his desires not been blunted by age and illness, they might yet have been for her. Even if his heart were now incapable of love, his tender friendship and his whole life were still dedicated to her. She knew that a return of the old passion was a thing that never happened in nature, she resigned herself to this fact and was fairly happy with what did remain, supplemented by her own love of study and work. The question now was whether such a sensitive heart as her own could go on being satisfied with the dull and peaceful sentiment of friendship. Was it right, even, to hope that it would be preserved for ever in a sort of vacuum?

It seems from this statement that Emilie's body and soul were by no means ticking together in harmony like Leibnitz's two clocks, but were in a sad state of confusion. Had she quite forgotten Maupertuis and all her other lovers? What was their relationship to that heart, unique in its constancy?

Longchamp records that during the winter of 1747–8 Emilie and Voltaire were quarrelling a great deal. The scientist Clairaut came every day to the rue Traversière to verify the findings in her translation of Newton; he and she would shut themselves up together in a room at the top of the house, only appearing for supper and then often very late. One day Voltaire, who was punctual by nature, sent up to say that supper was ready. Emilie told the servant to put the dishes on the table, as she was coming at once. This was duly done, time passed and the food began to get cold. Suddenly Voltaire lost his temper. He rushed upstairs, found Emilie's study door locked, kicked it in, and possibly saw that something other than mathematics was going on. He began to scream, saying that they were conspiring to kill him. Presently the three of them came down in silence and nobody spoke a word during the meal. When Clairaut had gone, Emilie talked Voltaire back into a good temper. After that she made an effort to be more punctual.

On another occasion the philosophers were having a heated argument while drinking coffee together. Voltaire leapt up from his chair, to illustrate some point, and in doing so he knocked Emilie's cup from her hand and smashed it to atoms. It was a beautiful piece of Dresden china, which he himself had given her, lined with gold and ornamented with figures in a landscape. Emilie, deeply upset, went to her own room. Voltaire gave the broken bits to Longchamp and told him to go and match the cup at M. la Frenay's china shop on the Ile de la Cité. Longchamp found nothing as fine, but he brought back half a dozen cups for Voltaire to choose from. The one he picked out cost ten louis. He tried to bargain, M. la Frenay held his ground and Voltaire had to pay in full. However, Emilie liked the cup, received it with smiles and all was well again.

In the New Year of 1748 they went to Cirey. All Paris was saying that Voltaire had been exiled, but there is no proof of this, and the reasons given for it varied wildly. Some said that the Queen and her children had insisted on it after the publication of a poem in which Voltaire exhorted both the King and Mme de Pompadour to keep their conquests. Others that he had spoken disrespectfully of the Queen's favourite gambling game, *cavagnole*, and called it tedious. He was not the only person who thought so; *cavagnole* was out of fashion and the courtiers grumbled and groaned when they were made to play it. 'Of course, naturally,' said Voltaire, 'if I had really said such a dreadful thing and been guilty of lèse-cavagnole, I would deserve any fate.' He denied that he was exiled, and probably was not, in the strictest sense of the word, but the feeling at Versailles had certainly become hostile to him. He said that he was leaving Paris because he was a mere planet in the solar system of Emilie, obliged to turn in her orbit.

He wrote to Cideville: 'My life is not as I should wish it to be; we are, in this world, like marionettes,' and to Mme Denis, 'I feel stupid and sad not to be able to live with you in a peaceful anonymity. Oh how dreary it is not to live with you in the same house!' Mme Denis was threatening to marry a military man she had known at Lille. Voltaire said she must please herself. If she married, his greatest hope was that the wedding service would be soon followed by a funeral (that of the husband). But he would not try to influence her one way or the other. Meanwhile, when she wrote to Cirey, '*bisogna scrivere discretamente perche le lettere sono tal volte aperte*'. '*La dame* is watching me as I write.'

The philosophers left Paris in bitterly cold weather, starting after supper. Emilie always travelled at night, to save time. She said that she could sleep but could not work on the road. She, Voltaire and her maid were wedged in their places by a variety of parcels and things thrown in at the last minute. There was not room in the coach for another pin. They were to make their first stop at the country house of M. de Chauvelin, one of the King's ministers, near Nangis (Seine-et-Marne). As their host was not there they sent Longchamp, on horseback, to acquaint the servants with their arrival and light fires in their rooms. At Nangis he found the inn shut up and everybody gone to a dance the other side of the town. An obliging neighbour went off to fetch the stable-boys, Longchamp ordered a change of horses to be made ready for Voltaire, and then asked the way to M. de Chauvelin's. They said it was a complicated road but they had a little white horse who knew it, they would lend him to Longchamp. After a certain turning, which they described, off the main road, he need only give the white horse his head. He did as he was told, and sure enough the faithful creature carried him to the house, which of course lay in total darkness. He knocked up the servants and told them to make the necessary preparations. They hurried to the poultry yard, killed a few pigeons and a chicken, and soon had them roasting on a spit. Then hours and hours went by with no sign of the travellers.

Meanwhile the two philosophers had been trotting along the high road from Paris to Nangis when they were violently woken from their first sleep. The back axle snapped in two and the coach fell on its side with a tremendous crash. Voltaire, buried beneath the two women and all the parcels, thought he was in danger of being smothered to death. The air was filled with his screams. He had to stay where he was a good long time however. One of the footmen was hurt in the accident, and the others had difficulty in extracting the passengers through the up-turned door of the coach. Finally they had to be pulled out by their legs, Voltaire last and screaming all the time. The four men they had with them, one of whom was out of action, were not able to right the coach and they had to send for help to the nearest village, several miles away. Cushions were laid on the snowy banks of the road and Voltaire and Mme du Châtelet sat on them, shivering with cold in spite of their furs. It was a night of brilliant stars. The country was flat, there were no trees or houses, and the firmament could be observed from one horizon to the other. Both very fond of astronomy, they had never before seen the map of the heavens so clearly displayed. They soon forgot the cold and all their troubles as they gazed around them, speculating on the nature, the course and the destination of thousands upon thousands of enormous globes hanging in space. They only needed a telescope to be perfectly happy. Too soon they were interrupted by the arrival of a band of peasants, complete with ropes and tools. The coach was righted, and the men patched up the axle as best they could, to be rewarded with twelve livres, which was far too little. They grumbled and argued furiously while the travellers and the luggage were being packed into their places again, but to no avail. However they had the last laugh. The coach advanced fifty yards and again collapsed on to the road, the right way up this time. Of course the discontented peasants now refused to help; they had to be bribed with enormous sums paid in advance, before they would set to work again. Finally, in broad daylight, the coach was put into running order and the journey resumed. Just as Longchamp was setting out to see what could have happened to them, the philosophers arrived at M. de Chauvelin's, fell voraciously on the pigeons and the chicken, went to bed and slept for hours.

They had left Paris at short notice, and were not expected at Cirey. Mme de Champbonin was not there to welcome them, or any other neighbours. This was soon rectified. *L'aimable champenoise* arrived with a niece, the whole neighbourhood flocked to them and rehearsals of a comedy were put in hand at once. A few days later, in the middle of a cheerful bustle, a coach drove into the courtyard. It was a very grand affair, displaying the arms of Stanislas, ex-King of Poland; from it emerged a black-habited man of God, a Jesuit priest, Père Menou. An unfamiliar face is always enlivening to a small society; the busy household welcomed him. If he could not act, he could occupy a seat and applaud, which really suited them better. He did so, and was such an appreciative audience that Voltaire pronounced him to be the most enlightened Jesuit he had ever met. How could anybody have foreseen that, more like the wizard in a fairy tale than a priest, he was going to cast a spell that would transform smiling Cirey into a place of mourning?

# Chapter Nineteen

## An Invitation

PÈRE MENOU was King Stanislas's chaplain and he brought an invitation from his master to the philosophers. Would they go back with him to Lunéville? He must have been the first and last Jesuit who ever wanted to import Voltaire into his own sphere of influence; he was driven to this rash act by the following circumstances.

King Stanislas, having been twice chased off the throne of Poland, was comfortably ending his days as the ruler of Lorraine. His Court was a toy model of Versailles. The royal palace was not in the capital, Nancy, but at Lunéville, a small garrison town some miles away. Like his son-in-law, Louis XV, Stanislas had country houses within an easy day's drive of his palace, where he could go with a few friends when he wanted to get away from the crowd of courtiers. He, too, was fond of building; Nancy, rebuilt by him, became one of the most beautiful small towns in Europe. The Place Stanislas there inspired the King of France to make the Place Louis XV (Concorde). Stanislas, like Louis, had a neglected Queen, and was governed by a beautiful Marquise. His cousin, the Duke Ossolinski, had the title, at Lunéville, of M. le Duc like the King of France's cousin, the Duc de Bourbon, at Versailles. At the beginning of his reign Stanislas had filled his Court and its offices with Polish refugees. In due course, however, his ancient mistress 'Mme la Duchesse' (Ossolinska) was replaced by the young Lorrainer Marquise de Boufflers, after which the atmosphere at Lunéville turned very French.

Stanislas was a merry old soul and the Lorrainers loved him, although they had been passionately attached to their own ruling family and were distressed by the fact that, on his death, their ancient duchy was to become a province of France. No two people could have been found to bridge the awkward period of transition so well as he and his 'Chancellor' the Marquis de La Galaizière, who was really the French intendant. In perfect harmony they ruled Lorraine together: the King was the figure-head, the Marquis did the work—and so it was in all things, including their liaison with Mme de Boufflers.

This laughing beauty, whose lovers dreaded her jokes even more than her infidelities, had been born and bred for the post of King's mistress. She was one of the eighteen children of the Princesse de Beauvau who had held it during the reign of Duke Leopold. Stanislas worshipped her, but he realized that, in his sixties, he could hardly expect to fulfil all the requirements of a lovely woman thirty years younger. So, at a certain moment, he would leave her room saying, 'My Chancellor must tell you the rest'. (This was the favourite story of Louis XV.) La Galaizière, too, loved her passionately. She was perfectly bewitching, and no unkind word has ever been said about her, either during her lifetime or since her death. Like the Marquise at Versailles, of whom she was very fond (and whose greatest friend was her sister the Mar-quise de Mirepoix), Mme de Boufflers had been well educated. She wrote light verse of merit and charm, and was an accomplished pastellist. She possessed every virtue except chastity; while there was a special place in her heart for the King, while the love of her life was La Galaizière, she had a regiment of other lovers. In 1748 she was at the beginning of a new affair. A year or two before, Pan-pan had been the favoured one, Mme de

Grafigny's Panpichon. But though both he and Mme de Boufflers cherished the memory of their love into extreme old age, Panpichon had one signal disadvantage as a lover: when his mistress was in his arms, desire for her would fade, only to be reborn in all its force when she was no longer there. In these circumstances it was no surprise to anybody that, while she kept a tender regard for Pan-pan, she should turn to his friend, Saint-Lambert.

The Marquis de Saint-Lambert has not been well treated by historians. The admirers both of Voltaire and of Jean-Jacques Rousseau have had reason to be unkind about him; his poetry has long been out of fashion; his title even has been disputed. But his contemporaries saw him as a fascinator. At Lunéville he was distinguished from the other courtiers by his manner, different indeed from theirs. King Stanislas, who loved pleasure and ease, had abolished all ceremony at his Court and its atmosphere was that of a large, rather silly, country-house party. The courtiers twittered and shrieked and romped from morning to night; practical jokes were encouraged. The horrid dwarf, Bébé, was the centre of everything, hiding in the women's skirts, losing himself in a cornfield, always bad-tempered, smasher of china, cruel to animals, but adored by Stanislas. He lived in a house three feet high and was dressed in the uniform of a hussar. 'Just imagine,' wrote President Hénault, 'his idiot of a mother spends her time praying that he will grow!'

In this exuberant society Saint-Lambert stood conspicuously aloof. He observed the antics around him with a sardonic eye, he never used exaggerated phrases, never flattered anybody, seldom laughed. There was something Byronic about him, and like Lord Byron he was a poet, though not so talented. He wrote about nature and the countryside. Mme du Deffand, who hardly ever spoke well of anybody except the members of her own clique, said that he was '*froid, fade et faux*' (cold, insipid and false) and of his poetry '*sans les roseaux, les ruisseaux, les ormeaux et leurs rameaux il aura bien peu de choses à dire*' which might be translated 'he would be lost without pines and vines and twining eglantines'. Diderot remarked that though his body might be in the fields his soul was in the town. All the same, he has his place among minor French poets and he became a member of the Académie-française.

He was capable of love and constancy. His affair with Mme d'Houdetot, after he had seduced her away from Jean-Jacques Rousseau, lasted fifty-two years. When she and M. d'Houdetot, who had lived comfortably together, wanted to celebrate their golden wedding, Saint-Lambert flew into a rage of jealousy and forbade it. In his youth he liked to capture hearts and to break up love affairs. Women generally loved him longer than he loved them, but not Mme de Boufflers, though their liaison, while it lasted, was extremely passionate. Stanislas and his Chancellor put up with an endless succession of infidelities, but she was at pains to keep this one from them —it was so serious.

Mme de Boufflers was the least grasping of women, she accepted fewer presents and favours than almost any other royal mistress on record, but it would have been foolish to throw away her brilliant position simply for lack of a little prudence, and she was not foolish. Besides, she was fond of her old King and loved La Galaizière. On the other hand, she and Saint-Lambert wanted more than an occasional hasty rendezvous; they liked to spend whole nights together, to go to sleep and wake up in each other's arms. This was rather difficult to arrange. Saint-Lambert was a captain in the regiment of Mme de Boufflers's brother Alexandre de Beauvau; he was often on garrison duty in the town of Lunéville but had no function in the royal household and therefore nc apartment in the château. He went there to pay his court, like the other officers. Mme de Boufflers's rooms were on the ground floor, with their own entrance to the street, but comings and goings were observed by the sentry and were never a secret for very long. However, she discovered a tiny empty room between her own apartment and the chapel. She managed somehow to get a bed put into it without the whole world knowing and here she and her lover spent delicious nights. Luckily, King Stanislas dropped with sleepiness by nine and was never in bed later than ten, a habit which had long been encouraged by his mistress.

When the Court moved to Commercy, one of the King's country houses, it became more difficult for the lovers to be together. Stanislas invited his special friends there but he had an unreasonable aversion to Saint-Lambert and never asked him. Every evening a supper-party was held in Mme de Boufflers's room; Saint-Lambert was not of it. Commercy had no forgotten corners, nowhere to hide a mouse. How could they manage? Of course they did: Mme de Boufflers always got what she wanted. There was an orangery which communicated with her rooms and at its other end with the house of the village priest. M. le Curé, like everybody else, was under her charm. She arranged with him that Saint-Lambert should wait in his parlour until the King had gone to bed. When the coast was clear, Mme de Boufflers blew out a lighted candle in her window as a signal that Saint-Lambert could now go to her through the orangery.

Alas! Mme de Boufflers was incapable of constancy. In 1747 Saint-Lambert went to the wars; when he returned he had been supplanted by a shadowy Vicomte d'Adhémar. Mme de Boufflers was finding it easier to conduct this liaison because King Stanislas rather liked d'Adhémar. Saint-Lambert suffered, and not in silence.

Torrents of rhymed reproaches flowed from his pen, and his demeanour became more melancholy and romantic than ever.

Mme de Boufflers and her King had most friends and all tastes in common with the exception of Père Menou and his spiritual exercises. She believed that Paradise was here on earth, while Stanislas was pious as only a Pole can be. The Father made him tremble with his strictures, delivered from the pulpit and in the confessional, on the sin, the mortal sin, of double adultery. Stanislas would come out of Church resolved to mend his ways. The Father had another hold over him. Like everybody with intellectual pretensions Stanislas felt obliged to compose French verses; Père Menou did for him what Jordan, and sometimes Voltaire, did for Frederick, he revised his work and put it into grammatical French. To please the Father, Stanislas built a Jesuit mission at Nancy, reserving a few exquisite rooms for himself. Here he would go, from time to time, for a retreat, while M. de La Galaizière and other adorers of the Marquise took advantage of his absence. The Father would then bring him into such a penitent frame of mind that Mme de Boufflers's dismissal seemed certain. But the moment Stanislas saw her again, his resolution melted away and he became more amorous than ever. The Marquise was a jewel, not to be discarded lightly; she was beautiful, clever and an excellent hostess, she set a brilliant tone at Lunéville and besides all that, he loved her. In her company his fear of hell-fire seemed ridiculous, and the delights of this earth paramount. As soon as she saw that he was at her feet again, the Marquise would begin coaxing and wheedling him to send away the confessor. Well, and why not? So priest and mistress used all their respective weapons to get rid of each other, and the poor old King was tormented between the two of them. At last he had an inspiration: he would keep them both.

Mme de Boufflers, easy going, all for a quiet life, asked
nothing better but the Father never gave up his design
of dislodging her. It was gradually borne in upon him
that things of the spirit alone were not likely to do so,
and that his best chance would be another woman. So he
began to look about for a suitable rival, not so easy to
find, however. She must be cheerful and amusing, beautiful and not too young, a noble Lorrainer by birth or
marriage so that she would be acceptable to the aristocrats who formed the little Court.

Did it come to him in a flash one wakeful night? Of
course, Mme du Châtelet. Why had he not thought of
her long ago? Where was she now? At Cirey! Too good
to be true. He suggested to King Stanislas that a visit
from Voltaire and his celebrated friend might be very
interesting. Stanislas was delighted at the idea and so
was the Marquise. She had known Emilie all her life,
and foresaw that she would liven up their little society.
As for Voltaire, he would be an ornament to any Court.
So Père Menou was hurried off to Cirey, with a royal
command. Voltaire and Mme du Châtelet, no longer
comfortable in their *tête-à-tête*, asked nothing better than
a visit to Lunéville. It suited Voltaire very well to go and
stay with the Queen's father, a move which would scotch
the rumours that he had been exiled by the Queen's
party at Versailles. So they abandoned the neighbours,
cancelled the theatrical programme, borrowed M. du
Châtelet's horses, which he had sent back from the front
to have a rest, and in less time than it takes to tell they
were on the road again to Lunéville.

# Chapter Twenty

## Lunéville

THEY WERE royally received. The Queen of Poland had died in 1746 and Mme du Châtelet was given her apartment on the ground floor, Voltaire was on the second floor, over the King, and his rooms communicated with Emilie's by a secret staircase. Père Menou soon saw that he had made a mistake in bringing them to Lunéville. Mesdames du Châtelet and de Boufflers became inseparable, twin sisters, adoring friends. Emilie had not the shadow of a design on Stanislas. What had he to give her? In her eyes it was more glorious to be the mistress of Voltaire than of the greatest King on earth. Her rank and precedence were undisputed; she did not mind her lack of fortune; if she wanted anything it was love. The King of Poland would have been less like a new lover than an old husband and of such she already had two.

The visit began with Voltaire falling seriously ill. Stanislas was all kindness and concern. Voltaire treated himself, as usual, with bed, starvation and tisane, and was on his feet again in a few days. He then threw himself into the production of comedies, wrote verses for all the women of the Court and kept the party in a cheerful stir. He broadcast enthusiastic letters describing the goodness of the King. How sweet is his so-called banishment, Lunéville is an enchanted palace, with a monarch who favours the poor exile in every way. *Mérope* has been given in Voltaire's honour, he forgot himself and wept at his own tragedy. Mme du Châtelet has acted three times already in Houdart de la Mothe's *Issé*. Nevertheless, reading between the lines of his letters, one sees that something was lacking. No doubt he missed Mme Denis, but that was not all. He missed the French Court and Louis XV.

King Stanislas was well-disposed towards the things of the mind. He loved Voltaire, was neither irritated nor embarrassed by him, never snubbed him, laid himself out to please. But, he was the ex-King of Poland, not the ruler of France. The courtiers were delightful, they were not snobs; they did not care (or not much) about precedence and birth; they never thought of sending Voltaire to Coventry. But they were provincials. There was freedom of speech but nobody to exchange it with. In short, Lunéville was not Versailles. Versailles may have had many silly and regrettable features but it was the hub of the universe, the palace of the most powerful King, the seat of the most important government in the world. The power and importance were in a decline but this was not, as yet, apparent. Society there was not confined to a handful of courtiers; nearly everybody of interest and influence came sooner or later. While frivolous young aristocrats were idling away their lives in green alleys and gilded temples, on the other side of the palace Marshals of France were clattering off to the front, Ministers and Ambassadors were arriving for audiences with the King. France was governed from Versailles. Lunéville was all make-believe, the society there was too frothy to be interesting. Mme de Boufflers, as she grew older, became a great reader and said that this was because she had to escape, somehow, from the eternal chattering which went on around her.

Voltaire would have liked to escape, he longed to go back to Paris, but he was kept in Lorraine by Mme du Châtelet. She was in her element at Lunéville. Her undoubted snobbishness was gratified by the honours paid

her there and the high precedence which her husband's
rank obtained for her. She had incessant gambling to
keep her soul in a healthy state. She became the leading
lady of a well-appointed theatre. She could show off her
clothes and jewels to more effect than at Versailles. When
she felt inclined to work she retired, self-importantly, to
her apartment and nobody was allowed to disturb her.
She did not realize that she was regarded as an amiable
joke by the whole company, though Voltaire had a pretty
shrewd idea of it. The anonymous author of a sort of
gossip column circulating at Lunéville said that she was a
'madwoman who knows more about atoms than about
her own family'. Voltaire remarked that this was nonsense. Why, she took any amount of trouble over her
family, she had got excellent commands in the army for
her husband and son and a splendid Italian duke for her
daughter. What more could she do?

Very soon after the arrival of Voltaire and Mme du
Châtelet at Lunéville, Père Menou's magic began to
work. As magic often does, however, it took a slightly
different course from that intended by the magician.
Emilie fell in love, and with a lover of Mme de Boufflers,
but not with King Stanislas. Saint-Lambert, seeing his
mistress in full fling with M. d'Adhémar, had continued
to suffer. When Mme du Châtelet arrived at Lunéville,
handsome, eager to please and high-spirited, he be-
thought him of that powerful love philtre, a dose of
jealousy. He made ostentatious advances to Emilie; it
was no trouble to him to do so, he found her attractive.
Mme de Boufflers, who laughed at everything, laughed,
but Mme du Châtelet did not. In a ferment of desire and
sensibility she fell into Saint-Lambert's arms and announced her intention of spending the rest of her life
with him. With him, Voltaire and M. du Châtelet of
course; Saint-Lambert was to be an addition not a substitute. Mme de Boufflers, still laughing, gave Emilie the

key of the hidden room with a bed in it and Saint-
Lambert was disconcerted to find that his parlour flirtation had become a full-dress love-affair.

Mme du Châtelet, excessive in everything, now behaved with an ardour embarrassing to contemplate.
She was forty-three (ten years older than Saint-Lambert), one of the most learned women ever produced by
our civilization, engaged on a task (the translation of
Newton) for which many scientists would find themselves
inadequate; she had two grown-up children; the greatest
writer of the day was at her beck and call. But her letters
to her new lover read like those of a clever, hysterical
schoolgirl. They begin with little notes on lace-edged
paper which Emilie would slip into Mme de Boufflers's
harp for the loved one to find during the evening party.
As time goes on they get longer, sadder and more senti-
mental, no jokes, no gossip, nothing but self-pity, love
and plans for the future. They are very dull.

Almost at once, Saint-Lambert fell ill in the little
secret room. He had fever and his body was covered with
a rash. Mme du Châtelet, who was quite used to illness,
though she had never known a day of it herself, drowned
him with tea, tisane and Seidlitz water, plied him with
roast chickens and partridges, and made him open his
window from time to time. She crept downstairs when
everybody else had gone to bed in order to watch him as
he slept. He got better, and soon Emilie was rewarded for
her attentions: 'I hope I did not agitate you too much
last night.' Pan-pan acted as go-between and the lovers
spent their time writing and exchanging letters. Saint-
Lambert wrote: 'It is very sweet to wake up and read
your charming letters and to know the happiness of
loving and being loved by you. I feel that I shall never be
able to do without your letters which are the joy of my
life. You have never been more tender, more lovable and
more adored.'

With one of Emilie's nature, so whole-hearted and possessive, no affair could keep a light touch for long, and as soon as Saint-Lambert was better she began to make scenes. He has treated her so coldly today, as if hardly giving her a thought, has never spoken of expedients for seeing more of her, has not even mentioned the subject. Why does he never look at her? Does he only care to be with her in company, does he not long to spend all his time with her? That is the test of love, every minute apart should be an agony. Why does he never go to her room where they can be alone together? The eggs she has cooked for him have grown cold with waiting, but she has not. Now she seems to have spoilt everything and made him cross. He must forgive and forget what she said last night and only remember the happy day they had. She is sorry now, she sees that she has been unfair, she only wishes she had taken more advantage of the time they have spent together to be happy in his love. She is too easily upset and she knows it. As we read these endless scribblings we wonder how the highly-strung Voltaire could ever have put up with her.

Saint-Lambert behaved rather well. Having aroused this unwanted passion, he did nothing unkind to try and check it, he waited for it to die down again. Emilie knew that she was more in love than he, but she was quite used to that. She only asked permission to go on loving and this Saint-Lambert graciously accorded. He even put off a journey to Italy when she implored him to do so.

As for Voltaire, he saw with satisfaction that Emilie was enjoying herself but perhaps did not realize that she was plunged in such a menacing joy. She, of course, with her mixture of logic and selfishness, never thought for a moment that she was behaving badly to him. He no longer made love to her and therefore could not expect her to be faithful. Besides, in spite of the burning, volcanic quality of her love for Saint-Lambert, her soul was not involved. She could never have written to him, as Voltaire wrote to Mme Denis, 'Sensual pleasure passes and vanishes in the twinkling of an eye, but the friendship between us, the mutual confidence, the delights of the heart, the enchantment of the soul, these things do not perish and can never be destroyed. I shall love you until I die.' Emilie's betrayal of Voltaire was spectacular; his of her was fundamental.

In May 1748 the party at Lunéville broke up for a while, for Stanislas to pay one of his periodical visits to his daughter the Queen. The two philosophers were to go to Paris, taking Cirey on the way, for the rehearsals of *Sémiramis*. Saint-Lambert rejoined his regiment at Nancy and Mme du Châtelet managed to spend a few happy days with him there while Mme de Boufflers kept Voltaire amused and unsuspicious at Lunéville. After this Emilie was more in love, and Saint-Lambert less. As soon as she and Voltaire had arrived at Cirey she began to be tormented by the thought of Mme de Boufflers, rather at a loose end at Lunéville (M. de Boufflers and La Galaizière having gone to Versailles with the King) and Saint-Lambert, also with nothing much to do, nearby at Nancy. She knew too well that Mme de Boufflers had but to say the word and Saint-Lambert would be her slave again. She could not settle down to her work, as she had planned, she could only pour out endless letters. 'This is too long,' she sometimes says. (Yes indeed, too long and much too plaintive.) She thinks of Saint-Lambert at Lunéville, hardly giving her a thought. The fact is he has no capacity for love, so what will he do with a heart like hers, now that it belongs to him? He must come to Cirey, otherwise she cannot believe all the things he told her at Nancy. In the end he did go, for twenty-four hours, and killed her suspicions for the time being. At Paris she felt calmer, because Mme de Boufflers had

joined King Stanislas at Trianon. Louis XV always lent
him this little palace for his visits to the Queen. However
they were only there another week, and it seemed rather
a horrid coincidence that, as soon as Mme de Boufflers
arrived back at Lunéville, Saint-Lambert rejoined the
garrison there. His letters became very short and the
writing (Mme du Châtelet noticed) very large, as though
he wanted to fill the pages in a hurry. He did address her
as '*Ma chère Maîtresse*', which was a little comfort.

'*Je vous adore, je vous adore.*' All the same, Emilie's
outpourings to the loved one were not particularly tactful. She is having a watch made for him with a secret
spring to contain her portrait. Should it be exactly like
the one she had given to Voltaire or would he prefer
something different? She sees from his reply that he
really has no feelings, Voltaire's watch will do, but that
he wants her, in the miniature, to wear the head-dress of
Issé. Very well, so it shall be. She hopes he will not be
angry, she is sending him an enormous bottle of nut-oil,
excellent for thinning hair. He must anoint his head like
a Pharisee. Abbé de Bernis is writing a poem on the
Seasons, how dreadful, the very subject Saint-Lambert
himself has chosen. Babet la Bouquetière must have heard
of it from somebody at Lunéville. Now Mme du Châtelet
has sent for Babet, who has read her the poem; it is very
dull and very much like Saint-Lambert's. No need to
answer so disagreeably and tell her to mind her own
business; surely it must be perfectly obvious that she
thought to do for the best; nobody would listen to a long
poem by Bernis for the fun of the thing. Now in her turn
she has to scold Saint-Lambert. It seems he has been
making trouble between her and Mme de Boufflers, and
this does not suit Mme du Châtelet at all. For one thing
Mme de Boufflers is a much better friend than he is a
lover—however, that is not the point. It is most important for M. du Châtelet to be given an official posi-

tion at Lunéville and his wife is counting on Mme de
Boufflers to arrange this. If he were passed over again,
as he has already been once, by King Stanislas, he and
Mme du Châtelet could not possibly stay on at Lunéville. They would have to leave Lorraine for ever, and go
and live at Cirey. As Saint-Lambert's love is not of the
quality to survive short meetings and long absences he
must see the absolutely vital necessity of M. du Châtelet's
appointment. She really must beg him to be careful to
keep Mme de Boufflers on their side.

The rehearsals of *Sémiramis*, with the actors still reading their parts, went very well. Voltaire was longing to
stay in Paris in order to produce the play himself, and
for other reasons, but of course Emilie's one idea was to
get back to her lover. As usual she had her own way.
Voltaire was borne off—like a parcel (*empaqueté*), he
said—ill, possibly dying, to Lorraine, where the Court
was at Commercy.

At Châlons-sur-Marne they had a disagreeable experience. Mme du Châtelet always took her own food
on journeys, she said to save time, but really to save
money. When they arrived at Châlons, however, she
felt she would like a cup of soup, so they stopped at the
inn. The innkeeper's wife, seeing the beautiful coach,
and hearing that it belonged to the Marquise du Châtelet,
brought the soup out herself in a china cup with a silver
lid. When Emilie had finished, Longchamp was told to
carry back the cup and settle the bill. To his horror the
woman demanded a louis. Longchamp thought he should
tell Emilie and when he did she flatly refused to pay.
Voltaire then took on the hostess, saying that such an
extortion would get her inn a bad name. She replied that
she had one tariff, whether for a whole dinner or a single
dish. The argument waxed very hot and a crowd collected. It was entirely on the hostess's side and began to
jeer and boo at the travellers. In the end, most un-

willingly, they had to pay the louis in order to get away, which they did to a crescendo of insults.

They arrived at Commercy on 27 June and here a cruel disappointment awaited Emilie. After nearly two months parted from her beloved she naturally thought of nothing but their passionate reunion. There was no sign of him, nor had he left a note or a message of any kind to reassure her. She was greeted with affection by everybody else, but from Saint-Lambert there was a dreary, disquieting silence. Instead of spending the night, as she had expected, in his arms, she spent it composing a letter of furious reproach. If he could not have contrived to see her at least he might have written. Variations on this theme covered several pages. However, the next day he appeared. As usual he was not of the house-party at Commercy, but was staying with M. le Curé; he could only join the others when Stanislas had gone to bed. Then he came, as of old, through the orangery and could easily make his way to Emilie's flat on the ground floor.

Life at the little Court was as cheerful and inane as usual. Voltaire's time was eaten up with the daily round of a country-house visit and with theatrical productions. Emilie counted on him to keep the King in a good mood until M. du Châtelet's appointment was settled. She was now soliciting the Comte d'Argenson, War Minister at Versailles, to promote her husband to Lieutenant-General, which would make it easier for Stanislas to do as she wished.

Voltaire still either was, or pretended to be, ignorant of the state of Emilie's heart and doubtless would have preferred to remain so. However, one evening at Commercy, he went to have a word with her before supper. There was no footman in her anteroom and he went straight into her boudoir, as he always did, without waiting to be announced. He found Emilie and Saint-

Lambert at a moment when it is preferable not to be interrupted. Voltaire flew into a violent temper and upbraided them in no measured terms. Saint-Lambert, cold and elegant, remarked that if Voltaire were displeased he could leave the room, leave Commercy and meet him anywhere, with any weapons that he chose. Voltaire had no intention of fighting. He stumped off furiously, went back to his own rooms and told Longchamp to buy or hire him a carriage as he was leaving that night for Paris. Having travelled to Lorraine in Mme du Châtelet's coach, he had not one of his own with him. Longchamp thought he had better know what all this was about. He pretended to go to the village but really went straight to Mme du Châtelet who told him exactly what had happened. She said that at all costs Voltaire must be prevented from leaving Commercy. Longchamp must make delays and as soon as Voltaire had simmered down a little she would go and have a word with him. So Longchamp waited till two in the morning and then told Voltaire that he could not beg, borrow or steal a carriage since such a thing did not exist in the whole of Commercy. Voltaire gave him a wallet of money and said that, as soon as it was daylight, he must go to Nancy and buy a vehicle of some sort. Longchamp went back to Mme du Châtelet, who was still at her writing-table. She asked what Voltaire was doing and when Longchamp told her that he had gone to bed but certainly not to sleep, she decided to go up and see him. Longchamp went back to his own room in Voltaire's flat and undressed. Presently there was a knocking at the door; he got up in his night-shirt to open it, and announced Mme du Châtelet. Voltaire saw that the man had been got out of his bed so he had no suspicion of a plot. Longchamp went back to his room which was next to Voltaire's and listened through the wall like anything.

The conversation began in English, with Mme du Châtelet repeating a pet name she had for Voltaire in that language. Presently they relapsed into French. 'So,' cried Voltaire, 'you expect me to believe all this after seeing what I saw with my two eyes. I have sacrificed my whole life to you—health, fortune, all laid at your feet and this is my reward! Betrayal!' 'No,' she answered, 'I still love you. But you must admit it's a long time now since you have been able to—I have no wish to kill you, nobody is more concerned with your health than I. On the other hand, I have my own to consider. As you can do nothing for it any longer it is not very reasonable of you to be so angry when I find one of your friends who can.'

Voltaire could not help laughing. 'Ah! Madame!' he said, 'of course you are in the right as usual. But you really should manage so that these things do not take place before my very eyes.' After this he calmed down. Mme du Châtelet kissed him and went back to her own room. The next day she had to deal with Saint-Lambert who still considered that he had been insulted and was determined to fight. Mme du Châtelet pointed out that Voltaire was too old and too famous for such an adventure, and after a long argument she talked Saint-Lambert into apologizing to the venerable bard. Of course Voltaire was mollified at once. 'No no, my child, I was in the wrong. You are still at the happy age when one can love and be loved. Make the most of it. An old, ill man like myself can no longer hope for these pleasures.' They made it up, and thereafter were very friendly.

Voltaire wrote to the Comte d'Argenson: 'I am here in a beautiful palace, a free man though my host is a king, with all my historical books and my references and with Mme du Châtelet; even so I am one of the most unhappy thinking creatures upon earth.'

And to Mme Denis: 'I spend my life in cogitating how I can spend the rest of my life with you.'

# Chapter Twenty-One

## Sémiramis

THERE is nothing so much calculated to soothe the heart and mend the troubles of a writer as the launching of a new work. Fortunately for Voltaire the rehearsals of *Sémiramis* were now well advanced and the play was to open in August. He had decided not to go to Paris for it, but Stanislas, who was off there himself, to see his daughter before the Court migrated to Fontainebleau, insisted on taking him. The King missed very little of the goings-on around him and no doubt he thought a change of scene would be good for Voltaire. So it was arranged that they should go together, leaving their mistresses behind. Mme de Boufflers announced that her doctor had ordered her to take the cure at Plombières, a watering-place in the Vosges mountains; Stanislas begged Mme du Châtelet, as a favour to himself, to go with her. It was the last thing Emilie wanted; she was, of course, dying to remain in an empty Lunéville with Saint-Lambert. But she could not very well say 'no' to the King.

Plombières had an enormous reputation from a medical point of view but nobody liked going there. A grim and gloomy place, always overcrowded with dyspeptic invalids, it was fearfully uncomfortable. Even the climate was bad. Eighteenth-century correspondence is punctuated with moans and groans from Plombières, or commiseration with friends obliged by their doctors to endure its hardships. Voltaire often told Frederick

243

that he had only established himself at Lunéville because his health demanded constant visits to Plombières. In fact he never went there at this time, though he had done so when he was younger.

Mme de Boufflers, who had never felt better in her life, had planned this excursion as a little honeymoon with d'Adhémar; Stanislas sent him to look after her. Relieved that her liaison with Saint-Lambert was over, he positively encouraged 'the insipid Viscount', as Emilie called him. Saint-Lambert was furious at being left behind and Mme du Châtelet's letters were not calculated to soothe his ruffled feelings. They began with the usual picture of the horrors of Plombières. She is vilely lodged in a house with fifty other people, making it almost impossible to work. Her bed is only separated from that of a dreadful old *fermier-général* by a curtain. But there is one compensation. Mlle de la Roche-sur-Yonne is also taking the waters. Mme du Châtelet has her coffee, her baths and all her meals with this royal princess (a Bourbon-Conti). So, even had Saint-Lambert been there he would have seen nothing of his beloved by day, since she believes that he is not in Mlle de la Roche-sur-Yonne's set? By night, the presence of the *fermier-général* would have been a distinct drawback to their enjoyment—indeed gallantry would be impossible in that over-crowded establishment. Finally, life at Plombières is so expensive that Saint-Lambert could never have afforded it. Without a pause, almost without a full stop, Mme du Châtelet proceeds from these reflections on Saint-Lambert's social position and the state of his purse to the wildest flights of passion: 'I have found that treasure for which, according to the Gospel, we must abandon everything.'

Saint-Lambert, not to be outdone in what he regarded as a literary exercise, replied that she would have to teach him to love her less. But he took his revenge. One

day when the post arrived, Emilie noticed with some
annoyance that he had written to Mme de Boufflers who
read the letter, laughed, and ostentatiously tore it into a
thousand pieces. With the next post he enclosed a note
for Mme de Boufflers in his letter to Emilie. Needless to
say, she steamed it open, and did not care for what she
found. 'I love you madly.' What did it mean? she asked
him in a torrent of reproaches. It meant that Saint-
Lambert still rather preferred Mme de Boufflers to his
other mistress.

The Plombières visit had only been meant to last a
week or so. Unfortunately, Mme de Boufflers was enjoying it as much as Mme du Châtelet was not. Snobbishness did not impel her to spend her time with Mlle de la
Roche-sur-Yonne; she found a delightful circle of friends
with whom to laugh, gossip and play *comète*. She was not
trying to translate Newton in a house where there were
fifty other people, packed like sardines. Stanislas had
arranged for her to have a charming room to herself,
with no *fermier-général* snoring away the other side of a
curtain and to this room the Vicomte d'Adhémar came
and went as he liked. Mme de Boufflers made up a cock-
and-bull story about her health, an aspect of it not
usually mentioned by women to men but discoursed upon
at length in Emilie's letters to Saint-Lambert. The
journey was put off, on account of '*ses prétendues pertes*',
from day to day. This was clearly done to annoy Emilie,
against whom Mme de Boufflers now turned. Emilie,
whose very existence at Lunéville depended on the favour
of Mme de Boufflers, did everything she could think of to
oblige her friend. But the harder she tried to please, the
more she seemed to be on the other woman's nerves. The
reason for this change of heart is not clear. Perhaps Mme
de Boufflers minded more than she seemed to about
Saint-Lambert, or possibly she thought that Emilie had
been paying too much attention to Mlle de la Roche-sur-

Yonne. It was no secret that the Queen of France would have liked her father to marry this elderly, ugly, dull but vastly rich Princess, and that Mlle de la Roche-sur-Yonne was willing. This would not have suited Mme de Boufflers at all. She had enjoyed herself much more since the Queen of Poland's death, and had no wish to share the honours at Lunéville with a new Queen. The danger was not great; Stanislas was happy as he was. He came back to Lunéville with a present for his mistress; he had persuaded Louis XV to appoint her lady-in-waiting to his daughters, Mesdames de France. Mesdames, who liked Boufflers no better than they liked Pompadour, and for the same pious reason, were displeased by this arrangement, the more so that Louis XV did not tell them about it himself. They learnt of it through the gushing letters of thanks which they received from their new lady.

*Sémiramis* was only moderately successful. A bad play, considering it was by Voltaire, was the general view. There was a ghost in it whose appearance never made the right impression and crowd scenes which were almost impossible to manage. Spectators were allowed on the stage at the Comédie-française; it was not until 1759 that this silly habit was forbidden by the police. At *Sémiramis* the stage was thronged with young men, some for and some against Voltaire; they got so much in the way of the actors that the play almost came to a standstill. The ushers had to cry out: 'Gentlemen, gentlemen, please make way for the ghost,' which was thought exceedingly funny by all except Voltaire. His enemies were now led by the veteran poet, Crébillon (not to be confused with 'young Crébillon' his son). He sometimes acted as literary censor for the government and had been one of the people who had caused the withdrawal of *Mahomet*. Ever since then Voltaire had goaded and tormented him and a mutual hatred flourished.

In order to counter-attack what he called '*les soldats de Corbullon*' (Crébillon), Voltaire engaged the services of the Chevalier de La Morlière. This curious person played a powerful role in the theatre-world: he could almost make or mar the success of a play. He was a large, impressive, dignified man with a worldly air and a literary way of talking. There was a certain aura of mystery about him, and he wore a foreign order which nobody had ever been able to place. He practically lived at the Comédie-française, could clap louder than anybody in Paris and was the inventor of the yawn as a way of showing disapproval. The Chevalier directed a *claque* of 150 men, some volunteers and some in his pay. Before the curtain went up on a first night they would assemble at the Café Procope and discuss their plan of action. As well as La Morlière, Voltaire rounded up all his own cronies and told Longchamp to bring anybody capable of effective applause. Voltaire himself knew how to make his presence felt in a theatre and the actors dreaded the nights when he was in front. He was a terrible fidget, jumping up and down throughout the performance. At any adverse demonstration, even little whispers or giggles, he would be on his feet screaming: '*Arrêtez, barbares!*' The first night of *Sémiramis*, which was more like a battlefield than an entertainment, was financially profitable. There was a house of 1,117 and the takings were 4,033 livres. Voltaire, as usual, gave his share to the actors. The play ran for fifteen nights.

The nervous strain of the battle of *Sémiramis* had made Voltaire very ill again. We know from Longchamp that he now quarrelled with Mme Denis. Longchamp had no idea that they were lovers and this shows how careful they were to keep their secret: never in the world has there been such a nosy-parker as he was. He speaks of a coldness between them without throwing any light on its reason. Mme Denis was always very promiscuous; at this time she was having affairs with at least two of her uncle's young literary protégés, Baculard d'Arnaud and Marmontel. Voltaire may have made some disagreeable discovery or possibly she issued an ultimatum to try and get him away from Emilie. Whatever the cause of the quarrel its effect was to make him long for Mme du Châtelet. He ordered his carriage and prepared to go back to Lunéville. His friends all besought him not to travel, ill as he was; but he had made up his mind and he left.

He arrived at Châlons-sur-Marne in an apparently dying condition, having touched no food on the journey. He refused to go to the inn which had charged a louis for a cup of soup, and stopped at the much more primitive Hôtel de la Poste. Longchamp had to carry him up the stairs to bed. The Bishop and the Intendant of Châlons, hearing that he was there, both hurried to him and begged him to stay with them, but he would not move. Having tried in vain to swallow some broth, he told Longchamp, who was by now thoroughly alarmed, not to leave him on any account but to stay and throw a little earth on his body. Death seemed imminent. The Bishop and the Intendant came back with a doctor but Voltaire could not speak to them. He only had the strength to push away the medicines they wished to administer. Longchamp wrote to Mme du Châtelet and to Mme Denis (with whom he was in correspondence) and acquainted them with his master's condition. After six days at Châlons, during which time Voltaire had eaten nothing, he decided that he did not wish to die there. He made Longchamp carry him down to his coach and they resumed the journey. Longchamp had to tie him on to the seat, where he lay like a corpse. At Saint-Dizier, while they were changing horses, he spoke, asking where they were. Just after the stop, they met one of Mme du Châtelet's men on the road; he had come for news of Voltaire. This seemed to cheer him up and when

at last he was comfortably in bed at the good inn at
Nancy, he drank a little soup. Longchamp, who had
never left him for a moment all this time, ordered his
own supper to be sent up to his master's room. When
Voltaire had seen him put down an entrée, half a shoulder of mutton, two roast thrushes and a dozen robins, he
suddenly felt hungry himself. He ate some robins and
drank a little wine in his water. He then went into a
sound sleep, only waking up at three the next afternoon.
They arrived at Lunéville later in the evening and his
cure was completed by the sight of Mme du Châtelet.

Now that all the Lunéville friends were joyfully reunited, Stanislas decreed a little holiday at Commercy.
As usual, Saint-Lambert was not invited. The King had
been so pleased to see Mme du Châtelet again, so particularly kind and welcoming, that she made a bold
decision. She asked for a private audience at which,
greatly to the King's embarrassment, she announced her
love-affair. Explaining that she could not enjoy herself
at Commercy without Saint-Lambert she begged an invitation for him. Stanislas was pleased with neither her
news nor her request. He hummed and hawed very
crossly, but finally said that Saint-Lambert could come.
'But which room will Your Majesty give him?' pursued
the shameless Emilie. This was too much for Stanislas
who said that he could stay with the Curé and use the
orangery as he always did. He then indicated that the
audience was over.

The Commercy visit was rather spoilt for Emilie by
Mme de Boufflers's bad temper and Voltaire's nerves.
Resigned as he was to her liaison with Saint-Lambert he
could not help making jealous scenes from time to time.
Even more tiresome, he was for ever scolding Emilie because she no longer got on with Mme de Boufflers, as
though it were her fault. She thought this was most un-

fair. She was happy, on the whole, with her lover, they went out riding together, and he supped every evening in her room; but the time she spent with the rest of the party was not particularly agreeable. The King, who was truly fond of her (he never wrote to Voltaire without a loving message for '*la chère Mme du Châtelet*') seems to have felt sorry for her, and it was at Commercy that, quite suddenly, he announced the appointment of her husband to the coveted post of Grand Maréchal des Logis de la Cour. Emilie was in the seventh heaven; nothing, now, could prevent her from living in Lorraine for the rest of her days.

If Voltaire was in a crotchety mood it was partly because he was engaged on one of those great fusses about nothing which he half enjoyed but which always affected his nerves. The Comédie-italienne had announced a parody of *Sémiramis*, and once more Voltaire demonstrated the fact that much as he loved teasing he could not bear to be teased. He was, at this very time, writing the tragedy *Catalina* with the avowed intention of baiting Crébillon and of showing up his play on the same subject as old-fashioned and silly. Voltaire sincerely felt that, while he himself was at liberty to stamp on other people's feelings, his own must be spared. He badgered all his friends to prevent the Italians from producing their parody, he even made Stanislas write to the Queen about it. Considering her feelings for Voltaire, she was not likely to do as he wished, and said as much. Not only had she been, for many years, whole-heartedly on the side of Monseigneur de Mirepoix in his disputes with Voltaire, not only did she have to put up with fulsome poems glorifying Mme de Pompadour, but now it seemed to her that the two philosophers were leading her old father down the road to hell. Under their influence, as the Queen supposed, Stanislas had written *Le Philosophe Chrétien*, a book which was clearly the work of an atheist. She saw, too, that Voltaire had allied himself with Mme de Boufflers against those who were trying to bring Stanislas to a decent marriage-bed. She could hardly contain her horror and loathing of him, while the Dauphin openly said that he ought to be tortured to death. So far from being inclined to forbid the parody, they were both keenly looking forward to applauding it. In the end the all-powerful Mme de Pompadour stopped it, though she read Voltaire a lesson about his exaggerated touchiness.

'Voltaire to Sir Everard Fawkener:
'Lunéville, at the Court of Lorraine 5 no^bre (1748).
'Dear Sir
'Yr letter has afforded me the most sensible satisfaction. For when my friendship to you began, t'was a bargain for life. Time that alters all things, and chiefly my poor tattered body, has not altered my sentiments. You acquaint me you are a husband and father and I hope you are an happy one. It behoves a secretary to a great general to marry a great officer's daughter, and really I am transported with joy to see the blood of Marlborough mixed with that of my dearest Fawkenear. I do present your lady with my most humble respects and I kiss your child. You are a lusty husband and I a weak batchelor as such unhealthy as you saw me, but some twenty years older. Yet I have a kind of conformity with you; for if you are attached to a hero so I am in the retinue of another; tho not so intimately as you are; my King has appoinnted me one of the ordinary gentlemen of his chamber. Yr post is more profitable. Yet I am satisfied with mine, because if it gives not a great income, it leaves me at my full liberty, which I prefer to Kings. The King of Prussia would once give me one thousand pounds sterl per annum to live at his court; and I did not accept of the bargain because the court of a King is

not comparable to the house of friend. I live these twenty years with the same friends and you know what power friendship gets over a tender soul and over a philosophical one. I find a great delight in opening my heart to you and in giving thus you an account of my conduct. I'll tell you that being appointed, too, historiographer of France I do write the history of the late fatal war which did much harm to all the parties and did good only to the King of Prussia. I wish I could show you what I have writ upon that subject. I hope I have done justice to the great Duke of Cumberland. My history shall not be the work of a courtier, not that of a partial man; but that of a lover of mankind.

'As to the tragedy of *Sémiramis* I'll send it you within a month or two. I'll rember alluvays with great pleasure I dedicated to you the tender tragedy of *Zaïre*. This *Sémiramis* is quite of an other kind. I have try'd, tho it was a hard task, to change our french *petits maîtres* into Athenians hearers. The transformation is not quite performed; but the piece has met with great applause. It has the fate of moral books, that please many without mending anybody.

'I am now my dear friend at the Court of King Stanislas, where I have passed some months with the ease and cheerfulness that I enjoyed once at Wandsworth; for you must know that King Stanislas is a kind of Fawkenear. He is indeed the best man living but for fear you should take me for a wanderer of courts and a vagabond courtier, I'll tell you I am here with the very friend whom I never parted from for these twenty years past. The lady du Chastellet, who comments Newton and is now about printing a french translation of it, is the friend I mean.

'I have at Paris some ennemies such as Pope had at London and I despise them as he did. In short I live as happy as my condition can permit.

'Nisi quod simul esses caetera laetus.

'I return you a thousand thanks my dearest and worthy friend. I wish you all the happiness you deserve and I'll be yours for ever. Voltaire.'

Back at Lunéville, where there was a larger society and more to do than at Commercy, the various frictions in the company were not so noticeable. They all threw themselves into a wild pursuit of pleasure. Stanislas, enjoying himself like a child, kept advancing the time of dinner so that he could cram more and more amusement into the afternoon. La Galaizière said that if he went on like this he would be dining the day before. Mme du Châtelet led the revels; she organized theatrical performances, readings out loud, scientific experiments and excursions. Everybody wrote verses to everybody else; Voltaire, Pan-pan, and Saint-Lambert were kept busy extolling the Court beauties, Stanislas and each other. Saint-Lambert wrote a play about two Iroquois who shared a wife, greatly to the advantage of all three. 'Erimée (the wife) was sweeter to Mouza but more passionate with Tolho.' Voltaire dedicated a poem to Saint-Lambert. 'It is for you to pluck the roses but the thorns are for me.' As usual, everything had settled down quite easily for Mme du Châtelet who was now the lucky possessor of two husbands and a lover. The only drawback to her happiness was that the lover did not really love.

Stanislas was having trouble again with Père Menou. The Jesuit realized what a fatal mistake he had made when he imported Voltaire. The courtiers had all taken to philosophy, the King hung upon Voltaire's lips and his greatest treat was a reading of the *Pucelle* or of the even more dangerously insidious *Contes Philosophiques*. Père Menou adjured Stanislas in and out of Church to bring the visit to an end, while the King, who had no

intention whatever of losing the chief ornament of his
Court, used delaying tactics. He stood up to his confessor
and had an answer to every argument. 'Voltaire is a
revolting hypocrite,' said the Father. 'Hypocrisy is the
tribute he pays to virtue,' replied the King. 'Is it not
better to have him here in a hypocritical mood, than to
see him making scandals somewhere else?'

However, at Advent Stanislas had a fit of piety. He
stopped the acting and the parties. Mme du Châtelet and
Voltaire took the hint and decided to absent themselves
for a while. She found that she had business to do at
Cirey, an ironmaster at one of the forges must be replaced, the forests visited, the rents collected and various
other things regulated before the New Year. So they
arranged to go there for Christmas and then on to Paris.
Loving farewells were said at Lunéville and fervent
promises exchanged. Saint-Lambert was never to write
less than once a day, while Emilie would spend her whole
life writing.

After supper, as always, the philosophers started on
their journey. The following morning at eight they
arrived at Châlons-sur-Marne, and went to pass the
time of day with their friend the Bishop. The carriage
was sent off for a change of horses and told to come back
in an hour. There was an agreeable house-party at the
Bishop's and Emilie suggested a game of cards. By the
time the carriage re-appeared she was immovably fixed
at the card table. It was raining and very cold and when
the postilions had waited in the courtyard a good long
while they threatened to go away altogether. Emilie sent
word that she would not be wanting them before 2.30.
But by 2.30 she had lost a large sum of money and was
determined to win it back. The rain was still drenching
down, men and horses were shivering with cold. The
postilions cracked their whips under the Bishop's windows and shouted threateningly. She pretended not to

hear and began another game. The Bishop, taking pity on the men, told them to unharness and put up the horses in his own stables. Voltaire was frantic at this waste of a day. Not until eight in the evening did they resume their journey; Emilie had been playing cards for twelve solid hours.

At Cirey she settled down to her Newton. She had been working on it and talking about it for a long time, and had written a preface which Voltaire said was a masterpiece. Now she must finish the translation and write the commentary. She knew that this would test her powers to their utmost capacity. She had engaged a professor, as she always did, to help her when she arrived at Paris, and she was now hoping to have several months of perfect quiet.

# Chapter Twenty-Two

## Miscellaneous Works

AFTER A few days at Cirey Voltaire saw that Emilie had something on her mind. Her usual tearing spirits had left her; she was low and obviously worried. She had reason to be. The assiduities of Saint-Lambert had had a most unexpected and unwelcome result. At nearly forty-four Mme du Châtelet was pregnant. As soon as she was sure of it, she told Voltaire. Though certainly not delighted by this news, he behaved angelically. His only thought was for Emilie, who was making herself ill with nerves and worry. He told her that everything would be all right, there was nothing supernatural about her condition; certainly no cause for despair. They would face the facts together and see what had better be done. Partly in order to cheer her up, he advised her to send for Saint-Lambert: he wrote himself, explained what had happened and asked him to come at once. Saint-Lambert got on a horse and was at Cirey a few hours after receiving Voltaire's letter. The three of them then examined the situation.

Grave as it was, they could not help seeing the funny side. The servants at Cirey, as servants do, knew everything and had half expected a scene, a duel perhaps, between the two men; they were not a little astonished when shrieks of laughter rang through the house. Longchamp, who was eavesdropping for all he was worth, says the whole affair was treated as an enormous joke. The great question was how to break the news to M. du

Châtelet. Emilie had lived on friendly but platonic terms with him for the last seventeen years. Had she better go and hide in some remote spot until all was over? But that would be so inconvenient and so dull. And if she did what would she call the child? Whom should she name as its father? Voltaire said it would have to appear among the miscellaneous works of Mme du Châtelet (*œuvres mêlées*). After hours of discussion, punctuated by hysterical laughter, they decided that *pater est quem nuptiae demonstrant*. So Mme du Châtelet wrote to her husband, who was at Dijon with his regiment and asked him to come and join them at Cirey. She baited the letter with the rents she had been collecting, she said she wanted to hand them over to him, and added that she was threatened with a lawsuit. She would be very glad to see him.

(When the wags at Versailles heard all this, which they did almost at once, they said: 'Why does Mme du Châtelet suddenly want to see her husband?' Answer: 'It is one of those cravings of a pregnant woman.')

The good Marquis came post haste. Never had he had such a reception, in his own house or anywhere else. His wife greeted him tenderly; all the most agreeable neighbours were gathered at Cirey; his tenants were waiting to give him a cheer; Voltaire and Saint-Lambert laid themselves out to please. The morning after he arrived he was sent off on a horse, to visit his farms and his forges. When he returned, with an excellent appetite, there was no question of the coachman's dinner. The whole company was waiting for him and they sat down to a large meal, consisting of his favourite dishes. Afterwards they played games; the supper which followed was as brilliant as if it had been at Versailles. On the second day this programme was repeated and the festivities exceeded anything ever known at Cirey. At supper, Mme du Châtelet, in a very low gown and all her diamonds sat next her husband, plied him with food and drink and made him tell stories of his various campaigns. Usually he was not allowed to speak of them at home, but this evening the whole table listened with bated breath. He was quite over-excited by the effect he was having on his guests and by the loving looks which Emilie flashed at him over her almost naked bosom. When he had come to the end of his repertoire, Voltaire took up the tale. Addressing himself entirely to du Châtelet he told curious stories as only he could tell them. More and more exhilarated, the Marquis became very gallant with his wife. Voltaire and Saint-Lambert, seeing that all was working out as they had hoped, exchanged satisfied nods and winks. At last, du Châtelet begged Emilie's permission to pay her his homage as a husband. She pretended to be very much surprised and rather shocked. She blushed, she bridled. He pressed the point, she refused, he insisted and she said she would think about it.

All this time the guests, led by Voltaire, kept up a convivial din, bursting occasionally into song. In due course, Emilie surrendered and, begging to be excused, host and hostess retired. The second honeymoon, thus begun, lasted for three weeks while the jollities continued in full swing. Then Emilie told her husband that their union was once more to be blessed. M. du Châtelet nearly fainted with joy. He announced the happy news to all assembled friends and went round his estate announcing it to the tenants. He was warmly congratulated, not to say applauded, and a party was given to celebrate his splendid achievement. After this, everybody went their separate ways—Voltaire and Mme du Châtelet to Paris, Saint-Lambert to Nancy, du Châtelet to Dijon and the gentlefolk of Champagne to their anonymous country lives.

Emilie's character in its extraordinary contrasts, her equal enthusiasm for serious and trivial matters, has never been so brilliantly illuminated as during the months of her pregnancy. Though she felt ill with sickness and headaches and also suffered from deep melancholia, she set herself the task of finishing Newton. At this time when a woman longs for the support of the man she loves, she even had the strength of mind to separate from Saint-Lambert in order to be able to work. She knew that she was going to die, as much as human beings ever know it, and she was determined to leave a monument to her fame. At the same time she flung herself into the worldly life of which she was so fond, and conducted her love-affair. Her letters to Saint-Lambert alone would have occupied the leisure and energy of an ordinary woman. Neither lover comes well out of them; Saint-Lambert is shown to have been cold, neglectful, not, in fact, loving; Mme du Châtelet possessive, self-pitying and a terrible nag. Greatly to her despair he was moving heaven and earth to get an army command which would take him away from Nancy, and the theme of many of her letters was: 'You want to be free to separate from me for ever if it suits you, and yet you keep the right to reproach me for this and that——'

She was very much occupied with where to have the baby. Her pregnancy, at her age, made her a figure of fun and she knew it. She also knew that, while M. du Châtelet had been pleased about it at first, the indiscretion of an acquaintance might soon spoil everything. Their son made no secret of his displeasure, he had no desire to share his fortune with this deplorable afterthought. Altogether, Emilie's position was delicate, and she looked for a shelter from all the chill winds that might blow upon herself and her baby. She decided that Stanislas had better provide it. She would give birth at Lunéville, in the Queen of Poland's apartment; nothing could possibly be more respectable. There was also the advantage that she would be near her lover (if, indeed, he were still in Lorraine); and her two husbands could also be in attendance. It seemed a good deal to ask of the old King that he should turn his late wife's bedroom into a ward for such a strange maternity, but Emilie was never shy of asking and generally got what she wanted. First of all she wrote to Mme de Boufflers, 3rd April 1749.

'I am pregnant and you may imagine my distress, my fears for my health—for my very life even—how ridiculous I feel it to have a baby at the age of forty [forty-four, really] and how much I mind on my son's account. Nobody knows yet, it shows very little, I think it must be in the fourth [month]. I haven't felt it move, but that won't be until four-and-a-half months. I am so thin that if I felt giddy or unwell, and if my breasts were not swollen I should think it was simply an irregularity. You can imagine how much I count on your friendship now, and how much I need it to console and help me to bear my condition. It would be very hard for me to be so long away from you and not to have you at my lying-in, yet how can I go to Lunéville and put everybody to so much trouble? I really do not know if I can ask the King, good as he always is, to let me have the Queen's small apartment which I used to occupy. The wing would not do because of the noise, the smell of the manure-heap and the fact that I would be too far from you and M. de Voltaire.'

After Easter Stanislas went to Trianon to see his eldest granddaughter, Mme Infante, who had come back from Spain, with her little girl, to visit her parents. He was accompanied, as usual, by the husband and lover of his mistress, the Marquesses de Boufflers et de La Galaizière. Mme du Châtelet asked if she could go and stay with him at Trianon and when permission was given she moved in with a mountain of trunks containing all her summer dresses. In about a fortnight she had extracted everything she wanted from the King. He said she could have the Queen's small apartment, and he would shut up the big one so that she would be entirely private. The *bosquet* near the Queen's terrace would be reserved for Emilie and when her time was near, she could take air and exercise there without being seen. Stanislas even promised to furnish a little summer-house where she could go and rest.

The matter of her lying-in off her mind, Mme du Châtelet went back to Paris and concentrated on Newton. No more social life, no supper-parties—she refused to see Mme du Deffand and indeed everybody except Voltaire and Clairaut. Clairaut went through each chapter of her book as she finished it to make sure that there were no careless mistakes; these were so easily made and overlooked that the manuscript was then given to a third party to correct. She translated the Latin into French, and amplified the demonstrations to bring the material within the grasp of French mathematicians. Her working hours were from eight, or at the latest nine, in the morning, to 3 p.m. when she had her coffee. At four she began again and went on until supper time at ten o'clock. After supper she chatted with Voltaire an hour or two and then worked until 5 a.m. She was feeling very well and thought the baby particularly lively, it jumped about so much.

'I don't love Newton,' she wrote to Saint-Lambert. 'I am finishing him because it is reasonable and honourable to do so, but I only love you.'

Voltaire was leading, as he always did in Paris, a life divided between intellectual activity and nervous upsets. A new play of his, *Nanine*, was put on at the Théâtre-français without making much of a splash. His correspondence with Frederick, which had flagged of late, began again, as loving as ever. Frederick was, of course, delighted at the discomfiture of his female rival. 'It seems that Apollo, as God of Medicine [*sic*], has ordered you to preside at Mme du Châtelet's lying-in.' Voltaire promised to go to Berlin as soon as it was over. He would see his King again, die happy, and be buried in Frederick's church with '*Ci-gît l'admirateur de Frédéric le Grand*' on his tombstone. Frederick replied that his proudest title would be '*Possesseur de Voltaire*'. Voltaire hinted that he would be irresistibly drawn to Berlin if he were presented with the Prussian order *Pour le Mérite*. The flirtation, in fact, was resuming its prickly course. Frederick told his sister Wilhelmine, 'We shall have Voltaire here this autumn, he is coming as soon as Mme du Châtelet has had her baby. It's doing him too much honour to father it on him; a certain Saint-Lambert enjoys the glory, her husband the shame and Voltaire the spectacle.' At about this time Frederick made his often-quoted remark to Algarotti: '*C'est bien dommage qu'une âme aussi lâche soit unie à un aussi beau génie. Il a les gentillesses et les malices d'un singe.*'*

Voltaire now had a quarrel with Richelieu which very nearly put an end to their age-old friendship. The Duke and he had arranged a little back-scratching with the object of gaining favour in the eyes of Louis XV. The French Academicians were to go to Versailles and congratulate their master on the recent peace treaty (Aix-la-Chapelle). Richelieu, a member of that body, which always includes two or three Dukes, had been chosen as spokesman and particularly wanted to shine. So he made Voltaire write the address for him to learn by heart and deliver as his own. 'If the Academy has chosen me to express its sentiments it must be because it is my good fortune to enjoy daily contact with the great soul and essence of all we admire. . . . It is the duty of my colleagues, Your Majesty, to acquaint future generations

* 'It is a great pity that such a despicable soul should be joined to such a beautiful genius. He has all the charming ways and all the malice of a monkey.'

of your triumphs over your enemies and over yourself, the good you do to the nations and the example you set to other Kings. . . .' This was not entirely insincere. Voltaire did in fact greatly admire Louis XV for the peace of Aix-la-Chapelle—by which France reaped practically no benefit from a series of glorious victories to her arms. The King had said that he was not a merchant and did not intend to bargain. Most of his subjects, however, thought this generosity misplaced and were very much annoyed with him for making such an unprofitable treaty.

Voltaire having written Richelieu's speech, the Duke, for his part, had engaged to present the King with Voltaire's *Panégyrique à Louis XV*, in Latin and the four civilized modern languages, French, Italian, Spanish and English, finely bound in blue morocco. In this Voltaire went much further. Louis XV, he said, was the greatest French King since Charlemagne and it was to be hoped that all the monarchs of the future would resemble him. As Louis XV never now spoke to Voltaire, or even looked in his direction, he did not dare present the *Panégyrique* himself.

On the appointed day, a party of Academicians went to Versailles: Richelieu, the Duc de Saint-Aignan, Mirabaud, Abbé d'Olivet, President Hénault, Abbé Alary, Hardion, Crébillon, the Bishop of Mirepoix, La Chaussée, Foncemagne, Cardinal de Soubise, Abbé Duresnel, Marivaux, the Bishop of Bayeux, Bignon, Abbé de Bernis, Abbé de la Villé, Duclos, Paulmy and Gresset. It included two great enemies of Voltaire, Crébillon and the Bishop of Mirepoix, and four great friends, Richelieu, d'Olivet, Bernis and Hénault. He himself was not present. The delegation was assembled in the Œil de Bœuf awaiting its audience when, to his horror, Richelieu heard somebody in the crowd reciting the very phrases that he had so carefully learnt and was just about to deliver. He was obliged to make up a new speech there and then and stammer it out under the mocking glances of his enemy, Maurepas, who knew quite well what had happened.

The Duke thought that this was one of Voltaire's monkey tricks; he was furious and riposted by sending the *Panégyrique* back to its author without comment. Voltaire, in his turn, flew into a wild rage. He tore down an *Apothéose du Duc de Richelieu* in gouache which always hung in his bedroom and trampled it to pieces. In the end the matter of the 'leakage' was cleared up. It was the usual story. Mme du Châtelet, it seemed, had read the address to Mme de Boufflers who had come to pick her up and take her to the Opera. Mme de Boufflers asked for a copy, had twenty more made and distributed them among her friends. Voltaire and Richelieu laughed together over this feminine indiscretion, all was forgiven and forgotten, and they never quarrelled again in the course of their long lives.

The *Panégyrique* was presented to the King by Mme de Pompadour. He was quite clever enough to see through its fulsome flattery and Voltaire complained that the only person who did not seem to like it was Louis XV.

## Chapter Twenty-Three

### 'C'est vous qui me l'avez tuée'

IN JUNE 1749 Mme du Châtelet had finished her work with Clairaut, though not her book. She and Voltaire set out for Cirey. The weather was bad, and on three days of that month there was hard frost. Voltaire said: 'We hear a great deal about St Martin's summer and always forget St John's winter.' (St John's Day is the 24th June.)

Saint-Lambert was supposed to meet them at Cirey. Emilie had told him to go there from Nancy with M. du Châtelet. But in the end he said he really could not risk spending several days alone with the Marquis and preferred to wait for Emilie in Lorraine. She and Voltaire only stayed a fortnight at Cirey and then went on to Lunéville. Voltaire says that Emilie now behaved like a man about to embark on a long journey. Sadly, but firmly, she put her affairs in order and began to take leave of her friends. She made up various parcels of letters and manuscripts, some of which she gave to Longchamp with directions for disposing of them in case of her death.

Saint-Lambert was very kind and affectionate during the last two months of Emilie's pregnancy, and so was Mme de Boufflers. In fact she was surrounded by love and it would have been a happy time but for her melancholy premonitions and her physical state. She became absolutely enormous and had a great deal of pain in her back. Everybody at Lunéville was worried about her, it

was thought most dangerous to have a child so late in life
and she seemed worn out by her exertions in Paris. Saint-
Lambert blamed Voltaire for having allowed her to work
so hard.

'When I am with you,' she wrote to Saint-Lambert,
who had gone to see the Prince de Beauvau at Haroué, 'I
can bear my condition, often, indeed, I hardly notice it,
but when I lose you everything goes blank. I walked to
my little summer-house today and my belly is so terribly
fallen, I am suffering such pain in my kidneys, I feel so
sad this evening, that it would not surprise me if I had
the baby tonight. I should be miserable, though you, I
know, would be pleased. My pains would be easier to
bear if you were here in the same house. I wrote you
eight pages yesterday. . . .'

Voltaire's nerves began to give way under the strain of
waiting for the baby to be born and he found an outlet
for them in a short but violent quarrel with M. Alliot, the
Controller of the Household at Lunéville. Alliot, a *fermier-
général*, was one of the remarkable Frenchmen whom
Louis XV had sent to administer Lorraine. By his honest,
clever and thrifty conduct of the treasury there he made
it possible for Stanislas, who was far from rich, to gratify
his taste for building. Nancy owes its beautiful monuments almost as much to Alliot as to Stanislas himself.
Mme Alliot, a pious *bourgeoise*, had already had a passage
with Voltaire. During a tremendous storm at Lunéville
she made it clear that in her view God would most likely
destroy all the courtiers with a thunderbolt to punish
them for associating with so much wickedness. 'Madame,'
said Voltaire, 'I have thought and written more good of
Him than you, who find Him so terrifying, could say in a
lifetime.'

Voltaire was sometimes too ill and often too bored to
dine with the rest of the party. He considered that the
food which was sent up to him on these occasions was

nasty and inadequate. Suddenly, on 29 August, he seized his pen and wrote a violent letter of complaint to Alliot. Voltaire has left everything to come and pay his court to the King. But he is a sick man, and unfortunately the times of meals often coincide with those of his worst pains. Also, in such freezing weather, it would be most dangerous for an invalid to leave his room in the mornings and evenings. Will M. Alliot see to it that in future he will be sent what is necessary, or must Voltaire complain to the King himself?

This letter went off to Alliot's office in the palace at 9 a.m. At nine-fifteen, having received no reply Voltaire wrote again. The King of Prussia is for ever asking Voltaire to go and live with him. At Berlin he is not obliged to beg for bread, wine and a candle. It is monstrous that an officer of the French Court, visiting the King of Poland, should be obliged to solicit these elementary attentions.

No reply. Voltaire gave it another half-hour and then wrote to Stanislas.

'29 August 1749, 9 3/4 hours.
'Sire, When one is in Paradise it is to God that one must address oneself. Your Majesty has allowed me to come and pay my court until the end of the autumn, at which time I shall be obliged to take my leave of Y.M. Your Majesty knows that I am very ill and that my work and my sufferings keep me in my own apartment. I am obliged to beg Your Majesty to give orders that I shall receive the usual amenities granted to foreigners at your court. Since the time of Alexander kings have nourished men of letters, and when Virgil was with Augustus, Allyotus, the Court Chamberlain, issued him with bread, wine and a candle. I am ill today and have neither bread nor wine for my dinner. I have the honour to be with profound respect, Sire, Your Majesty's very humble etc.
V.'

At last Voltaire received a reply from Alliot, to whom
Stanislas had passed on his letter.

'You have got dinner in your own room, Monsieur.
You have soup, wine and meats; I have sent you fire-
wood and candles. And now you are complaining to the
Duke and to the King, with equal injustice. His Majesty
has sent me your letter, without comment, and for your
sake I hesitate to tell him how much you are in the
wrong. There are certain rules in this house to which
you will be so good as to conform. Nothing leaves the
cellar without a note from myself of the same day. If
this is tiresome for anybody, it is for me. What difference
can it make to you, so long as you get what you ask
for?

'I say to you that you have lacked nothing, and you say
that you have lacked everything.

'You are the first person who has ever complained
about the treatment here of foreigners, if you count
yourself such. I have sent you everything you have
asked for, and I tell you again you are quite wrong to
grumble.

'You mention the French Court as a model. It has
its rules and we have ours, but ours have nothing to
do with the French Court and you know that as well
as I.

'I am very sorry, on your own account, that you have
seen fit to take these steps, and I hope you feel how much
they are out of place.

'I do not agree with you that Allyotus, Court Chamberlain, gave bread, wine and a candle to Virgil.

'I do so for M. de Voltaire because he is a poor man,
but Virgil was powerful and kept an excellent table of his
own, where he entertained his friends and was happy
with them. No comparison is possible. And, by the way,
Virgil worked to please himself and for the glory of his

times; M. de Voltaire does so out of sheer necessity and to satisfy his needs. So, what is given to one from decency could not even have been offered to the other, for fear of a rebuff.'

For once in his life Voltaire was silenced by this letter, which brings to an end the exchange of notes that summer morning.

Four days later, Mme du Châtelet was sitting, as usual, at her writing-table when she felt something. This something was a little girl. Emilie barely had time to call her maid, the maid barely had time to hold out her apron and receive the child, who was then put on a large book, while her mother arranged some papers and went to bed. Soon they were both sleeping like dormice. The birth which had been so much dreaded was as easy as that. Voltaire wrote to all the friends describing this event in letters radiant with joy and relief. It has been much easier for Mme du Châtelet to have a baby than for him to write *Catalina*. She is so well that she has only gone to bed because it is usual to do so, and is only not writing herself to announce the news because that is not usual. But to Mme Denis he made it all sound rather tedious. 'Mme du Châtelet has had her baby and I have lost a whole week.'

For several days Mme du Châtelet was perfectly well. Everybody assembled in her room and the jolly communal life flowed round her. The baby was put out to nurse. Then Emilie began to have some fever. There was a heat-wave, for the first time that summer. She never liked hot weather and it added, now, to her discomfort. She asked for an iced drink, very popular at Lunéville, made of almonds. They all tried to dissuade her, but she would have it and drank a large quantity. It seemed to have a bad effect, stopping a natural function of the body necessary to a woman in her state. The King's doctor came and ordered a treatment which succeeded fairly well. The next day she had palpitations and trouble with her breathing. On 10 September two more doctors were called in, from Nancy. They gave her some medicine to calm her; she seemed better and disposed to sleep. Voltaire and du Châtelet went off to sup with Mme de Boufflers, leaving Saint-Lambert, Mlle du Thil, Longchamp and Mme du Châtelet's maid in the sick-room. Saint-Lambert sat talking to Emilie but he thought she was falling asleep so he left her and went across the room to join Longchamp and the two women. Suddenly there was a noise from the bed like snoring, punctuated by hiccups after which Mme du Châtelet lay quite still. They tried to revive her by making her smell vinegar, slapping her hands and moving her feet, but to no avail. She was dead. 'She never knew the horror of death; that was left to us,' said Voltaire.

Mme de Boufflers and her supper party heard that Mme du Châtelet was worse; they rushed to her room where they learnt the truth. There was a terrible silence followed by unrestrained weeping and sobbing which went on for a long time. Somebody led the husband away, by degrees the others went to bed until only Voltaire, Saint-Lambert and Longchamp were left. Voltaire, like a man in a dream, wandered to the outside door leading to the terrace. Here he staggered, fell, rolled down the steps and began beating his head on the stone pavement. Longchamp and Saint-Lambert, who had followed, ran to him and lifted him up. Seeing Saint-Lambert through his tears, Voltaire, said, gently and sadly, '*Ah! Mon ami! C'est vous qui me l'avez tuée.*'* Suddenly, as though waking from his dream he cried in a terrible voice: '*Eh! Mon Dieu, Monsieur, de quoi vous*

---

* 'Ah, my friend, it is you who have killed her for me.'

*avisiez-vous de lui faire un enfant?'*\* The two men, exhausted by emotion, then parted and went each to his own room.

The next day Mme de Boufflers sent for Longchamp. She told him that it was very important for her to have a cornelian ring set in diamonds that Mme du Châtelet always wore. Longchamp slipped it off the dead woman's finger and took it to Mme de Boufflers. She pressed a secret catch and removed a miniature of Saint-Lambert which was inside the stone, after which Longchamp put the ring back among Mme du Châtelet's effects. He was worried about Voltaire—who was in a black misery—and thought that if he told him about the miniature it might help to cure him by making him angry. Voltaire clasped his hands, raised his eyes to heaven and said that women were all the same. 'I replaced Richelieu, Saint-Lambert has driven me out. It is the natural order of things, one nail knocks out another, and so it is, in this world.'

Emilie was far too vivid and vital a person to die with her death, and it was many weeks before she began to fade from the consciousness of Voltaire. By day he shut himself up writing innumerable letters about her, at night he would wake from a troubled sleep and wander from room to room calling her. In the first extremity of his grief he even spoke of entering a monastery. 'My tears will never stop flowing.' 'I only hope to join her soon.' 'It is not a mistress I have lost but half of myself, a soul for which my soul seems to have been made.' 'I love to find her again, as I talk to her husband and her son.' To d'Argental: 'I come to weep out the rest of my unhappy existence in your arms.' He was tormented, now, to think of the light-hearted, joking way in which, so few days before, he had announced the birth of the child to their friends: 'I was very far from suspecting the

\* 'What gave you the idea of getting her with child?'

slightest danger.' Mme du Châtelet herself, always con-
scious that this pregnancy had its ridiculous side, had
decreed the tone she wished him to take. (She knew her
compatriots. At Versailles they were saying: 'How like
that pretentious Mme du Châtelet to die in childbirth at
her age.') Voltaire said: 'The unhappy little girl who
caused her death had no interest for me.' This poor baby
herself died a few days later, regretted by nobody. Had
she lived, she would certainly have been shut up in a
cold, damp convent and never heard of again.

Stanislas, very sad, gave Mme du Châtelet a state
funeral, and then did all he could to keep Voltaire with
him. But Voltaire felt that he must get away from
'abominable Lunéville, the cause of her death' as soon as
he could. He also clung very much to du Châtelet at this
time. When the funeral was over, the two men and
Emilie's son went to Cirey. At first Voltaire felt com-
forted there, but in a day or two the atmosphere of a
house which he and Emilie had embellished together,
where they had been so happy for years and where he
had expected to die in her arms made his grief more real
and terrible than ever. Cirey, he said, had become 'un
objet d'horreur' to him. In a mad desire to get away for
ever he had all his possessions, which included much of
the furniture in Emilie's rooms as well as that in his own,
piled on to wagons and sent to Paris. He and du Châtelet
were prevented by some inhibition from discussing this
matter and in the end the arrangement suited neither of
them. Du Châtelet would have been glad to buy the furniture, as it was needed at Cirey, and Voltaire had
nowhere to put it. The house in the rue Traversière,
which he now took over entirely, was already furnished.
Later on, Voltaire went to see du Châtelet's sister and
settled his accounts with the Marquis. He had lent him
40,000 livres for the rebuilding of Cirey. Of this, du
Châtelet had engaged to pay back 30,000 but he had

never done so and Voltaire had had no interest on it. In the end du Châtelet paid 10,000 and Voltaire let him off the rest saying that friendship was more to him than money.

In spite of Voltaire's grief it was, as usual, easy to amuse him and he would shriek with laughter at a joke. He had perfectly clear intentions about his future, which was bound up with Mme Denis. On the day of Emilie's death, he wrote to his niece:

'Lunéville, 10 September.
'My dear child, I have just lost a friend of twenty years. For a long time now, you know, I have not looked upon Madame du Chastellet as a woman, and I am sure that you will enter into my cruel grief. It is frightful to have seen her die in such circumstances and for such a reason. I am not leaving Monsieur du Chastellet in our mutual sorrow. I must go to Cirey, there are important papers. From Cirey I shall come to Paris to embrace you and to seek, in you, my one consolation, the only hope of my life.'

From Cirey he wrote, 'My dear heart', and said: 'You can see by my present grief that I have a soul which is made to love; you are far dearer to me than a person for whom, as you know, my only feeling was that of gratitude. Give me your heart and regret me, one day, as much as I am regretting Madame du Chastellet.'

Voltaire could not bear to stay at Cirey, but was not in a hurry to get to Paris. He spun out the journey, making various excuses to Mme Denis. He had to go slowly, he had lent his fast carriage to Emilie's son who had smashed it up. He said he could not face, as yet, the curiosity of his Paris acquaintances, their sympathy and the endless mortuary discussions which French people think suitable at these times. So he went to the Bishop of Châlons and other friends and only arrived at the rue Traversière a month after Emilie's death. He had stayed two nights with Mme de Champbonin before leaving Champagne for ever.

# *Epilogue*

---

DU CHÂTELET lived to be seventy. He never married again. Emilie's son was created a Duke and was Ambassador to London 1768–70. He was guillotined at the age of sixty-six. His son also died in the Revolution, in prison, and the family became extinct. Voltaire set up house with Mme Denis and lived another twenty-nine years. After his death she married a man ten years her junior. Saint-Lambert set up house with M. and Mme d'Houdetot and lived another fifty-four years.

Emilie's translation of Newton was published by Clairaut in 1756. Her correspondence with Voltaire, which is known to have been bound up in eight large morocco volumes, is generally thought to have been destroyed by Saint-Lambert after her death. There is no shadow of proof that this was so, but Saint-Lambert is known to have burnt all Jean-Jacques Rousseau's letters to Mme d'Houdetot. Another story is that these volumes lay about at Cirey until the Revolution, when they disappeared. Mr Besterman still has hopes that one day they will turn up, to be included in his great edition of Voltaire's correspondence.

# BIBLIOGRAPHY

MOST of the information in this book comes from Voltaire's Correspondence, edited by Theodore Besterman. This edition, indispensable to any student of Voltaire, is not yet complete but it covers the death of Mme du Châtelet. It contains already twice as many letters as any of the other editions and also gives those of various members of Voltaire's circle.

Other printed sources are:

BEUCHOT. *Œuvres de Voltaire* 1829-40, 72 vols.

GUSTAVE DESNOIRESTERRES. *Voltaire et la Société Française au 18ième Siècle.* Paris 1868, 8 vols.

EUGÈNE ASSÉ. *Lettres de la Marquise du Châtelet.* Paris 1806.

*Lettres Inédites de Madame la Marquise du Châtelet à M. le Comte d'Argental.* A Paris MDCCCVI.

*Catalogue of the Collection of Autograph Letters and Historical Documents formed between 1865 and 1882; by Alfred Morrison.* 14 vols.

IRA WADE. *Studies on Voltaire including hitherto unpublished papers of Mme du Châtelet.* Princeton University Press 1947.

MADAME LA MARQUISE DU CHÂTELET. *Institutions de Physique.* Paris 1740.

LONGCHAMP et WAGNIÈRE. *Mémoires sur Voltaire.* Paris 1826. 2 vols.

LA MARQUISE DE CRÉQUY. *Souvenirs.* Paris 1840. (These *mémoires* are partly apocryphal and must be treated with reserve.)

GASTON MAUGRAS. *La Cour de Lunéville au XVIII Siècle.* Plon 1925.

LA BAUMELLE. *Vie de Maupertuis.* Paris 1856.

JOHN LOUGH. *Paris Theatre Audiences in the 17th and 18th Centuries.* O.U.P. 1957.

JEAN STERN. *Voltaire et sa Nièce Madame Denis.* La Palatine 1957.

LORD MORLEY. *Voltaire.* Macmillan 1872.

*Cambridge Modern History.* C.U.P. 1934.

LORD CHESTERFIELD. *Miscellaneous Works.* London 1777.

SAINTE-BEUVE. *Causeries du Lundi.* Paris N.D.

BERTRAND RUSSELL. *History of Western Philosophy.* Allen & Unwin 1955.

CARLYLE. *History of Friedrich II called Frederick the Great.* Chapman & Hall 1903.

WILLIAMS. *The Fascinating Duc de Richelieu.* 1910.

HILLAIRET. *Gibets, Piloris et Cachots du Vieux Paris.* Editions de Minuit 1956.

W. H. BARBER. *Leibnitz in France.* O.U.P. 1955.

Unpublished sources are various letters of Mme du Châtelet at the Musée Voltaire, Geneva, and 240 letters from Voltaire to Mme Denis, which have only just come to light, and are in the possession of Mr Besterman.

# INDEX

(See under 'Voltaire' for references to his individual works)